Sturm und Drang

The German Library: Volume 14
Volkmar Sander, General Editor

STURM UND DRANG

The Soldiers, The Childmurderess,
Storm and Stress, and *The Robbers*

Edited by Alan C. Leidner

CONTINUUM • NEW YORK

1992
The Continuum Publishing Company
370 Lexington Avenue, New York, NY 10017

The German Library
is published in cooperation with Deutsches Haus,
New York University.
This volume has been supported by a grant from the
Marie Baier Foundation.

Printed in the United States of America

Library of Congress Cataloging-in-Publication Data

Sturm und Drang / edited by Alan C. Leidner.
    p.   cm. — (The German library ; v. 14)
    Includes bibliographical references (p.   ).
    Contents: Introduction / Alan C. Leidner — The soldiers / Jakob
Michael Reinhold Lenz ; translated by William E. Yuill — The
childmurderess / Heinrich Leopold Wagner ; translated by Betty Senk
Waterhouse — Storm and stress / Friedrich Maximilian Klinger ;
translated by Betty Senk Waterhouse — The robbers / Friedrich
Schiller ; translated by F. J. Lamport — Preface to The robbers /
translated by Alan C. Leidner.
    ISBN 0-8264-0704-8 (cloth). — ISBN 0-8264-0705-6 (paper)
    1. German drama—18th century—Translations into English.
2. English drama—Translations from German.   I. Leidner, Alan C.
II. Series.
PT1258.S78   1992
832'.608—dc20   91-24555
                                                              CIP

Acknowledgments will be found on page 305,
which constitutes an extension of the copyright page.

Contents

Introduction

In the first scene of Friedrich Maximilian Klinger's *Storm and Stress* (*Sturm und Drang,* 1777), Wild tells Blasius and La Feu:

> I want to have myself stretched over a drum so as to take on new dimensions. How my heart aches again. Oh, if I could but exist in the barrel of this pistol until a hand blasted me into the air. Oh, indecision! How far you lead mankind, and how far astray!

The urge to be jarred into a life of greater decisiveness and expanse—to take on larger dimensions—finds wide expression in the literary tradition to which Klinger's play gave a name. The sources of this urge are a matter of debate, but every account of Sturm und Drang must begin by noting Germany's lack of a common nationality. By the eighteenth century, the land was a patchwork of some three-hundred tiny states, most ruled by German *Fürsten,* not princes in the sense that their power stemmed from a royal house, but sovereigns in their own right. The eighteenth-century German, as Justus Möser (1720–94) pointed out, had no real fatherland with which to identify, at most only a principality, a bishopric, or "father city." Thus Klinger's Wild, whose explosive frustration stems in large part from his sense of a life lived on too small a scale.

But why the 1770s? This is a more difficult question, and to begin to answer it, one first needs to look at the overall landscape of the European Enlightenment. The rise of the middle class meant a rigorous new critique of society, and the stage became a forum for this critique: Louis Sébastien Mercier (1740–1814) recommended that drama be used to activate audiences politically. As it came into its own, the middle class fashioned itself as a segment of society more "human" because it was more atuned to emotions than the aristocracy was. Yet as writers soon learned, unearthing the resources of the inner life was not an easy process: Rousseau's *Confessions,* for example, written in the 1760s, end with depression and paranoia. The new subjectivism also required expressive theories of art capable of overthrowing French neoclassicism, which prescribed the traditional unities of time, place, and action as well as a high-born tragic hero. Writers announced that they found a precursor in Shakespeare, a "genius" whose work seemed to be the essence of originality and emotional power. With its treatment of all classes of society, its colorful language, and its masterful character portrayal, Shakespearean drama was held up as the antidote to a tired eighteenth-century dramatic tradition.

In Germany, especially since Lessing, there was the feeling among writers that a renewal of German literature could play a role in lifting Germans above the cultural disunity of *Kleinstaaterei*. Pride in the German heritage was particularly strong after the Seven Years' War (1756–63), which confirmed Prussia's role as a military power and made many Germans feel as if their lives might not always be lived on a small scale. The Prussian victory seems also to have reinforced the aristocracy's own self-importance as the ruling class, leading to further class distinctions. Still, interest in the collective heritage of Germany had been growing since the middle of the century and showed no sign of abating. In the 1750s and 1760s, Johann Georg Hamann (1730–88) defended the native culture of the *Volk* and maintained that language, the root of all our experience, was richer in images and more powerful prior to the "abstract" eighteenth century. The Danish military officer Heinrich Wilhelm Gerstenberg (1737–1823) in his *Briefe über die Merkwürdigkeiten der Literatur* (Letters on noteworthy aspects of literature, 1766–67), rejected French neoclassicism and held up Shakespeare as a model for the new German writer, while Hamann's student Johann Gottfried von Herder (1744–1803) maintained in his essays "Shakespeare" and "Oßian" (The German Library, volume 11) that great literature relies not on immutable rules, but on the specific culture out of which it rises. Herder's message would reach Sturm und Drang writers in Strasbourg when, in the winter of 1770–71, he ridiculed Goethe's rococo poems and drew his attention not only to the work of Hamann and native German folk poetry, but also to Laurence Sterne, Oliver Goldsmith, and James Macpherson.

Although most writers of Sturm und Drang viewed themselves as opponents of the Enlightenment, as H. A. Korff pointed out in 1923, Sturm und Drang—especially with its interest in integrating the individual into a viable society—is in fact a continuation of the

Enlightenment. Nevertheless, the tradition makes its own distinctive contribution to eighteenth-century culture, bringing attention to the power of the environment as well as to the contradictory and self-defeating attitudes present in every segment of society. Its vivid and insightful portraits of both violence and depression, and its open plot structures, are ahead of their time. Whereas, like the Enlightenment itself, Sturm und Drang is not a tradition with a unified philosophy or literary program, certain patterns still persist. It is sometimes said, for example, that its protagonists are either passive and often melancholy victims of their environment or people of action and explosive frustration who fail. (Both characteristics can be found in Wild's own paradoxical "active passivity.") This twofold aspect of the tradition finds expression in J. M. R. Lenz's idiosyncratic essay "Notes on the Theater" (*Anmerkungen übers Theater*, 1774, The German Library, volume 83), where Lenz redefines the distinction between tragedy and comedy as he reverses Aristotle's primacy of plot over character. In his view, tragedy deals with an individual who creates events by "turning the whole machine" of the play; comedy, on the other hand, presents the deterministic, machinelike environment in which the individual is hopelessly enmeshed. "In my opinion the central idea of a comedy would be an *event*," writes Lenz, "and of a tragedy a *character*." German dramatists, Lenz reasons, whose culture is a blend of high and low, must write "comically and tragically at one and the same time."

Whereas the status of the French culture into which Rousseau was born was never in question, the same could not be said for Germany, and perhaps for this reason contemporary German versions of individualism are quite different. Writers of the German 1770s found themselves creating the singleminded, violent *Kraftmensch,* first depicted by Goethe in his drama *Götz von Berlichingen mit der eisernen Hand* (Götz von Berlichingen with the iron hand, 1773). Götz is a sixteenth-century "free knight" whose virtues of loyalty and independence come up against the new bureaucratic and intrigue-ridden government of the court. German dramatists even found ways to create violent individuals who could, at the same time, enjoy the feeling that they were still part of a larger moral order. Karl Moor's rebellion, for example, in *The Robbers* (*Die Räuber,* 1781) clearly grows from love of his father and from his own piety, and Schiller's play ends as Karl attempts to restore the higher order that he feels he has offended.

Yet is this higher order that of a particular community, or of some realm unconditioned by time and place? It turns out that Sturm und Drang goes in both these directions at once, and often we observe characters leaping quickly from a concern with the particular circumstances of their existence to a concern with absolutes. Thus, while Herder may have recommended that writers go to the culture of the *Volk* to find Germany, Wild still longs for "the eternal high emotion" (act 2, scene 1), and Goethe's *Faust*, the first draft of which belongs to Sturm und Drang, makes the Renaissance magician a seeker after absolute truth. Sometimes explained as an escape from a "German misery" that Friedrich Engels saw in eighteenth-century class relations, Germany's taste for the infinite and unconditioned had, in fact, been around to buoy up its fragmented culture for centuries. Still, as many of these writers realized, their attraction to unconditioned realms led away from the development of a specific community of people who could deal with others and enjoy shared traditions. J. M. R. Lenz rejects unconditioned absolutes summarily, saying that he would rather deal in specific social practices than embrace vague ideals. And Wild realizes already in the first scene of *Storm and Stress* that in rushing around trying to be "everything," he has, so far, found "Nowhere peace, nowhere respose."

The struggle to get a grip on their own identity from the inside out and increase the import and momentum of their lives turned writers of Sturm und Drang into philosophers of character and the characteristic. Gerstenberg admired Shakespeare for his attention to character; Goethe, whose zeal to locate a general German character led him in 1771 to the erroneous conclusion that Gothic architecture originated in Germany, would write: "The only true art is characteristic art"; Lenz defended "the characteristic" against the artist who "orbits an imaginary idea of beauty"; and Klinger admired those who had achieved "balance of character." Yet as they discovered, character is not a quality that can burst on the scene all at once in the actions or language of a *Kraftmensch*, or in Wild's image of the pistol shot: it needs traditions. And whereas it sometimes seems in this literature as if the only widening of character possible is one that reached upward toward the infinite, over and over again it becomes clear that what these writers want is the feeling that they are part of a larger whole, with specific traditions and practices that seem like second nature. As I think the following four examples show, Sturm und Drang is not only concerned with character—or individualism—per se, but also with the conditions of existence that make character possible.

Jakob Michael Reinhold Lenz (1751–92) was born in the village of Seßwegen, (now Casvaine, Estonia), the son of a Protestant clergyman, and grew up in Dorpat (now Tartu). In 1771 he gave up his study of theology and philosophy at the University of Königsberg for the opportunity to travel to Strasbourg, where he wrote the essay "Notes on the Theater" (1774) and the dramas *The Tutor* (*Der Hofmeister*, 1774), *The New Menoza* (*Der neue Menoza*, 1774), *Pandaemonium Germanicum* (1775), and *The Soldiers* (*Die Soldaten* 1776). Lenz spent most of 1776 in Weimar (Goethe, for reasons that are unclear, appears to have had him expelled from town), then, in 1777, experienced the first of a number of schizophrenic attacks that essentially put an end to his literary career. The periodic recurrence of his mental illness thwarted earnest attempts to begin other careers in Germany and Russia (after 1780), and he was found dead in a Moscow street on the morning of June 4, 1792.

The subject of *The Soldiers* is the humiliation of townspeople by soldiers; specifically, it treats the soldiers' seduction of young middle-class women. Marie's ruination is, as the Countess sees it, a result of the ban on soldiers' marriages, and the Colonel's idea for a solution to the problem—a state-sanctioned corps of prostitutes to accompany the soldiers—comes across as a parody of Lenz's inability both to end the play and to find a satisfying solution to the problem. Nothing is harder to observe than the ordinary, and what we get in Lenz is a well-observed world where one's identity is fluid—and hopelessly entangled in the social and linguistic environment. Rapidly changing scenes are presented in a mosaiclike fashion rather than being linked by a linear plot line. A comedy by Lenz's definition, *The Soldiers* depicts an unadmirable, self-divided figure with no power over her surroundings, and who adopts without thinking whatever mode of speech helps her cause at the time. In the first scene, we see Marie writing a letter to her fiancé Stolzius's mother in the style of her father, the merchant, yet when Stolzius's reprimand arrives in act 2, scene 3, we see that she can also use the aristocratic language of Desportes. At the same time she is the victim of the linguistic ploys of others, believing, for example, in act 1, scene 6, that Desportes's four-line Petrarchan love lyric expresses his true feelings about her. Lenz's recognition of the power of the environment, including the linguistic environment, and his use of naturalistic and uncommunicative dialogue, open form, the grotesque, and tragicomedy anticipate the drama of Büchner, Grabbe, Hauptmann, Wedekind, Brecht, and Dürrenmatt.

Heinrich Leopold Wagner (1747–79) was born in Strasbourg, where he studied law and was a member of the literary circle around Johann Daniel Salzmann (1722–1812), a group to which Lenz also belonged. At the time of his death at age thirty-two he had served for three years as a dramatist, producer, translator and lawyer for the well-known itinerant theater company of Abel Seyler. The German translator of Mercier's influential *Du théâtre ou nouvel essai sur l'art dramatique* (On the theater; or, a new essay on the dramatic arts, 1773; German translation 1776), Wagner is best known for two plays, *Die Reue nach der Tat* (The remorse after the deed, 1775) and *The Childmurderess* (*Die Kindermörderin*, 1776).

The Childmurderess is formally one of the most traditional plays of Sturm und Drang, with a tightly structured plot and few changes of setting. Missing is the irony and fatalism of Lenz. But this depiction of a middle-class life invaded by the aristocracy prefigures the drama of naturalism a century later with its boldly drawn characters and their wide linguistic range, from the colorful language of Meister Humbrecht to the dialect of the jailers. Wagner also characterizes his figures well through gestures, costumes, and stage settings. The rape of Evchen Humbrecht in a bordello was an indelicate topic to depict so realistically, thus in Wagner's day the play was performed only without the first act. When Evchen despairs, goes mad, and kills her child, it is clear that the culprit is actually her social environment, and her father's last speech, in which he exclaims, "the whole world is growing too narrow for me" prefigures a similar statement by Meister Anton at the end of Hebbel's *Maria Magdalena* (1844). Still, *The Childmurderess* does not yet present a completely determined world, and often it seems as if the problems it treats are less a matter of the rigidity of the old norms than simply the failure of Evchen's parents to apply them properly. Gröningseck's betrayal by his fellow officer Hasenpoth may represent Wagner's realization that, despite the progressive attitude of one aristocrat, society is not yet ready to overlook the barriers between classes. Goethe later maintained that Wagner stole the idea for a child-murder drama from him, and there are several similiarities between *The Childmurderess* and *Faust*. But child murder, a widely discussed topic in the eighteenth century, was already a frequent subject of popular fiction, and all the major Sturm und Drang writers—Klinger, Wagner, Goethe, Friedrich "Maler" Müller (1749–1825), Schiller, and Lenz—dealt with the theme.

Friedrich Maximilian Klinger (1752–1831), the son of a town constable, was born in Frankfurt and studied law in Giessen with the financial support of Goethe's family. After spending a short time in Weimar followed by a year and a half with the Seyler troupe, he fought as an officer on the side of Austria in the War of the Bavarian Succession (1778–79). In 1780 he moved to Russia, where he had a distinguished career as an officer, and where he continued to write, though in a restrained, classical style. Besides *Storm and Stress,* his early plays include *Otto* (1775), *Das leidende Weib* (The suffering wife, 1775), *Die Zwillinge* (The twin brothers, 1776), *Die neue Arria* (The modern Arria, 1776), and *Simsone Grisaldo* (1776).

Storm and Stress by no means provides the realistic depiction of eighteenth-century German society that we find in Lenz and Wagner; instead, we are in a vaguely rendered revolutionary America. Evident is the superficial influence of Shakespeare: the feud between the two houses derives from *Romeo and Juliet,* while the names Berkley, Bushy, and La Feu are borrowed from *Richard II* and *All's Well That Ends Well.* In this play, wrote Klinger, "the deepest tragic emotion continually alternates with laughter and joviality," and in fact, *Storm and Stress* weaves scenes of anger and urgency with scenes of conciliation, parody, and general levity—such as in act 3, scene 8, when Caroline tells Wild, who is courting her from a tree, that she is afraid that the branch will break. La Feu is parodied for his pastoral sentimentality, Blasius for his boredom and melancholy. Least parodied, perhaps, is Caroline, who along with the "primitive" Young Moor, was a favorite of the play's first audiences. "The rolling, threatening eyes, the fixedness, the unshakableness, the resolution" that Berkley admires in his son is also what Klinger himself, who found his home in the military, seemed to value. Like so many plays of the tradition, *Storm and Stress* ends with a reconciliation as it is suddenly revealed that the feud between the families of Bushy and Berkley was incited by an unnamed third party who deliberately turned them against each other.

Friedrich Schiller (1759–1805) was born in Marbach and educated at duke Karl Eugen of Württemberg's Karlschule in Stuttgart, where he had a brief career as a regimental surgeon. Most of the work on *The Robbers* was done in 1779 and 1780, and after leaving his regiment without permission to see its 1782 premiere, Schiller was forbidden by the duke to write more plays. He deserted and continued writing, living in various cities before settling in Jena as a professor of history in 1788–89. After his Sturm und Drang plays *The Robbers* and *Intrigue and Love* (*Kabale und Liebe*, 1783), he went on to become a major poet and to write his famous essays and dramas of Weimar classicism.

The Robbers depicts a fraternal rivalry, a theme already treated by Johann Anton Leisewitz (1752–1806) in *Julius von Tarent* (1776) and in Klinger's *Die Zwillinge*. Franz Moor, angry at his second-born status in a system honoring the right of primogeniture, acts entirely without regard to social or moral considerations, and his views on God in act 5 represent the most blasphemous attack on religion in German literature up to that time. But the play provides more than a contrast of two brothers. Like Klinger's *Storm and Stress*, *The Robbers* hinges on a misunderstanding: Karl, deceived by Franz into believing that his father's love has turned to hate, becomes a disillusioned, self-righteous *Kraftmensch*. Audiences could measure the depth of Karl's disappointment—perhaps even his underlying virtue—by the extent of his violence. When the misunderstanding is cleared up, Karl regrets his crimes and gives himself up to the civil authorities. The disapproval of Goethe, Wieland, and the majority of German critics notwithstanding, *The Robbers* is a masterful work of social dynamics that takes deep German patterns of sensibility into account: behind Karl's urge for autonomy lurks the desire for a community of values. As in so much Sturm und Drang drama, the larger need expressed in this literature is for a community that reflects back flatteringly on individuals and promises them more of a sense of identity, import, and momentum than was currently available. *The Robbers* would go on to have a wide influence, inspiring writers from Wordsworth and Coleridge to Nietzsche and Dostoevsky.

A. C. L.

Sturm und Drang

THE SOLDIERS

A Comedy

Jakob Michael Reinhold Lenz

CHARACTERS

WESENER, *a jeweler in Lille*
MADAME WESENER, *his wife*
MARIE   ⎫
            ⎬ *their daughters*
CHARLOTTE ⎭
STOLZIUS, *cloth merchant in Armentières*
His MOTHER
DESPORTES, *a nobleman from Hainaut in French service*
COUNT VON SPANNHEIM, *his colonel*
CAPTAIN PIRZEL
EISENHARDT, *regimental chaplain*
MAJOR HAUDY
LIEUTENANT RAMMLER
LIEUTENANT MARY
COUNTESS DE LA ROCHE
COUNT DE LA ROCHE, *her son*
MADAME BISCHOF
Her COUSIN, *and others*

The setting is Flanders.

Act One

Scene 1

Lille. Marie, Charlotte.

MARIE *(with her chin in her hand, writing a letter):* Sister, do you know how to spell "Madame"? *M-a-d: Mad; d-a-m: dam; m-e: me.*

CHARLOTTE *(sitting and spinning):* That's right.

MARIE: Listen, I'll read it to you, and you tell me if it's all right: "Dear Madame. We've arrived safe back in Lille, thank goodness." Is this right? *Arriviert. A-r: ar; r-y-v: viert. Arriviert.*

CHARLOTTE: That's right.

MARIE: "We cannot think how we have merited the kindness with which you overwhelmed us; wish, however, we were so situated . . ." Is that correct?

CHARLOTTE: Read on to the end of the sentence, can't you?

MARIE: "As to repay your esteemed courtesy and favors, but seeing as it isn't in our power, can only crave continuation of same."

CHARLOTTE: *We* can only crave.

MARIE: Oh, leave me alone, do! Why must you keep interrupting?

CHARLOTTE: *We* can only crave continuation of same.

MARIE: Oh, why do you go on so? Papa writes like that too, you know. *(folds the letter and prepares to seal it)*

CHARLOTTE: Well, finish reading, then.

MARIE: The rest is none of your business. You always want to make out you're smarter than Papa: only the other day Papa said it wasn't polite to keep writing "we" and "I" and all that. *(seals the letter)* Here, Steffen, *(gives the servant money)* take this letter to the post office.

CHARLOTTE: It's just that you didn't want to read me the last bit; I expect you've put something nice in it for Monsieur Stolzius.

MARIE: That's none of your business.

CHARLOTTE: Well, I never! Do you think I'm jealous, then? I could have written just as well as you, but I didn't want to take away from you the pleasure of showing off your fine hand.

MARIE: Listen, Lottie, stop teasing me about Stolzius, or else I'll go straight down and complain to Papa.

CHARLOTTE: Well, just think of that! What do I care: he knows anyway that you're in love with him, and you can't bear anyone else even to mention his name.

MARIE: Lottie! *(bursts into tears and runs downstairs)*

Scene 2

Armentières. STOLZIUS *and his* MOTHER

STOLZIUS *(with a bandage round his head):* I'm not well, Mother.

MOTHER *(stands for a moment looking at him):* Well, I do believe you've got that wretched girl stuck in your head, that's why it hurts so much. You haven't had a cheerful moment since she went away.

STOLZIUS: Seriously, Mother, there's something not right with me.

MOTHER: Well, if you speak nicely to me, perhaps I can cheer you up a little. *(takes a letter from her pocket)*

STOLZIUS *(jumps to his feet):* She's written to you . . .!

MOTHER: Here, you can read it. *(Stolzius snatches the letter from her hand and pores over it)* But listen, the Colonel wants that cloth measured out for the regiments.

STOLZIUS: Let me answer the letter, Mother.

MOTHER: I'm talking about the cloth, dummy, that the Colonel ordered for the regiments. Come along. . . .

Scene 3

Lille. Marie, Desportes.

DESPORTES: What are you doing there, divine Mademoiselle?

MARIE *(has a pile of blank paper in front of her on which she is scribbling, quickly puts her pen behind her ear):* Oh, nothing, nothing, sir. *(smiling)* I'm far too fond of writing.

DESPORTES: If only I were so happy as to see one of your letters, even a single line from your fair hand.

MARIE: Oh, I beg your pardon. I don't have a fair hand, I'm quite ashamed to show you anything I've written.

DESPORTES: Anything that comes from such a hand is bound to be fair.

MARIE: Oh, Baron, pray stop. I know that these are simply empty compliments.

DESPORTES *(kneeling down):* I swear to you, never in all my life have I beheld a being more perfect than you, mademoiselle.

MARIE *(knitting, with her eyes fixed on her work):* My mother told me, you know. . . . Look how two-faced you are.

DESPORTES: Two-faced! Me? Can you believe that of me, divine Mademoiselle? Is it two-faced to sneak away from my regiment, having sold my half-year's furlough, and risk being thrown into jail when I return, if they find out I'm not with my parents, as I said I was? Is that two-faced? Just to have the bliss of seeing you, my paragon!

MARIE *(looking down at her work again):* But Mother has often told me I'm not properly grown up yet, I'm at an age when girls are neither pretty nor homely.

WESENER *(enters):* Well, well, look who's here! Your humble servant, Baron. How come we have the honor of your presence once again? *(embraces him)*

DESPORTES: I'm only here for a week or two to visit a relative of mine who has come up from Brussels.

WESENER: I'm sorry I wasn't at home. My little Marie will have bored you, I fear. How are your esteemed parents; I hope they received the snuffboxes?

DESPORTES: No doubt. I haven't been home. I expect we have another account to settle, little father?

WESENER: Oh, time enough for that; it isn't the first time, after all. Your lady mother didn't come down for our carnival last winter.

DESPORTES: She is not too well. Were there many dances?

WESENER: So-so. A fair number. You know I never go to any, and my daughters don't either.

DESPORTES: But is it fair, Wesener, to deny your daughters all such pleasures? Is it healthy to do that?

WESENER: Oh, if they work hard they'll be healthy enough. There's nothing the matter with my little Marie, thank heaven, and she always has fine pink cheeks.

MARIE: Yes, Papa won't hear different, and sometimes I get such a tight feeling sitting indoors that I don't know what to do with myself. I feel so on edge.

DESPORTES: You see, you allow your daughter no entertainment, and that will turn her melancholic one of these days.

WESENER: Nonsense, she has entertainment enough with her friends; when the lot of them get together you can't hear yourself speak.

DESPORTES: Allow me the honor of escorting your daughter to the theater some time. They're putting on a new piece today.

MARIE: Oh, Papa!

WESENER: No! No, definitely not, Baron! I trust you will not take it amiss, but my daughter is not in the habit of going to the play: it would only cause talk among the neighbors—and with a young gentleman from the military, at that!

DESPORTES: You can see I'm in civilian dress. Who will recognize me?

WESENER: *Tant pis!** Once for all, it's not a proper thing with any young gentleman, whoever he may be. She's not even been confirmed yet, and she should go to the theater and act the grand lady! In short, Baron, I'll not allow it.

MARIE: But, Papa, if nobody knows the Baron by sight.

WESENER *(softly):* Hold your tongue, can't you? Nobody knows him? So much the worse if nobody knows him. Your pardon, Baron, gladly as I'd do you the favor . . . in all other matters I am at your service.

DESPORTES: By the way, my dear Wesener, won't you show me some of your brooches, please?

WESENER: At once! *(exit)*

DESPORTES: Shall I tell you something, my angel, my divine Marie? We'll play a trick on your father. We can't do it today, but the day after tomorrow they're putting on a splendid piece, *La chercheuse d'esprit,* and the curtain raiser is *Le déserteur.*† Haven't you a good friend somewhere here?

MARIE: Frau Weyher.

DESPORTES: Where does she live?

---

*So much the worse!

†*La chercheuse d'esprit* (The seeker of wit) is a comic opera by Charles-Simon Favart (1710–92), first performed in 1741. *Le déserteur* (The deserter) is probably the drama by Louis-Sebastien Mercier (1740–1814), first performed in 1770.

MARIE: Right on the corner by the fountain.

DESPORTES: I'll go there, and you come too, and then we'll go off to the play together. (Wesener *returns with a large cardboard box full of brooches.* Marie *smiles and makes a sign to* Desportes)

WESENER: Here you are: all different prices. This one's 100 livres, this one's 50, and this one's 150.

DESPORTES (*inspects one after the other and shows the box to* Marie): Which would you recommend? (Marie *smiles, and as soon as her father is engrossed in unpacking the brooches, she makes signs to* Desportes)

WESENER: Look, this one sparkles splendidly, upon my word.

DESPORTES: You're right. (*holds it up beside* Marie's *head*) Look at that against such lovely brown hair, what a splendid effect! Listen, Monsieur Wesener, it suits your daughter so well, won't you be so kind as to let her keep it?

WESENER (*hands back the brooch with a smile*): Pardon me, Baron, but that would never do. . . . My daughter has never in her life accepted presents from gentlemen.

MARIE: (*her eyes fixed on her knitting*): I couldn't have worn it anyway; it's much too big for my hairstyle.

DESPORTES: Then I'll send it to my mother. (*wraps up the brooch carefully*)

WESENER (*wrapping up the remaining brooches, mutters something to* Marie): You're just a trinket yourself! You'll never wear a thing like that on your head, that's no fashion for the likes of you. (*She says nothing and goes on with her knitting*)

DESPORTES: I'll take my leave then, Monsieur Wesener! We'll settle up before I go.

WESENER: Time enough for that, Baron, time enough for that. Be so kind as to honor us with another visit sometime.

DESPORTES: By your leave. Farewell, Mademoiselle Marie! (*exit*)

MARIE: Well I never, Papa, how you do go on!

WESENER: I've gone and done something not to your liking again, eh? What do you know of the world, you silly chick?

MARIE: He's a real good-hearted gentleman, the Baron.

WESENER: Because he pays you a few compliments and all that sort of thing. One's as bad as the next, and don't you try to tell me anything about the young gentry of the military. They're in and out of all the inns and coffeehouses telling each other tales, and before you know where you are, a poor girl is the talk of the town.

Yes, and Mademoiselle This or Mademoiselle That is no better
than she ought to be, and I know of this one and that one, and
she'd like to have him where she wants him. . . .

MARIE: Papa! *(begins to weep)* You're always so coarse!

WESENER *(pats* Marie's *cheek):* You mustn't mind me. You're my
only joy, you little fool, that's why I worry about you.

MARIE: If only you'd let me worry about myself. After all, I'm not a
child any more.

Scene 4

Armentières. Count von Spannheim (the Colonel) *at table with his
chaplain,* Eisenhardt; *the* Colonel's *cousin, a* Young Count; *the*
Young Count's tutor; Major Haudy; Mary; *and other officers.*

YOUNG COUNT: Do you think we shall have a good troupe of actors
here again soon?

HAUDY: It would be highly desirable, especially for our younger
gentlemen. They say Godeau* meant to come to Armentières.

TUTOR: Indeed, it can't be denied, the stage is a well-nigh indispens-
able amenity for a garrison, *c'est-à-dire*† a stage on which good
taste prevails, as for example the French stage.

EISENHARDT: I cannot see the benefit of it.

COLONEL: You're saying that, Chaplain, simply because you have
those two white tabs there under your chin. I know you really
think otherwise in your heart of hearts.

EISENHARDT: I beg your pardon, Colonel. I've never been a hypocrite, and if that were a necessary vice for our calling, then I
imagine army chaplains at least would be exempt from it, since
they have to do with the more sensible sort of men. I am fond of
the theater myself and I like to go and watch a good play, but I do
not for that reason believe it is such a beneficial institution for the
officer corps.

HAUDY: For God's sake, parson or preacher or whatever you call
yourself, just you tell me what excesses are not forestalled or
prevented by the theater. After all, officers must have some pas-
time or other.

---

*There does not seem to be an historical actor or theater manager named Godeau.
†That is to say.

EISENHARDT: No need to be so heated, Major! Say, rather, what excesses have not been instigated among officers by the theater.

HAUDY: Nothing but talk and, what's more, beside the point. In short, sir, *(plants both elbows on the table and leans forward)* I tell you here and now, a single play—even supposing it were the worst sort of farce—promotes more benefit, not only among officers but in the nation as a whole, than all the sermons that you and your like have ever preached or are ever likely to preach.

COLONEL *(angrily):* Major!

EISENHARDT: If I labored under some prejudice in favor of my office, Major, I would lose my temper. But as it is, let us leave all that aside, for I do not reckon you or many of these gentlemen capable of judging aright the proper function of our office as long as you live. Let us confine ourselves to the theater and the amazing benefits it is alleged to have for the gentlemen of the corps. Pray, answer me one question: what do these gentlemen learn from the theater?

MARY: Oh, Lord, do we always have to be learning something? We enjoy ourselves, isn't that enough?

EISENHARDT: Would to God that you *did* only enjoy yourselves, that you *didn't* learn anything! But in fact you emulate what is represented on the stage and inflict calamity and blight upon our families.

COLONEL: My dear Chaplain, your zeal is praiseworthy, but it smacks of the cassock, if you don't mind my saying so. What family has ever been ruined by an officer? No doubt a wench or two that deserve no better are put in the family way.

HAUDY: A whore will always turn out a whore, no matter whose hands she falls into; if not a soldier's whore, then a preacher's whore.

EISENHARDT: It vexes me, Major, that you keep on dragging preachers into the argument because it prevents me from answering you in a really forthright way. You might imagine something of personal rancor in what I say, and if I grow heated it's due to the subject of our discourse, not to your sneers and insults concerning my office. That can neither gain nor lose by all your witty conceits.

HAUDY: Talk, talk, talk; blather away! That's what we're here for, who's stopping you?

EISENHARDT: What you were saying a moment ago is an idea

worthy of the soul of a Nero or an Oglei-Oglu*—which even in such a context might have aroused horror when it was first stated. A whore will always turn out a whore! Are you so intimately acquainted with the opposite sex?

HAUDY: You're not the man to instruct me, sir.

EISENHARDT: You owe your acquaintance with them to the master-pieces of your art, perhaps, but permit me to inform you, a whore will never turn out a whore unless someone makes her a whore. The urge is in all human creatures, but every female knows that she owes her entire future happiness to this urge, and will she sacrifice that if she is not tricked into it?

HAUDY: Am I talking about respectable girls?

EISENHARDT: It is precisely the respectable girls who are bound to tremble at your plays. That's where you acquire the art of destroy-ing their respectability.

MARY: Who would harbor such evil thoughts!

HAUDY: You're a damned uncivil tongue when you speak of officers, sir. God damn it, if anyone else were to talk to me like that . . .! Do you think, sir, we cease to be gentlemen the moment we enter the service?

EISENHARDT: I wish you much joy of your convictions. But as long as I observe kept mistresses and the ruined daughters of respect-able families, then I cannot retract my opinion.

HAUDY: That deserves a bop on the nose!

EISENHARDT *(stands up):* Sir, I, too, bear a sword!†

COLONEL: Major, please! Pastor Eisenhardt is not at fault, what do you expect of him? And the first man who offends him . . . be seated, Chaplain, he shall give you satisfaction. *(Exit* Haudy) But you go too far, Pastor Eisenhardt, all the same. There's not an officer who doesn't know full well what honor requires of him.

EISENHARDT: If he has time enough to think of it. But in our latest plays isn't it the case that the most dastardly crimes against the hallowed rights of fathers and families are represented in such glowing colors, the most venomous deeds rendered so innocuous that a villain stands before us as if he'd come straight down from heaven? Is that not calculated to encourage, is it not calculated to stifle every scruple conscience may have assimilated from the parental home? Deceiving a watchful father, instructing an inno-

*The name is unclear.
†Eisenhardt is reminding Haudy that, as regimental chaplain, he, too, is an officer.

cent maiden in the practice of the vices—these are the tasks accomplished and rewarded on the stage.

HAUDY *(in the entrance hall with other officers, as the door opens momentarily)*: That confounded preacher. . . .

COLONEL: Let's be off to the coffeehouse, Chaplain, you still owe me my revenge at chess . . . And, Adjutant, would you request Major Haudy not to leave his quarters today. Tell him I shall return his sword to him personally tomorrow.

Scene 5

Lille. Wesener *sitting at supper with* Madame Wesener *and* Charlotte, *their elder daughter.* Marie *enters, dressed in all her finery.*

MARIE *(throws her arms round her father's neck)*: Oh, Papa, Papa!

WESENER *(with his mouth full)*: What is it, what's the matter with you?

MARIE: I cannot keep it secret from you: I've been to the play. What a thing it is, to be sure!

(Wesener *pushes his chair back from the table and turns away his face)*

MARIE: If only you'd seen what I've seen, you wouldn't be angry, Papa. *(sits on his lap)* Dear Papa, such goings-on, it was, I shan't be able to sleep all night, it was such fun! The Baron *is* kind!

WESENER: What? It was the Baron that took you to the play?

MARIE *(somewhat timidly)*: Yes, Papa, dear Papa!

WESENER *(shoves her off his lap)*: Away with you, you tramp! Do you mean to become the Baron's mistress?

MARIE *(with her face half-turned away, half-weeping)*: I was at Madame Weyher's . . . and we were standing at the door . . . *(stammering)* and then he spoke to us.

WESENER: Yes, go on lie! Lie the Devil's ear off! Out of my sight, you godless creature!

CHARLOTTE: I could have told Papa it would come to this. They've been carrying on together secretly all the time, the Baron and her.

MARIE *(weeping)*: Hold your tongue, can't you!

CHARLOTTE: Well, I never! Not for you, I won't! Tries to order people about and carries on the way she does. . . .

MARIE: You just watch yourself, you and that young Monsieur Heidevogel of yours. If I behaved half as bad as you. . . .

WESENER: Will you be quiet, both of you! Go to your room this instant, you shan't have any supper, you wicked creature! *(Exit Marie)* And you be quiet, too, I don't suppose you're any angel either. Do you think no one sees why Monsieur Heidevogel comes here so often?

CHARLOTTE: It's all Marie's fault. *(weeps)* The godforsaken strumpet, she just wants to get decent girls into trouble because that's the way her own mind works.

WESENER *(very loudly)*: Hold your tongue! Marie is far too high-minded to talk about you like that, but you're jealous of your own sister. Seeing you haven't her looks you might at least have a more respectable way of thinking. Shame on you! *(to the maid)* Take it away, I can't eat any more. *(pushes away his plate and napkin, throws himself into an armchair, and sits plunged in thought)*

Scene 6

Marie's *bedroom.* Marie *is sitting on her bed, has the brooch in her hand, and is looking at herself in a mirror, lost in thought. Her father comes in, she gives a start and tries to hide the brooch.*

MARIE: Oh, Lord!

WESENER: Now then, don't be such a child. *(strides up and down the room a couple of times, then sits down beside* Marie*)* Listen, Marie! You know I'm fond of you; be frank with me; it will not be to your disadvantage. Tell me, has the Baron said anything to you about love?

MARIE *(with an air of mystery)*: Papa! He's in love with me, he really is. Just look: he gave me this brooch.

WESENER: What the dickens! Damn it all! *(takes the brooch from her)* Didn't I tell you not to. . . .

MARIE: But, Papa, I can't be so rude and refuse him. I can tell you, he carried on like a madman when I said I wouldn't take it. *(goes over to the cabinet)* Here are some verses he wrote about me. *(gives him a piece of paper)*

WESENER *(reading aloud)*:
Sublimest object of my chastest passion soaring,

I cannot cease from loving thee, adoring
With never-dying faithfulness imbued
This fairest orb of day with ev'ry morn renewed.
"This fairest orb of day"—ha, ha, ha!

MARIE: Wait, I'll show you something else. He gave me a little heart, too, set with stones in a ring. *(goes back to the cabinet and takes out the ring. Her father glances at it carelessly)*

WESENER *(reads again)*: "Sublimest object of my chastest passion soaring." His intentions are honorable, I can see that. But listen, Marie, mark what I say. You mustn't accept any more presents from him. I don't like him giving you all these presents.

MARIE: It's his kind heart, Papa.

WESENER: And give me that brooch. I'll give it back to him. Leave it to me, I know what's good for you. I've lived longer in this world than you have, my girl, and you can go to the theater with him again, but take Madame Weyher with you and don't let on that I know about it. Tell him he must keep it secret and that I would be very angry if I knew. But for heaven's sake, girl, take no more presents from him.

MARIE: I know my papa wouldn't give me bad advice. *(kisses his hand)* You'll see, I'll follow your advice to the letter. And I'll tell you everything, you can depend on it.

WESENER: Well, all right, then. *(kisses her)* You might end up a real lady yet, you silly child. You never know your luck.

MARIE *(in a subdued tone)*: But Papa—what will poor Stolzius say?

WESENER: You mustn't scare off Stolzius right away, d'you hear? Now, I'll tell you how to word your letter to him. In the meantime sleep well, little monkey.

MARIE *(kisses his hand)*: Good night, Pappushka! *(when her father has gone she sighs deeply and goes to the window, unlacing her bodice)* My heart is so heavy. I do believe we shall have thunder tonight. If the lightning were to strike. . . . *(casts her eyes up to heaven, places her hands on her breast)* Dear God, what have I done wrong, then? Stolzius . . . I love you still . . . but if I can make my fortune . . . and Papa himself advises me to . . . *(pulls the curtain to)* If it strikes, then it strikes: I'd not be sorry to die. *(blows out the lamp)*

Act 2

Scene 1

Armentières. Haudy *and* Stolzius *walking by the River Lys.*

HAUDY: You mustn't let yourself be bullied right from the start, my
dear friend! I know Desportes; he's a scoundrel who's only out to
enjoy himself. But that doesn't necessarily mean he's out to lure
away your fiancée.

STOLZIUS: But the gossip, Major! The town is full of it and all the
countryside as well for miles around. I could jump into the river
this minute just to think of it!

HAUDY *(takes his arm):* You mustn't take it so much to heart. The
Devil knows, everybody has to put up with gossip! I'm your best
friend, you can be sure of that, and I'd certainly tell you if there
was any danger. But there is none, you're just imagining it. Make
sure, though, that the wedding can take place this winter, while
we're still in garrison here, and if Desportes causes you the
slightest trouble, I'll have his blood, I promise you. Meanwhile,
take no notice of the gossip; you must know that the most respectable girls are the most talked about; it's natural that the young
fools who haven't had their way with them should try to get their
own back.

Scene 2

Coffeehouse. Eisenhardt *and* Pirzel *on a sofa in the foreground,
drinking coffee. In the background a group of officers chatting and
laughing.*

EISENHARDT *(to* PIRZEL*):* It's laughable the way people swarm
round that poor Stolzius like flies round a honeypot. One plucks

at him here, another nudges him there, this one goes walking with him, that one takes him into his cabriolet, another plays billiards with him: like bloodhounds on the scent! And how remarkably his cloth trade has prospered since it became known that he's to marry the good-looking young lady who passed through here not long ago.

PIRZEL *(seizes* Eisenhardt's *hand, vehemently):* Why is that, Pastor? Because people don't think! *(Strikes a highly picturesque pose, half-turned toward the group in the background.)* A perfect Being exists. Either I can insult this perfect Being—or else I cannot insult Him.

ONE OF THE GROUP *(turning round):* Off again, is he?

PIRZEL *(eagerly):* If I can insult Him, *(turns to the group)* then He would cease to be the most perfect Being.

ANOTHER OF THE GROUP: Yes, indeed, Pirzel, you're absolutely right, absolutely right.

PIRZEL *(turns quickly to* Eisenhardt): If I cannot insult Him. . . . *(Seizes his hand and stands quite motionless in deep thought)*

TWO OR THREE OF THE GROUP: Hang it all, Pirzel, are you speaking to us?

PIRZEL *(turns solemnly toward them):* My dear comrades, you are venerable creations of God, hence I cannot but respect you and venerate you; I, too, am God's creation, so you must hold me equally in respect.

ONE OF THE GROUP: If you take our advice, you'll do just that!

PIRZEL *(turns again to the chaplain):* Now. . . .

EISENHARDT: Captain, I am entirely of your opinion on every point. Only the question was, how can we get it into people's heads that they should leave poor Stolzius in peace and not cast jealousy and suspicion into two hearts that otherwise might have rendered each other eternally happy.

PIRZEL *(who has meanwhile sat down, jumps up again hastily):* As I had the honor and pleasure of telling you, Chaplain, that's because people simply don't think. Think, think what man is— that's what I say. *(seizes his hand)* Look, that's your hand, but what is it, in fact? Skin, bones, clay! *(taps his pulse)* There, there, that's where it is—this is just the sheath, the blade's in there, in the blood, in the blood. . . . *(looks round suddenly because of the commotion caused by* Haudy, *who enters shouting at the top of his voice)*

HAUDY: I've got him, boys! He's as mild as mother's milk! *(roars at the top of his voice)* Madame Roux! Get some glasses rinsed and brew us a good punch! He'll be here any moment. Do me a favor and treat the fellow courteously.

EISENHARDT *(leans forward)*: Who, Major, if I may ask?

HAUDY *(without looking at him)*: Nothing: a good friend of mine. *(The whole company throngs around* Haudy)

AN OFFICER: Have you quizzed him? Will the wedding be soon?

HAUDY: You must let me handle this, fellows, otherwise you'll ruin my pitch. He trusts me, I tell you, like the prophet Daniel, and if any of you puts his oar in, then the whole thing's screwed up. He's jealous enough as it is, poor soul; Desportes has given him a cruel lot to think about, and it took me all my time to stop him jumping into the river. My dodge is to make him trust the woman; he must know her and realize she's not one of the impregnable kind. That's just to let you know, so you don't put the man off.

RAMMLER: What are you talking about! I know him better than you do, he's got a pretty sharp nose, believe you me!

HAUDY: And you've got an even sharper one, I can see.

RAMMLER: You think the way to get on his good side is to say flattering things about his fiancée. You're wrong: I know him better, it's just the opposite. He pretends to believe you, takes note of everything you say, and never lets on. But if we can make him suspicious of the woman, he'll think we're being open and aboveboard with him. . . .

HAUDY: You and your airy-fairy schemes! D'you want to make the fellow crazy? Don't you think he's got enough maggots in his head as it is? And if he leaves her in the lurch, or strings himself up— where are you then? A man's life is no bagatelle, is it, Chaplain?

EISENHARDT: I want no part in your council of war.

HAUDY: But you must admit I'm right.

PIRZEL: My worthy brothers and comrades, do no man wrong. A man's life is a legacy with which he is endowed. But no one has the right to dispose of a legacy bestowed on him by someone else. Our life is such a legacy. . . .

HAUDY *(seizes* Pirzel *by the hand)*: Yes, Pirzel, you're the finest fellow I know! *(sits down between* Pirzel *and* Eisenhardt) But the Jesuit here, *(embraces* Eisenhardt) he's itching to be cock of the walk himself. . . .

RAMMLER *(sits down on* Eisenhardt's *other side and whispers in his ear):* Chaplain, you'll see what a trick I'll play on Haudy. *(Stolzius enters.* Haudy *jumps up)*

HAUDY: Ah, my dear fellow, come along! I've ordered a good glass of punch for the two of us. That wind went through us like a knife. *(leads him to a table)*

STOLZIUS *(taking off his hat, to the others):* Gentlemen, you'll pardon my being so bold as to come to your coffeehouse; it was on the Major's insistence.

(They all take off their hats politely and bow. Rammler gets up and comes over to join Haudy *and* Stolzius*)*

RAMMLER: Your humble servant: we're signally honored!

STOLZIUS *(raises his hat once more, rather distantly, and sits down beside* HAUDY*):* There's such a bitter wind out there, I do believe we shall have snow.

HAUDY: I believe so, too. *(filling a pipe)* You do smoke, don't you, Monsieur Stolzius?

STOLZIUS: A little.

RAMMLER: I can't think what's happened to our punch, Haudy. *(stands up)* What can that confounded Roux woman be doing all this time.

HAUDY: Mind your own business! *(shouts at the top of his voice)* Madame Roux! Bring some candles! And our punch—where is it?

STOLZIUS: Oh, Major, I should be heartily sorry to cause you any inconvenience.

HAUDY: Not a bit of it, dear friend. *(offers him the pipe)* Truly, that breeze off the Lys does one no good at all!

RAMMLER *(sits down at their table):* Have you had any word from Lille lately? How is your fiancée? *(Haudy glares at him;* Rammler *remains seated with a bland smile on his face)*

STOLZIUS *(in embarrassment):* I . . . humbly beg your pardon, sir . . . I know nothing of a fiancée, I haven't one.

RAMMLER: Mademoiselle Wesener from Lille, is she not your intended? Desportes wrote and told me you were betrothed.

STOLZIUS: Then Monsieur Desportes must know more of the matter than I do.

HAUDY *(smoking):* Rammler is never done jabbering: he's no idea what he's talking about or what he's after.

ONE OF THE GROUP: I assure you, Monsieur Stolzius, Desportes is a man of honor.

STOLZIUS: I never doubted it in the least.

HAUDY: A lot you people know about Desportes! If anyone knows him, then it's me. His mother put him under my wing when he joined the regiment, and he's never yet done anything without consulting me. But I assure you, Monsieur Stolzius, Desportes is a man of feeling and religion.

RAMMLER: We were schoolmates together. Never seen a man in my life who was so shy with women.

HAUDY: That's true, he's right there. Desportes is incapable of uttering a single word the moment a female gives him an encouraging look.

RAMMLER (*adopting a studied air of guilelessness*): I do believe, in fact—if I'm not mistaken—yes, it's true, he still writes to her. . . . On the very day of his departure I read a letter he had written to a young lady in Brussels, a girl he was quite astonishingly infatuated with. He will probably marry her quite soon, I should think.

ONE OF THE GROUP: The only thing I can't make out is what he's doing in Lille all this time.

HAUDY: God damn it! What's happened to our punch? Madame Roux!

RAMMLER: In Lille! Oh, I'm the only one who can explain that, for I'm privy to all his secrets. But it's not something I care to say in public.

HAUDY (*irritably*): Spit it out, you fool! What are you trying to hide it for?

RAMMLER (*laughing*): I can only say so much: he's waiting for a certain person there he means to ride off with secretly.

STOLZIUS (*stands up and lays down the pipe*): Gentlemen, I beg to take my leave of you.

HAUDY (*startled*): What's this? Where are you off to, my dear friend? We shall have our punch any minute now.

STOLZIUS: Please do not be offended, but something has just come over me all of a sudden.

HAUDY: But what? The punch will do you good, I assure you.

STOLZIUS: I do not feel well, my dear Major. You will excuse me . . . permit me . . . but I cannot stay here a moment longer, or else I shall faint. . . .

HAUDY: It's the Rhine air*—or was the tobacco too strong?

---

*This oversight, in which Lenz mentions the Rhine air, underscores the fact that the plot originated in his Strasbourg experiences.

STOLZIUS: Good-bye! *(exit, swaying on his feet)*

HAUDY: That's done it! You asses!

RAMMLER: Ha, ha, ha! *(thinks for a moment, striding about the room)* You stupid devils, didn't you see I fixed it all on purpose? What did I tell you, Chaplain?

EISENHARDT: Leave me out of this sport, I beg of you!

HAUDY: You scheming cockatoo! I'll wring your neck!

RAMMLER: And I'll smash your arms and legs and chuck them out of the window! *(struts about in melodramatic fashion)* You don't know what feints I've still got up my sleeve.

HAUDY: Yes, you're full of feints, the way an old sheepskin's full of lice. You make me sick with your scheming!

RAMMLER: And I'll parry. I'm more than a match for the whole bunch of you here when it comes to Stolzius, if I once put my mind to it.

HAUDY: Listen, Rammler! You've got more wit than is good for you; you're too clever by half. You're like a bottle that's filled too full: when you turn it upside down, not a single drop comes out because they're all jammed together. Get away with you: when I have a wife I'll give you leave to bed with her—if you can talk her into it.

RAMMLER *(striding rapidly up and down):* You'll see, the lot of you, what I make of that Stolzius! *(exit)*

HAUDY: The fellow gives me a bellyache with his fool ideas. All he can do is wreck other people's plans.

ONE OF THE GROUP: That's true. He has his finger in every pie.

MARY: He's always got his head stuffed with plots and crafty schemes; he thinks other people are as incapable of living without such things as he is. Not long ago I happened to ask Reitz privately whether he wouldn't lend me his spurs for the following day. If he didn't chase me around for the rest of the day, begging me for God's sake to tell him what we meant to do! I believe there's a statesman gone to waste in him!

ANOTHER OFFICER: The other day I stopped in front of a house to read a letter in the shade. He jumped to the conclusion it was a love letter that had been thrown down to me and kept on prowling round the house until midnight. I thought I'd split my sides! There's an old Jew of sixty lives in the house, and Rammler had posted sentries all over the place to spy on me and give him a signal if I went in. I bribed one of the fellows, and he told me the whole thing for three livres. I thought I'd die laughing!

ALL: Ha, ha, ha! And he thought there was a pretty girl in the house!

MARY: Listen! If you want a good laugh, let's warn the Jew that there's someone prowling around with an eye on his ducats.

HAUDY: That's an idea! Come on, let's go right away. It will be a riot! And you, Mary, put it into his head that the most beautiful woman in all Armentières lives there and that Gilbert told you in confidence he was going to pay her a visit tonight.

Scene 3

Lille. Marie *in an armchair, weeping, a letter in her hand. Enter* Desportes.

DESPORTES: What's wrong, my golden Marie, what's the matter with you?

MARIE *(tries to hide the letter in her pocket):* Oh!

DESPORTES: For heaven's sake, what sort of letter is that to cause you such tears?

MARIE *(more composed):* Just look at what that fellow Stolzius has written: as if he had a right to scold me! *(weeps again)*

DESPORTES *(reads the letter silently):* The impertinent ass! But tell me, why do you correspond with such a cur!

MARIE *(dries her eyes):* I can only say, Baron, it's because he's asked for my hand, and I'm half-promised to him.

DESPORTES: Asked for your hand? How dare he! Wait, I'll give that ass an answer to his letter.

MARIE: Yes, my dear Baron! And you wouldn't believe what I have to put up with from father; he's never done telling me I oughn't to spurn my good fortune.

DESPORTES: Your good fortune? With a lout like that? What can you be thinking of, my dearest Marie—and what can your father be thinking of? I know the man and his circumstances, as it happens. To put it in a nutshell; you're not cut out to marry a commoner.

MARIE: No, Baron, nothing will come of all this! Those are simply vain hopes you're trying to beguile me with. Your family will never consent to it.

DESPORTES: That is my concern. Do you have pen and ink? I'll reply to the cur's letter, just you wait!

MARIE: No, I'll write myself. *(sits down at the table and arranges writing materials;* Desportes *comes and stands at her shoulder)*

DESPORTES: Then I'll dictate to you.

MARIE: No, you shan't. *(Writes)*

DESPORTES *(reading over her shoulder):* "Monsieur . . ." Bumpkin, put there. *(dips a pen in the inkwell, and makes as if to write)*

MARIE: *(covering the paper with her arms):* Baron!

(They begin to tease each other; as soon as she takes her arm away, he makes as if to write. After much laughter she smears his face with the pen. He runs over to the mirror to wipe the ink off, she goes on writing)

DESPORTES: I've still got my eye on you.

(He comes nearer, she threatens him with her pen, finally she puts the paper away in her pocket. He tries to stop her and they wrestle with each other. Marie *tickles* Desportes, *he begins to yell at the top of his voice and finally falls breathlessly into an armchair)*

WESENER *(enters):* Now, then, what's all this? We'll have people in from the street any moment, at this rate.

MARIE *(getting her breath back):* Papa, just imagine what kind of letter that ill-bred lout Stolzius has written to me. He calls me an unfaithful girl! Just think, as if we'd herded pigs together. But I'll give him the sort of answer he doesn't expect, the boor.

WESENER: Show me the letter! *(Enter Mademoiselle Zipfersaat.)* Oh, look who's here—Mademoiselle Zipfersaat! I'll read it downstairs in the shop.

MARIE *(curtsying mischievously all round* Mademoiselle Zipfersaat*):* Mademoiselle Zipfersaat, allow me to present a baron who is mortally enamored of you. Here, Baron, this is the young lady that we talked about so much and that you took such a mortal fancy to at the play the other day.

MADEMOISELLE ZIPFERSAAT: I don't know what's got into you, Marie!

MARIE *(dropping a deep curtsy):* Now you can declare your love!

(Marie runs off, banging the door behind her. Mademoiselle Zipfersaat *is embarrassed and goes over to the window.* Desportes, *having cast a contemptuous glance at her, keeps a lookout for* Marie, *who opens the door briefly every now and then. Eventually she puts her head round the door)*

MARIE *(mockingly):* Well, are you nearly finished?

*(Desportes *tries to stick his foot in the door,* Marie *chases him away*

with a large pin; he shouts and suddenly runs off to get at Marie *through a door on the other side of the stage.* Mademoiselle Zipfersaat *goes off in high dudgeon, while shouts, screams, and giggles come from the room next door.* Wesener's old mother *creeps into the room, spectacles on her nose, sits down in the window nook and begins to knit, singing—or rather screeching—in a hoarse old voice.)*

WESENER'S MOTHER:

A maiden young is like the dice
And lies as she is tumbled,
The little rose from Hennegau*
Goes soon to Our Lord's table.

(Counts the stitches)

Why smile you then so gay, my child,
A cross you soon must carry;
The little rose from Hennegau,
They say, is soon to marry.
Oh, child of mine, how sad am I,
While still your eyes are smiling,
For soon a thousand tears you'll cry,
That stain your cheeks beguiling.

(In the meantime the laughing and teasing continues in the next room. The old woman goes in to rebuke them)

---

*Hainaut, the greater part of which is now a province of Belgium.

Act 3

Scene 1

Armentières. Aaron's *house.* Rammler *enters with a number of heavily cloaked men, whom he posts at various points.*

RAMMLER *(to the last of his men):* If anyone goes in, then cough. I'll hide under the steps so I can creep up after him. *(Crawls into hiding under the steps)*

AARON *(looks out of the window):* Got, vot iss zis for a plotting going on before my very house?

(Mary, wrapped in an overcoat, comes down the lane, stops below Aaron's window and whistles softly)

AARON *(calls down to him sotto voce):* Iss it you, sir? *(Mary gives a signal)* I vill at once open ze door. *(Mary goes up the steps. Someone coughs softly.* Rammler *follows* Mary *on tiptoe without* Mary *looking round.* Aaron *opens the door, and* Rammler *slips in behind* Mary. *The scene changes to* Aaron's *bedroom. It is very dark.* Mary *and* Aaron *are whispering to each other.* Rammler *prowls around them, darting back every time they make a movement)*

MARY: He's in here somewhere.

AARON: Oi vai!

MARY: Keep quiet and he'll do you no harm; let him do what he wants with you, even if he ties you up. I'll be back in a minute with the two watchmen. He'll pay for it all right. Lie down on the bed.

AARON: But vot if he take my life, eh?

MARY: Don't worry, I'll be back in a moment. He can't be convicted unless he's caught in the act. The watchmen are downstairs all ready, I'll just go and fetch them in. Lie down. *(Goes out.* Aaron *lies down on the bed.* Rammler *creeps nearer to him)*

AARON *(his teeth chattering):* Adonai! Adonai!*

RAMMLER *(to himself):* I do believe it's a Jewess. *(aloud, trying to imitate* Mary's *voice)* Oh, my darling, how cold it is outside.

AARON *(more and more faintly):* Adonai!

RAMMLER: You know me, don't you? I'm not your husband, I'm Mary. *(takes off his boots and tunic)* I think we shall have snow, it's so cold.

*(*Mary *rushes in with a crowd of officers carrying lanterns; they burst into loud laughter.* Aaron *starts up in terror)*

HAUDY: Have you gone crazy, Rammler? What lewdness are you up to with the Jew?

RAMMLER *(stands as if petrified. After a while he draws his sword):* I'll make mincemeat of you, the whole damned lot of you! *(runs out in confusion. The others laugh even louder)*

AARON: Got knows, I been half-dead already! *(stands up. The officers rush out in pursuit of* Rammler. Aaron *follows them)*

Scene 2

Stolzius's house. He is sitting, a cloth around his head, at a table with a lighted lamp on it. He has a letter in his hand. His Mother is standing beside him.

MOTHER *(suddenly losing her temper):* Won't you get off to bed, you godless creature! What's the matter with you! You were far too good for that slut! What are you grieving for, why are you whining over that . . . soldier's whore!

STOLZIUS *(in a towering rage, getting up from the table):* Mother!

MOTHER: What else is she then? And you, too, hanging round such trollops!

STOLZIUS *(catches hold of both her hands):* Dear mother, don't malign her, she's innocent, that officer has turned her head! Look how she used to write to me. It's enough to drive me out of my mind! A good-hearted girl like that!

MOTHER *(stamps her foot):* A slut like that! Go to bed, I order you! What's going to come of all this, how will it all end? I'll show you, young man, that I'm your mother!

STOLZIUS *(striking his chest with clenched fist):* My little Marie!

---

*Adonai is Hebrew for Lord.

No, she's not my Marie anymore, she's not what she was! *(jumps up)* Leave me alone!

MOTHER *(weeping)*: Where are you off to, you godforsaken boy?

STOLZIUS: That fiend who corrupted her, I'll. . . . *(falls exhausted onto his chair, holding his hands)* Oh, you shall pay for this, you shall pay for this! *(coldly)* One day is just like another; what doesn't come to pass today will come to pass tomorrow, and what comes slowly still comes surely. What does it say in the song, Mother? If a little bird carried away a single grain of sand from a mountain every day, in the end it would carry off the whole mountain.

MOTHER: I believe you're delirious! *(feels his pulse)* Lie down, Karl, I beg you, for heaven's sake! I'll tuck you in, what will come of it all, God in heaven? You're all in a fever . . . and all for the sake of a strumpet like that. . . .

STOLZIUS: At last, at last . . . every day a tiny grain of sand, a year has ten, twenty, thirty, a hundred . . . *(Mother tries to lead him away)* Leave me alone, Mother, I'm quite all right.

MOTHER: Come along, come along! *(dragging him away)* Fool! I shan't leave you, believe me. *(exeunt)*

Scene 3

Lille. Mademoiselle Zipfersaat; *a maid from* Wesener's *house.*

MADEMOISELLE ZIPFERSAAT: She's at home, but won't see anyone? Well, I must say! Has she turned so proud?

MAID: She says she's busy, she's reading a book.

MADEMOISELLE ZIPFERSAAT: Tell her I've some news for her that she wouldn't miss for the world.

(Marie enters with a book in her hand)

MARIE *(offhandedly)*: Good morning, Mademoiselle Zipfersaat. Why didn't you sit down?

MADEMOISELLE ZIPFERSAAT: I only came to tell you that Baron Desportes has run away.

MARIE *(in great excitement)*: What's that you say?

MADEMOISELLE ZIPFERSAAT: You can believe me all right; he cleared out owing my cousin over seven hundred livres, and when they went into his room they found all his things gone and a note on the table saying they needn't bother to follow him, he had taken his discharge and was off to join the Austrians.

MARIE *(runs out sobbing and calls her father)*: Papa, Papa!

WESENER: What's the matter?

MARIE: Come up here quickly, dear Papa!

MADEMOISELLE ZIPFERSAAT: There, you see what these officers and gentlemen are like, I could have told you so all along.

WESENER *(enters)*: Well, what is it? . . . Your servant, Mademoiselle Zipfersaat.

MARIE: Papa, what shall I do? That Desportes has run away!

WESENER: Now, then, who's been telling you such fairy tales?

MARIE: He's seven hundred livres in debt to young Monsieur Zipfersaat, the silk merchant, and he left a note on the table saying he'll never come back to Flanders as long as he lives.

WESENER *(very angry)*: What sort of confounded evil gossip is this. . . . *(striking himself on the chest)* I'll go surety for that seven hundred livres, you understand, Mademoiselle Zipfersaat? And for as much again, if you want. I've done business with that family for over thirty years, but it's all the fault of those jealous good-for-nothings. . . .

MADEMOISELLE ZIPFERSAAT: My cousin will be delighted, Monsieur Wesener, if you take it upon yourself to save the Baron's good name.

WESENER: I'll go with you this moment. *(looks for his hat)* I'll stop their mouths: how dare they bring my house into disrepute! Understand?

MARIE: But Papa. . . . *(impatiently)* Oh, I wish I had never set eyes on him!

(Exeunt Wesener *and* Mademoiselle Zipfersaat*)*

MARIE *(throws herself into the armchair; after sitting plunged in thought for a moment she calls timidly)*: Lottie! Lottie!

(Enter Charlotte*)*

CHARLOTTE: Well, what do you want, calling me like that?

MARIE *(goes up to her)*: Lottikins! My dearest Lottikins! *(strokes her chin)*

CHARLOTTE: Heaven help us, what's all this about?

MARIE: You *are* my dearest, kindest Charlotte, aren't you?

CHARLOTTE: I suppose you want to borrow money from me again.

MARIE: I'll do whatever you want.

CHARLOTTE: Oh, come on! I'm not going to waste my time on you. *(makes as if to go out)*

MARIE *(stops her):* But listen . . . just a moment . . . can't you help me write a letter?

CHARLOTTE: I haven't time.

MARIE: Just a couple of lines. I'll let you have my beads that cost six livres.

CHARLOTTE: Who do you want to write to, then?

MARIE *(shamefacedly):* To Stolzius.

CHARLOTTE *(starts to laugh):* Is your conscience pricking you?

MARIE *(half-crying):* Don't. . . .

CHARLOTTE *(sits down at the table):* Well, what do you want me to write to him, then? You know I don't like writing.

MARIE: My hands are trembling so. . . . Write at the top—or all in one line, if you like: "My very dear friend."

CHARLOTTE: "My very dear friend . . ."

MARIE: "In your last letter you gave me the opportunity, as was only proper, since my good name had been called in question . . ."

CHARLOTTE: "Called in question . . ."

MARIE: "Nevertheless you mustn't look too closely at everything I say, but have regard to my heart, that . . ." Wait a moment, what shall I write now?

CHARLOTTE: How should I know?

MARIE: Tell me, what's the word I want?

CHARLOTTE: How should I know what you want to write to him?

MARIE: "That my heart and . . ." *(begins to weep and throws herself into the armchair)*

CHARLOTTE *(looks at her and laughs):* Well, what am I to write to him?

MARIE *(sobbing):* Write whatever you like.

CHARLOTTE *(writes and then reads aloud):* "That my heart is not as fickle as you may think." Is that all right?

MARIE *(jumps up and looks over her shoulder):* Yes, that's right, that's right! *(embracing* Charlotte.) Dear old Lottie!

CHARLOTTE: Watch out, let me finish writing!

(Marie *walks up and down once or twice; then suddenly she rushes up to* Charlotte, *snatches the paper from her, and tears it into fragments)*

CHARLOTTE *(furious):* What are you doing? You tramp! Just when I have my very best idea! That's just the sort of *canaille* you are!

MARIE: *Canaille vous même!* *

---

*Canaille: Riffraff, scoundrel; *canaille vous même:* riffraff yourself.

CHARLOTTE *(threatens* Marie *with the inkwell):* You . . . !

MARIE: You're just trying to upset me all the more when I'm unhappy enough as it is!

CHARLOTTE: You tramp! What did you want to tear it up for, just when I was writing so well?

MARIE *(heatedly):* Don't you swear at me!

CHARLOTTE *(half-crying also):* Why did you tear it up, then?

MARIE: Do you want me to tell him lies? *(begins to sob passionately and throws herself down, burying her face in a chair)*

(Wesener enters. Marie looks up and rushes to him, throwing her arms round his neck)

MARIE *(trembling):* Papa, dear papa! What's the news? For heaven's sake, tell me!

WESENER: Don't be so foolish, he's not vanished from the face of the earth. You do carry on so!

MARIE: But if he's gone. . . .

WESENER: If he's gone, he'll have to come back, that's all. I believe you've taken leave of your senses and you're trying to drive me crazy as well! I've known his family longer than just since yesterday; they won't want any scandal. Now then, send up to our attorney and see if he's at home. I'll have that credit I signed for Desportes certified, and also the copy of the *Promesse de Mariage,* and I'll send all the papers to his parents.

MARIE: Oh, Papa, dear papa! I'll run up myself this very minute and fetch him. *(rushes off helter-skelter)*

WESENER: May God forgive me, but that girl could make Louis XIV himself lose heart! But it really is too bad of Monsieur le Baron, I'll see he gets a warm reception from his father. Just wait! Where is she then? *(goes after* Marie)

Scene 4

Armentières. Promenade by the old moat. Eisenhardt *and* Pirzel *strolling.*

EISENHARDT: Mary means to spend his furlough in Lille; what might that signify, I wonder? He has no relatives there, as far as I know.

PIRZEL: He's not a man of much discernment. Flighty, flighty! But the lieutenant colonel: there's a man for you!

EISENHARDT *(aside):* Ah, me! How can I haul him back out of his metaphysics? *(aloud)* In order to understand human beings, in my estimation, one ought to begin with women.

(Pirzel *shakes his head violently)*

EISENHARDT *(aside):* He has far too much of what the others lack! Oh, the profession of arms and its appalling ban on marriage: what caricatures it makes of people!

PIRZEL: With women, you say! That's like beginning with sheep. No, what a human being is . . . *(lays his forefinger against his nose)*

EISENHARDT *(aside):* He'll philosophize me into the grave! *(aloud)* I have observed that one can scarcely step outside the city gates this time of year without seeing a soldier caressing a wench.

PIRZEL: That's because people don't think.

EISENHARDT: But doesn't thinking interfere with your drill sometimes?

PIRZEL: Not a bit of it, it's quite automatic. The other fellows aren't thinking either, they've got visions of pretty girls in front of their eyes the whole time.

EISENHARDT: That must make for rather odd battles. A whole regiment with its wits bemused can hardly fail to perform prodigies of valor.

PIRZEL: All automatic!

EISENHARDT: Yes, but you march automatically as well. The Prussian bullets must sometimes have given you a rude awakening from your sweet dreams. *(They walk on)*

Scene 5

Lille. Mary's quarters. Mary, Stolzius *dressed as a soldier.*

MARY *(sketching, looks up):* Who's there? *(looks hard at Stolzius, then stands up)* Stolzius?

STOLZIUS: Yes, sir.

MARY: Where the dickens have you sprung from? And in that tunic? *(turns Stolzius around)* You've changed; you've grown so haggard and pale! You could have told me a hundred times you were Stolzius and I wouldn't have believed it.

STOLZIUS: That's the mustache, sir. I heard you needed a servant, and seeing as the Colonel knows me well he gave me his permission to come here and at least help you enlist a few recruits and to serve you.

MARY: Bravo! You're a first-class fellow! And I'm glad you're in the King's service. What's the good of that humdrum cheapjack's life anyway? And you're in a position to afford some little extras, live decently, and get on in the world. I'll take care of you, you can depend on that. Come along, I'll see about a room for you; you shall spend the winter with me, I'll square things with the Colonel.

STOLZIUS: As long as I pay someone to do my guard duties, no one can lay a finger on me. *(exeunt)*

Scene 6

Lille. Madame Wesener, Marie, Charlotte.

MADAME WESENER: It's a disgrace, the way you carry on with him. I can't see where the difference is, you treat him just like you treated Desportes.

MARIE: What else can I do, Mama? If he's Desportes's best friend and the only one who can get us news of him.

CHARLOTTE: If he didn't give you so many presents you'd be quite different with him.

MARIE: Am I supposed to throw his presents back in his face? I have to be civil to him because he's the only one who still writes to Desportes. If I scare him off, we'll be in a fine pickle. Desportes gets hold of all the letters that Papa writes to his father, and they never reach him, you know that.

MADAME WESENER: Once and for all, you're not to go out driving with that man! I won't have it!

MARIE: Then you come too, Mama! He's ordered a horse and cabriolet. Are they to be sent away again?

MADAME WESENER: What's that to me?

MARIE: Then you come, Lottie. What am I to do now? Mama, you know what I put up with for your sake.

CHARLOTTE: Cheeky into the bargain!

MARIE: You be quiet!

CHARLOTTE *(under her breath):* Army whore!

MARIE *(behaves as if she hadn't heard* Charlotte, *carries on preen-*

ing herself in front of the mirror): If we offend Mary, then we have only ourselves to blame.

CHARLOTTE *(aloud, marching out of the room):* Army whore!

MARIE *(turns around from the mirror):* Look, Mama! *(clasping her hands)*

MADAME WESENER: Who can help you? It's the way you behave.

(Enter Mary)

MARIE *(puts on a cheerful expression: goes up to him with the greatest gaiety and friendliness):* Good morning, Monsieur de Mary! Did you sleep well?

MARY: Supremely well, mademoiselle! I saw last night's fireworks all over again in my dreams.

MARIE: It was beautiful.

MARY: It must have been, if it had your approval.

MARIE: Oh, I am no expert in these matters, I'm merely repeating what I heard you say. *(he kisses her hand; she drops a deep curtsy)* We're in dreadful disarray; my mother will be ready in a moment.

MARY: Madame Wesener? You mean to come with us?

MADAME WESENER *(drily):* What's that? Is there no room for me?

MARY: Oh, yes. I shall climb up behind, and my man can run on ahead.

MARIE: Tell me, your servant has a strong resemblance to a certain person that I used to know; he wanted to marry me.

MARY: And you turned him down. I expect Desportes was partly to blame for that.

MARIE: He got back at me.

MARY: Shall we? *(he offers his arm to Marie, she curtsies and points to her mother; he gives Madame Wesener his arm, and Marie follows them out)*

Scene 7

Philippeville. * Desportes *alone in his shirtsleeves in a room with green wallpaper, writing a letter, a lighted candle in front of him.*

DESPORTES *(muttering to himself as he writes):* I'll have to keep her sweet, otherwise there will be no end to this letter writing, and sooner or later one of them will fall into my father's hands. *(reads his letter)* "Your esteemed father is angry with me because I have kept him waiting so long for his money; please pacify him until I have a chance to reveal everything to my father and persuade him to give his consent so that you may be mine, my darling, for ever and ever. Remember, I am greatly worried lest he should have intercepted some of your letters, for I see from your last that you must have written many that I never received. And that might well wreck all our plans. I beg you not to write to me until I have sent you a new address where I can safely receive your letters." *(seals the letter)* If only I could make Mary fall in love with her, so that she could forget me! I'll write and tell him he mustn't stir from my side once I have made my adorable Marie happy; they'll become good friends, just wait! *(strides up and down deep in thought, then goes off)*

Scene 8

Lille. Countess de la Roche's† *residence.* Countess, Footman.

COUNTESS *(looks at her watch):* Has the young gentleman not come home yet?

FOOTMAN: No, madame.

COUNTESS: Give me the key to the front door and go to bed. I shall open the door to him myself. How is young Catherine?

FOOTMAN: She had a high fever this evening.

COUNTESS: Go in to her again and see whether the governess is still

---

*Philippeville is now in southern Belgium.

†Lenz told the popular contemporary author Sophie von La Roche (1731–1807) that he based the character of Countess de la Roche on her because he felt that La Roche possessed the sensitivity necessary to understand and help reconcile social differences.

awake. Tell her I'm not going to bed. I'll come and take her place at one o'clock. *(Exit* Footman)

COUNTESS: Must a child cause his mother pain right to the grave? Were you not my son, and had I not endowed you with a heart so full of tender feeling. . . . *(Loud knocking at the door.* Countess *goes out and then returns with the* Young Count)

YOUNG COUNT: But, Mother, where's the footman? These confounded people, if only it weren't so late I'd send for the watch and have them break every bone in the fellow's body!

COUNTESS: Gently, gently, my son! Supposing I were as impatient with you as you are with this blameless man?

YOUNG COUNT: It's absolutely insufferable!

COUNTESS: I sent him to bed myself. Isn't it enough that the fellow has to look after you the whole day long? Is he to lose his night's sleep, too, on account of you? I do believe you'd have me look upon our servants as beasts of burden.

YOUNG COUNT *(kisses her hand):* Dear mother!

COUNTESS: I must talk to you seriously, young man! You are beginning to darken my days with care. You know I have never attempted to curb you; I have shared in your concerns as your friend, never as your mother. Why have you begun lately to make a secret of your *affaires de cœur*,* when formerly you concealed none of your youthful follies from me, since I, too, am a woman and was always able to give you the best of advice. *(looks at him severely)* You're becoming a rake, my son!

YOUNG COUNT *(weeps, kisses his mother's hand):* Dear mother, I swear that I have no secrets from you. You happened to meet me after supper with Mademoiselle Wesener; you drew conclusions from the hour and from the manner in which we were conversing. . . . She's an amiable girl, nothing more.

COUNTESS: I do not seek to know more. The moment you have reason to believe you are obliged to conceal something from me . . . but remember that you will have yourself to blame afterwards for the consequences of your actions. Mademoiselle Anklam has relatives here, and I know Mademoiselle Wesener does not enjoy the best of reputations—through no fault of her own, I understand: they say the poor child was led astray.

YOUNG COUNT *(kneeling down):* Exactly, dear mother! It's her

---

*Affairs of the heart.

misfortune, in fact . . . if you but knew the circumstances. Yes, I must tell you everything, I feel I am involved in the girl's fate. . . . And yet . . . how easily was she deceived, a carefree, open, blameless heart! It grieves me, Mama, that she did not fall into worthier hands.

COUNTESS: Leave compassion to me, my son. Believe me, *(embraces him)* believe me, my heart is no more obdurate than yours. But compassion is for me less perilous. Listen to my advice, do what I say. For the sake of your peace of mind, don't go back there again, leave the town, go to Mademoiselle Anklam . . . and be assured no harm will befall Mademoiselle Wesener here. In me you are leaving her a most affectionate friend. Do you promise me you will do as I say?

YOUNG COUNT *(looks long and lovingly at her):* Yes, Mama, I promise to do everything you ask. Just one word before I go. She is the victim of misfortune, poor girl, that much is certain.

COUNTESS: Don't worry. *(patting his cheek)* I believe you; you need not convince me of that.

YOUNG COUNT *(rises to his feet and kisses her hand):* I know you. . . . *(exeunt)*

Scene 9

Lille. Madame Wesener, Marie.

MARIE: Let me be, Mama! I mean to tease him.

MADAME WESENER: Get along with you! What? He's forgotten you, he hasn't been here for three days, and everybody says he's fallen in love with that little Madame Duval in the Rue de Bruxelles.

MARIE: You wouldn't believe how obliging the Count is to me.

MADAME WESENER: Oh, come! They say he's already promised.

MARIE: Then I'll tease Mary about the Count. He's coming again this evening after dinner. If only Mary could see me and the Count sometime when he's with that Madame Duval of his. *(a Footman enters)*

FOOTMAN: Countess de la Roche begs to know whether you are at home.

MARIE *(in great confusion):* Oh, heavens, the Count's mother! Tell her . . . Mama, tell me, what should he say?

(Madame Wesener gets up to go)
MARIE: Say it will be a great honor. . . . Mama, Mama, say something!
MADAME WESENER: Can't you open your mouth? Say it will be a great honor for us, although we're in a dreadful mess here.
MARIE: No, no, wait a moment, I'll come down to the carriage myself.
(Marie goes downstairs with the Footman. *Exit Madame Wesener)*

Scene 10

Countess de la Roche *and* Marie *enter.*

MARIE: Excuse us, madame, everything's in great confusion.
COUNTESS: My dear child, pray do not trouble yourself in the slightest on my account. *(takes* Marie's *hand and sits down on the sofa with her)* Look upon me as your very best friend. *(kissing her)* I do assure you, I take the most sincere interest in everything that can possibly affect you.
MARIE *(wiping her eyes):* I do not know how I have deserved this exceptional favor you show me.
COUNTESS: Do not speak of favors, I beg of you. I am glad we are alone; I have a great many things to tell you that are near my heart, and a number of things to ask you as well. (Marie *listens attentively with a joyfully expectant expression)* I love you, my angel! I cannot but confess this love. (Marie *kisses the* Countess's *hand fervently)* Your whole manner has something so frank and so engaging that your misfortune is doubly painful to me. Do you know, my dear new friend, that there is much talk of you in the town?
MARIE: I know all too well that there are spiteful tongues in every place.
COUNTESS: Not just spiteful tongues, virtuous tongues are talking of you as well. You are unfortunate, but you may console yourself with the thought that you have not incurred your misfortune through any vice. Your only fault was lack of acquaintance with the ways of the world: you did not acknowledge that disparity which prevails between the different classes of society; you have

been reading *Pamela,* the most pernicious book that a person in your station of life can possibly read.*

MARIE: I have never even heard of the book.

COUNTESS: Then you have placed too great a trust in what young gentlemen have told you.

MARIE: There is only one person I trusted too much, and it is not yet certain that he has been unfaithful to me.

COUNTESS: Good, my dear young friend! But tell me, pray, how did you come to look for a husband above your station? Your appearance, so you thought, could carry you further than other girls of your acquaintance. Oh, dear young friend, that is precisely what should have rendered you more circumspect! Good looks were never the means to found a good marriage, and no one has more cause to tremble than the possessor of a fair countenance. A thousand perils masked with blossoms, a thousand worshipers and not a single friend, a thousand pitiless seducers!

MARIE: Oh, Madame, I know very well that I am homely.

COUNTESS: Enough of this false modesty! You are beautiful, heaven has inflicted the penalty of beauty upon you. You have met people above your station who made you promises. You saw no difficulty in rising to a higher level, you despised the playmates of your youth, you felt it unnecessary to acquire other amiable qualities, you shrank from hard work, you treated young men of your own class with contempt and were detested in return. Poor child! How happy you might have made some respectable citizen, had you only imbued these unblemished features, this engaging manner with a modest and charitable spirit: how you would have been cherished by your equals, emulated, and admired by your betters! But you sought the envy of your peers. Poor child, what were you thinking of, and for what wretched fortune did you seek to exchange these merits? To become the wife of a man who would on your account be detested and despised by all his family! And to hazard your entire happiness, your entire honor, even your life on such an ill-starred game of chance! What were you thinking of, what were your parents thinking of? Poor misguided child, victim of vanity! *(clasps* Marie *to her breast)* I would have given my life's blood to prevent this happening!

MARIE *(weeping on the* Countess's *hand):* But he loved me!

---

*Samuel Richardson's epistolary novel of moral—and Romantic—sentiment, *Pamela; or, Virtue Rewarded* (1740/41; German tr. 1742).

COUNTESS: The love of an officer, Marie! Of a man who is hardened to every kind of debauchery and infidelity, who ceases to be a good soldier the moment he becomes a faithful lover, who swears to his king that he will not be any such thing and has himself hired on this understanding. And you thought you were the one person in the world who could keep him faithful—in spite of the wrath of his parents, in spite of family pride, in spite of his oath, in spite of his character, in spite of the whole world. That is, you sought to turn the world upside-down—and now that you see you have failed, you want to carry out your plan with others, and do not see that what you take for love in them is nothing but compassion with your fate, or something worse. (Marie *falls on her knees in front of the* Countess, *hides her face in the* Countess's *lap, and sobs)* Make up your mind, dearest child! Unhappy girl, there is still time, you may still escape the pit, I'll risk my life to draw you back from the brink! Abandon all your designs on my son; he is promised already, Mademoiselle Anklam has his hand and his heart. But come and live with me. Your honor has suffered a severe blow; this is the only way to restore it. Be my companion, and resolve to shun male company for a whole year. You shall help me bring up my daughter. Come, we shall go to your mother straightaway and ask her permission for you to come with me.

MARIE *(raises her head pathetically from the* Countess's *lap)*: Madame, it is already too late.

COUNTESS *(hastily)*: It is never too late to be sensible. I'll furnish you with a thousand livres for your dowry; I know your parents have debts.

MARIE *(still on her knees, almost falling over backwards, with clasped hands)*: Oh, Madame, permit me to think it over . . . to put it to my mother.

COUNTESS: Very well, my dear child, do your best. You will have entertainment enough in my house. I'll have you instructed in sketching, dancing, and singing.

MARIE *(falls forward on her face)*: Oh, too, too generous Madame!

COUNTESS: I must leave: your mother would find me in a strange state of mind. *(goes off quickly, looks back from the door at Marie, who is still on her knees, as if in prayer)* Farewell, child! *(exit)*

Act 4

Lille. Mary, Stolzius.

MARY: Let me tell you frankly, Stolzius, if Desportes doesn't marry the girl, I'll marry her myself. I'm madly in love with her. I've done my best to turn my thoughts elsewhere, as you well know, with that Duval woman . . . and then I don't care for that business with the Count, and what with the Countess taking the girl to live with her now . . . but still, all that—is neither here nor there, I can't get the foolish notion out of my head.

STOLZIUS: Doesn't Desportes write anymore, then?

MARY: To be sure he writes! Only the other day his father tried to force him into a marriage and locked him up for a couple of weeks on bread and water. *(striking his head with his fist)* And when I think how she went for a stroll in the moonlight with me not long ago and told me about her troubles, how sometimes she jumped up in the middle of the night to look for a knife when gloomy thoughts came over her.

(Stolzius trembles)

MARY: I asked her if she loved me. She said she loved me more tenderly than any of her friends and relatives and pressed my hand against her breast.

(Stolzius turns his face toward the wall)

MARY: And when I asked her to give me a kiss, she said, if it were in her power to make me happy, she'd do it for sure. But I would need leave from Desportes. *(seizes hold of* Stolzius *roughly)* Devil take me, man, if I don't marry her, if Desportes leaves her in the lurch!

STOLZIUS *(very coldly)*: They say she's very well in with the Countess.

MARY: If only I knew a way to talk to her. Go and make inquiries!

Scene 2

Armentières. Desportes *in prison,* Haudy *visiting him.*

DESPORTES: I'm glad I'm in jail, no one will find out I'm here.
HAUDY: I'll tell our comrades not to breathe a word.
DESPORTES: Mary mustn't find out, that's the most important thing.
HAUDY: Nor must Rammler. He sets himself up as such a great friend of yours: he says he joined the regiment a few weeks after you on purpose to allow you the seniority.
DESPORTES: The idiot!
HAUDY: Listen, we had another joke with him not long ago that will make you laugh your head off. You know that Gilbert lodges with an old hunchbacked, cross-eyed widow, just for the sake of her good-looking cousin. He gives a concert in the house once a week just to please this wench. Our Rammler gets drunk one night; he thinks the cousin sleeps in the house so he creeps away from dinner and in his usual crafty way sneaks into the widow's bedroom, strips, and lies down in the bed. The widow, who's had a bit to drink too, lights her cousin home to where she lives just nearby. We all think Rammler has cleared off home; she goes upstairs to her room, is about to get into bed, and finds our gentleman there in a great state of confusion. He excuses himself and says he didn't know where the lavatory was, she carts him downstairs without much ado, and we almost split our sides. He begged us for God's sake not to tell a soul about it. But you know what Gilbert is like, he told the girl the whole story, and she put it into the old woman's head that Rammler's in love with her. As a matter of fact, he has rented a room in her house—perhaps to make sure she keeps her mouth shut. And now you'd have the laugh of your life to see him and the old one together in company. She simpers and ogles him and twists up her lopsided wrinkled old mug. You could die laughing, and him with his red hawk's beak and his eyes popping out of his head—you can't even think about it without laughing yourself to death!

Scene 3

Lille. A garden at the residence of Countess de la Roche. Countess *in an avenue.*

COUNTESS: What can be the matter with the girl that she's gone down into the garden so late? I fear, I very much fear she has an assignation. She does her sketching absentmindedly, plays the harp absentmindedly, she's always woolgathering when her language master tells her something . . . Hark, I can hear someone . . . yes, she's up in the summerhouse, and somebody's talking to her from the road. *(puts her ear to the hedge)*

MARY'S VOICE *(offstage):* Is it fair to forget all your friends, everything you once cared for?

MARIE'S VOICE *(offstage):* Oh, dear Monsieur Mary, I'm sorry enough for it, but it must be so. I assure you, the Countess is the sweetest lady on God's earth.

MARY *(offstage):* But it's as if you were in a nunnery. Won't you ever come back into the world? You know that Desportes has written; he's inconsolable, he wants to know where you are and why you don't reply to him.

MARIE *(offstage):* Really? Ah, I must forget him; tell him that and say that he must forget me.

MARY *(offstage):* But why? Heartless girl! Is it fair to treat your friends like this?

MARIE *(offstage):* There's no other way. Oh, God, I can hear someone in the garden down there! Farewell, farewell! Cherish no false hopes. . . . *(climbs down)*

COUNTESS: So, Marie! You have assignations!

MARIE *(gives a terrified start):* Oh, Madame . . . it was a relative of mine . . . my cousin . . . and he's only just discovered where I am. . . .

COUNTESS *(gravely):* I heard everything.

MARIE *(half on her knees):* Oh, God, forgive me, just this once!

COUNTESS: You're like that sapling there in the evening breeze, girl: every breath of wind sways you. What are you thinking of; do you think you can pick up the threads of your affair with Desportes here under my very eyes? Do you think you can have secret meetings with his friends? Had I known that, I would never have bothered with you.

MARIE: Pardon me, just this once!

COUNTESS: I shall never pardon you when you act against your own best interests. Begone!

(Marie *goes off in despair*)

COUNTESS: I cannot tell whether I am right to rob the girl of her romance, in all conscience. What charms does life retain if our imagination does not introduce them? Eating, drinking, occupations without future prospects, without pleasures of our own making, this is naught but death delayed. She feels that and only pretends to be cheerful. If only I could discover something that would couple her imagination with my prudence, that would make her heart obey me, not just her reason.

Scene 4

Armentières. Desportes *striding rapidly up and down with a letter in his hand.*

DESPORTES: If she comes here, I'm a ruined man—disgraced, a laughingstock among my fellow officers (*sits down and writes*) What's more, my father mustn't see her. . . .

Scene 5

Wesener's *house.* Wesener, Countess's footman.

WESENER: Marie has run away from home? She'll be the death of me yet! (*rushes off, followed by the* Footman)

Scene 6

Mary's *quarters,* Mary; Stolzius, *pale and disheveled.*

MARY: Let's go after her then, damn it! I'm to blame for all this. Run down and fetch horses!

STOLZIUS: If only we knew where. . . .

MARY: Armentières! Where else can she have gone? (*exeunt*)

Scene 7

Wesener's *house.* Madame Wesener *and* Charlotte *in cloaks.* Wesener *enters.*

WESENER: It's no good. She's nowhere to be found. *(clasps his hands)* God! Who knows where she may have drowned herself!
CHARLOTTE: But who can tell, Papa. . . .
WESENER: Not a sign! The Countess's messengers have come back, and it's barely half an hour since she was missed. There's a horseman ridden out by each of the city gates, and she can't have vanished from the face of the earth in so short a time.

Scene 8

Philippeville. Desportes' gamekeeper *with a letter from his master in his hand.*

GAMEKEEPER: Oh, ho! Here's a fine quarry heading for my snare! She's written to the master to say she'll come straight to him in Philippeville. *(looks at the letter)* On foot . . . poor child! I'll give you refreshment!

Scene 9

Armentières. A concert in the house of Madame Bischof. *A number of ladies in a circle around the orchestra, among them* Madame Bischof *and her cousin* Mademoiselle Bischof. *Various officers, among them* Haudy, Rammler, Mary, Desportes, *and* Gilbert, *standing in conversation with the ladies.*

MADEMOISELLE BISCHOF *(to* Rammler): And you have moved in here as well, Baron?
*(*Rammler *bows without speaking and blushes violently)*
HAUDY: He's taken up his lodging on the second floor, right opposite your cousin's bedchamber.
MADEMOISELLE BISCHOF: So I heard. I congratulate my cousin.
MADAME BISCHOF *(squints and smiles in coquettish fashion):* Heh,

heh, heh! The Baron would not have moved in here if Monsieur Gilbert had not recommended my establishment so warmly. In any case, I treat all my gentlemen in such a way that they can have no cause to complain of me.

MADEMOISELLE BISCHOF: That I well believe; you get on very well together, I'm sure.

GILBERT: All the same, there's a little something between the two of them, otherwise Rammler wouldn't have come to stay here.

MADAME BISCHOF: Really? *(holds her fan in front of her face)* heh, heh, heh! Since when, then, Monsieur Gilbert, since when, then?

HAUDY: Since our last *soirée musicale,** you know, madame.

RAMMLER *(tugs Haudy's sleeve):* Haudy!

MADAME BISCHOF *(strikes Haudy playfully with her fan):* Naughty Major! Must you blurt out all our little secrets?

RAMMLER: Madame! I cannot think how we come to be so familiar, I must ask you. . . .

MADAME BISCHOF *(very annoyed):* Really, sir? So now you give yourself airs, do you? Anyway, you should esteem it a great honor that a lady of my years and my character should be so familiar with you. Just think how he must fancy himself, the young gentleman!

ALL THE OFFICERS: Hey, Rammler! . . . Fie, Rammler! . . . It isn't right to treat the lady so!

RAMMLER: Hold your tongue, madame, or I'll break every bone in your body and toss you out of the window!

MADAME BISCHOF *(stands up, furiously):* Come here, sir! *(seizes his arm)* Come here, this minute, you just try to lay a finger on me!

ALL THE OFFICERS: Up to bed, Rammler! There's a challenge for you!

MADAME BISCHOF: If you get above yourself, I'll throw you out of this house, d'you know that? And it's not all that far to your commanding officer! *(begins to weep)* Just think, such impertinence in my own house, the impudent lout. . . .

MADEMOISELLE BISCHOF: There now, cousin, the Baron didn't really mean it. He was only joking. Hush now!

GILBERT: Have some sense, Rammler, I beg of you. What honor is there in insulting an old woman?

RAMMLER: The whole damn lot of you can . . .! *(rushes out)*

*Literally, "musical evening."

MARY: Isn't that a riot, Desportes? What's the matter with you? You're not laughing.

DESPORTES: I have dreadful pains in my chest. This catarrh will be the death of me.

MARY: He kills me, that crackpot Rammler! Did you see how he turned black-and-blue in the face from sheer fury? Anybody else would have played up to the old hag.

(Stolzius *comes in and tugs at* Mary's *sleeve*)

MARY: What's up?

STOLZIUS: I hope you don't mind, Lieutenant. Can you step outside for a moment?

MARY: What's up, then? Have you heard something?

(Stolzius *shakes his head*)

MARY: Well, then. *(comes downstage with* Stolzius*)* Tell me here.

STOLZIUS: The rats got at your best embroidered shirt last night and gnawed it. When I opened the linen cupboard, a couple of them leaped out in my face.

MARY: What does it matter? Put down some poison.

STOLZIUS: I have to have a sealed note from you.

MARY *(irritably):* Why do you have to come to me just now?

STOLZIUS: I haven't time in the evening, Lieutenant: I have to be there when the uniforms are issued.

MARY: Here, take my watch; you can seal the note with my seal. *(Exit* Stolzius. Mary *returns to the company. An orchestra starts up*)

DESPORTES *(who has withdrawn into a corner of the room):* I think of her all the time. To hell with the thought! What can I do about it if she ends up one of them? It's all her own fault. *(comes back to the others and falls into a dreadful fit of coughing. Mary thrusts a piece of licorice into his mouth; he gives a start. Mary laughs)*

Scene 10

Lille. Wesener's *house.* Madame Wesener, *the* Countess's footman.

MADAME WESENER: What's that? You say the Countess is so affected that she's taken to her bed? Please convey our most humble respects to the Countess and her daughter. My husband has gone to Armentières, because they wanted to put seals on everything in the house on account of the bail, and he's heard that Baron Desportes is supposed to be there with his regiment. We are truly sorry that the Countess has taken our misfortune so much to heart.

Scene 11

Stolzius *prowling backwards and forwards in front of an apothecary's shop. It is raining.*

STOLZIUS: What are you trembling for? My tongue is so feeble, I fear I shan't be able to utter a single word. He'll guess at once from my face what I mean to do. . . . And must those who suffer wrong tremble, and only those who are guilty of wrongdoing be cheerful? Who knows where she's starving now under some hedge? In with you, Stolzius! If not for him, then for your own sake! And that is all you're after! *(goes into the shop)*

Act 5

Scene 1

On the road to Armentières. Wesener, *resting.*

WESENER: No, I'll not take the stagecoach, even if I have to lie here the rest of my life! My poor child cost me enough even before she went to the Countess's; she was always keen to act the grand lady, and I must make sure that her brothers and sisters have no occasion to reproach her for it.* My business too has been at a standstill for two years now. . . . Who knows what Desportes is doing to her, what he's doing to all of us . . . because she's bound to be with him. We must simply put our trust in God. *(sits lost in thought)*

Scene 2

Marie *on another road to Armentières, resting under a tree; she takes a piece of dry bread from her pocket.*

MARIE: I always thought a person could live on bread and water alone. *(gnaws at the bread)* Oh, if only I had a single drop of the wine I so often threw out of the window, the wine I used to wash my hands in when the weather was hot. *(writhes on the ground)* Oh, it hurts . . . well, I'm a wretched beggar. . . . *(looks at the piece of bread)* I cannot bring myself to eat it, God knows. Better to starve *(throws the bread away and drags herself to her feet)* I'll crawl as far as I can, and if I drop dead, so much the better.

*That is, if Marie spends all of Wesener's money, there will be none left for the other children.

Scene 3

Mary's *quarters.* Mary *and* Desportes *are sitting in uniform at a small table set for supper.* Stolzius *in the background putting out napkins.*

DESPORTES: I tell you, she was a whore from the start, and she only took up with me because I gave her presents. As a matter of fact, I was up to my ears in debt on her account, you wouldn't believe it: she'd have done me out of house and home if I'd carried on much longer. To cut a long story short, brother, before I know where I am, I get a letter from the wench, she's going to come to me in Philippeville. Now, just imagine the row, if my father had set eyes on her!

(Stolzius *switches the napkins around so as to have an excuse for lingering in the room*) What was I to do? I wrote to my gamekeeper; he was to meet her and keep her under house arrest in my quarters until I came back to Philippeville myself and took her back secretly to the regiment. For the moment my father set eyes on her she'd be done for. Now, my gamekeeper's a sturdy, lusty fellow; time will weigh heavily on their hands, what with being shut up there together. . . . I'll wait and see what he makes of her. *(laughs mockingly)* I let him know on the quiet that I wouldn't mind!

MARY: Look here, Desportes, that's not decent!

DESPORTES: What d'you mean, not decent? What do you want me to do? Isn't she well enough provided for if my gamekeeper marries her? A wench like that. . . .

MARY: She was in the Countess's good graces. And I'm damned if I wouldn't have married the girl myself if that young Count hadn't ruined my pitch, because he was in her good graces as well.

DESPORTES: You'd have got a fine slut round your neck, then!

(Exit Stolzius*)*

MARY *(calls after* Stolzius*):* See that Monsieur Desportes gets his wine soup right away! I don't know how it was the man got to know her: I believe she wanted to make me jealous because I'd been giving her the cold shoulder for a day or two. All that wouldn't have made any difference, but once I went to see her, it was in the hottest of the dog days, and because of the heat she had nothing on but a thin, thin shift of muslin, and you could see her lovely legs right through it. Every time she crossed the room and the shift fluttered out behind her . . . look, I'd have given my immortal soul to spend the night with her! Now, just imagine, as luck would have it, the Count has to turn up that very day—well, you know the girl's conceit. 'She carried on with him like mad, either to annoy me, or else because girls like that have no notion what they're about when a gentleman of the better class favors them with a friendly look. (Stolzius *comes in, puts a dish in front of* Desportes, *and stations himself, pale as death, behind* Desportes' *chair*) I felt like red-hot iron and then suddenly as cold as ice. (Desportes *gulps down the soup*) I lost all my appetite for her and from that moment I've never been able to feel affection for her. Mind you, when I heard she'd run away from the Countess. . . .

DESPORTES *(eating):* Why are we talking about that boor? Let me tell you, brother, you'll do me a favor if you never mention her name again. The very thought of her bores me to death! *(pushes the plate away)*

STOLZIUS *(behind* Desportes' *chair, with distorted features):* Really? (Mary *and* Desportes *look at him in amazement)*

DESPORTES *(clutches his chest):* I've got dreadful pains . . . Oh!!

(Mary, *his eyes riveted on* Stolzius, *says nothing)*

DESPORTES *(flings himself into an armchair):* Oh!! *(writhing in agony)* Mary!

STOLZIUS *(leaps toward* Desportes, *seizes him by the ears, and presses his face against his own; in bloodcurdling tones):* Marie! Marie! Marie!

(Mary *draws his sword and is about to run* Stolzius *through)*

STOLZIUS *(turns around calmly and snatches the sword from* Mary's *grasp):* Spare yourself the trouble, it's done already. I shall die happy now that I can take him with me.

MARY *(leaves his word in* Stolzius's *hand and rushes out):* Help! Help!

DESPORTES: I've been poisoned!

STOLZIUS: Yes, poisoned, you seducer! And I am Stolzius, whose bride you made a whore of. She was my bride. If you can't live without ruining women, why must you turn to those who can't resist, who believe every word you say? You are avenged, my Marie! God cannot condemn me! *(sinks to the floor)*

DESPORTES: Help! *(writhes on the floor and dies also)*

Scene 4

Wesener *walking by the River Lys, lost in thought. Twilight. A female figure wrapped in a cloak plucks at his sleeve.*

WESENER: Leave me alone—I am not interested in such things.

WOMAN *(in a barely audible whisper):* For God's sake, sir, whatever you can spare.

WESENER: To the workhouse with you! There are wanton strumpets enough and to spare in these parts; if a man were to give to them all, he'd have his hands full and his pockets empty.

WOMAN: Sir, I've gone three days without a bite of bread; be kind and take me to an inn where I can have a sip of wine.

WESENER: You wanton creature! Aren't you ashamed to make such a proposal to a respectable man? Begone! Run after your soldiers! *(Woman goes away without replying)*

WESENER: Somehow she sighed so deeply! How heavy my heart is! *(takes out his purse)* Who knows where my own daughter is begging alms at this moment? *(runs after the woman and offers her a coin with a trembling hand)* Here's a franc for you . . . but mend your ways!

WOMAN *(begins to weep):* Oh, God! *(takes the money and collapses, almost fainting)* What good is that to me?

WESENER *(turns away, wiping tears from his eyes. He addresses her in great agitation):* Where are you from?

WOMAN: That I may not say. But I am the daughter of a respectable man.

WESENER: Was your father a jeweler?

(Woman remains silent)

WESENER: Your father was a respectable man? Stand up. I'll take you home with me. *(tries to help her to her feet)* Does your father live in Lille, by any chance? *(At these last words the woman throws her arms round* Wesener's *neck)*

WESENER *(cries out):* Oh, my daughter!

MARIE: Father!

(Both collapse on the ground; a crowd of people gathers, and they are carried off)

Scene 5

The Colonel's *quarters.* Count von Spannheim *(the* Colonel), Countess de la Roche.

COUNTESS: Have you seen the unhappy pair? I haven't the heart. The very sight of them would kill me.

COLONEL: It made me ten years older. And to think that such a thing should happen in my corps! But, Madame, what can we do? It is the fate that heaven ordains for certain mortals. I'll pay all the man's debts and another thousand livres to compensate him. Then I'll see what can be done through an appeal to the villain's father on behalf of the family he has ruined and made destitute.

COUNTESS: Worthy man! Accept my warmest gratitude in these tears. She was the finest, the most lovable creature! What high hopes I had begun to cherish for her! *(she weeps)*

COLONEL: These tears do you honor. They soften my heart as well. And why should I not weep, a man who is obliged to fight and to die for his fatherland, to see a citizen of that fatherland and his entire family plunged into irrevocable ruin by one of my subordinates.

COUNTESS: These are the consequences of celibacy among our soldiers.

COLONEL *(shrugs his shoulders)*: How can it be helped? Even Homer said, I believe, that a good husband is a poor soldier, and experience confirms it. A particular idea has often occurred to me when I read the story of Andromeda.* I look upon soldiers as the monster to whom from time to time an unhappy female must be sacrificed, in order that all other wives and daughters may be spared.

COUNTESS: What do you mean?

COLONEL: If only the king would found an establishment of soldiers' paramours; it's true they would have to consent to give up the exalted notions that women have of perpetual union.

COUNTESS: I much doubt whether any woman of honor could consent to that.

COLONEL: They would have to be Amazons. In this matter, it seems

---

*In Greek mythology, Andromeda was an Ethiopian princess put out to be sacrificed to a sea monster to atone for her mother's vanity.

to me, one noble sentiment balances the other: the delicacy of womanly honor and the idea of martyrdom for the nation.

COUNTESS: How little you men know of the heart and the aspirations of women!

COLONEL: It is true the king would have to do everything in his power to render this class of society glorious and honorable. On the other hand, he would save recruiting expenses, and the children would belong to him. Oh, I only wish someone could be found to promote this idea at court: I would soon make sources of support known to him. Those who defend the nation would in this case be its fortune; the outer security of the nation would not cancel out its inner well-being, and in a society hitherto thrown into turmoil by us the peace and prosperity of all and universal bliss would be joined in one embrace.

(Curtain.)

Translated by William E. Yuill

THE
CHILDMURDERESS
A Tragedy
Heinrich Leopold Wagner

CHARACTERS

MARTIN HUMBRECHT, *a butcher*
FRAU HUMBRECHT
EVCHEN HUMBRECHT, *their daughter*
LISBET, *their maid*
MASTER HUMBRECHT
MAJOR LINDSTHAL
LIEUTENANT VON GRÖNINGSECK
LIEUTENANT VON HASENPOTH
LANDLADY *of the Yellow Cross*
MARIANEL, *a maid at the Yellow Cross*
FRAU MARTHAN, *a washwoman*
PUBLIC PROSECUTOR
TWO JAILERS
CLERK

The action takes place in Strasbourg over a period of nine months.

Act 1

A seedy room at the Yellow Cross, an inn.

(How this room is furnished is to be gathered from the dialogue itself. Off to the side is a door that leads to another room)
(Lieutenant von Gröningseck leads Frau Humbrecht by the hand into the room. Evchen, Frau Humbrecht's daughter, follows. The women are wearing dominoes; he, a large wolf's fur coat. All are in masks.)

MARIANEL *(sets a lamp on the table. As she leaves):* Have you ordered already? *(Lieutenant signals yes. Exit Marianel)*

FRAU HUMBRECHT *(removing her mask):* Captain! Can you assure me . . .

VON GRÖNINGSECK *(tosses off his mantle, mask and hat):* Of everything, my dear Frau Humbrecht! Of everything! A kiss, my little one, that is my right after a ball. *(pulls Evchen's mask off as well)* Don't be so bourgeois! A kiss, I say! *(kisses her. To Frau Humbrecht)* Now, now, I am not yet a captain, and I don't want to pretend to be what I'm not.

FRAU HUMBRECHT *(curtsies):* As you wish, Major! Serve me!

VON GRÖNINGSECK: Bravo! Bravo! Much better! Ha, ha, ha!

EVCHEN: Oh, Mother, don't try to play the grand lady. Major is higher than captain; you really don't know anything. The lieutenant has already been boarding with us a whole month—

VON GRÖNINGSECK: A month and three days, my child! I have counted every minute.

EVCHEN: Imagine! Does time hang so heavily on your hands then?

VON GRÖNINGSECK: Not yet! But it might very well soon, Evchen, if you don't—

EVCHEN: Evchen! Since when did you become so familiar?

VON GRÖNINGSECK: Don't quarrel, Evchen! Don't quarrel! You

mustn't take anything I say tonight the wrong way. I have had a bit too much to drink.

FRAU HUMBRECHT: What I wanted to ask, Lieutenant, is if you can assure me that this is a respectable establishment.

VON GRÖNINGSECK: May the devil tear me alive, Frau Humbrecht, if everybody of the *beau monde** doesn't come here daily. Just look around, see how shabbily the room is furnished?

FRAU HUMBRECHT: Exactly!

VON GRÖNINGSECK: Exactly, of course, exactly! That implies that all the good rooms are already taken. Do you believe then—*pardieu!*†—that Lieutenant von Gröningseck would normally enter such a pigsty? Three chairs and a table that you wouldn't dare touch! *(lurches forward, knocking the lamp and the table over. The lamp goes out)*

FRAU HUMBRECHT: My God, the lamp! Lieutenant, the lamp!

VON GRÖNINGSECK *(mimicking her):* The lamp! The lamp! Don't worry, this isn't the only damn lamp! Where's the candlestick? *(searches)*

EVCHEN: Here, I have it.

VON GRÖNINGSECK: Where? Where?

EVCHEN: Here, for heaven's sake! You're reaching right past it. Honestly!

FRAU HUMBRECHT: What is it? What's the matter?

VON GRÖNINGSECK: Oh, nothing, nothing. *(takes the candlestick and goes to the door) Holà, des flambeaux!*‡ *(An old woman holds a lighted candle out to him, without really letting herself be seen. He lights his own by it)*

EVCHEN *(wiping her hands on her handkerchief):* Lord, now my hands are all covered with tallow. *(secretly throws a threatening look at* von Gröningseck; *he smiles)*

FRAU HUMBRECHT: If there's nothing else—

VON GRÖNINGSECK *(rights the table, places the lamp on it):* That was, *ma foi,*§ a capital joke! Just as I was talking about the crippled dog, the scoundrel fell to the floor. We would have missed the best part. *Le diable m'emporte, c'est charmant, c'est*

---

*The fashionable world.
†My God!
‡Hey, a light!
§Indeed. Literally, "(by) my faith."

*divin!** Just look at the frame there: half bed, half sofa. I do believe
it's some army cot they stole from an old folks' home. Ha, ha, ha!
I bet you didn't have a bridal bed as pretty as this, Frau
Humbrecht! To be sure, there's only a straw sack *(tests it with his
hand)*, but well-stuffed—resilient!

FRAU HUMBRECHT *(somewhat angry):* See here, Lieutenant! In front
of my daughter—

VON GRÖNINGSECK: I must kiss you. Are you looking askance,
Evchen? Once more, back to Evchen for fun! So! All good things
come in threes. *(lets go of* Evchen; *offers her his hand; looks
fixedly into her eyes; softly to her)* That was punishment for your
tactless "Honestly!" *(*Evchen *laughs, shakes hands)*

FRAU HUMBRECHT *(during this pantomime):* I could just eat him up,
the little fool. You have to be good to him whether you want to or
not. He's like quicksilver: first here, then there.

MARIANEL *(enters):* Do you wish to be served now?

VON GRÖNINGSECK: But of course, *pardieu!* The sooner the better,
and the more the better.

FRAU HUMBRECHT: Come, Eva! I must slip my domino off a bit; I'm
getting so warm.

EVCHEN: Me too, Mother. *(takes the lamp from the* maid *and goes
with her mother to the adjoining room)*

VON GRÖNINGSECK: So much the better *(softly)* for me! *(calls after
them)* Should I act as chambermaid? I certainly know how to deal
with this.

FRAU HUMBRECHT: Oh, yes! That would be lovely. No, a personal
chambermaid would be much too aristocratic for us.

EVCHEN: We can manage without you, Mr. Bluecoat! *(pushes him
away from behind her Mother and shuts the door)*

VON GRÖNINGSECK: So how the hell did you wind up here, Marianel? Aren't you working at the coffeehouse on the corner any
more? That little room there was very cozy.

MARIANEL: I'm glad you brought that up, you little devil! Really
glad. You still owe me Christmas money. Pay up now or I'll tell
them all about you.

VON GRÖNINGSECK: I? Owe you? Didn't I always give you your little
taler when—

---

*The devil take me—it's charming, it's divine!

MARIANEL: Yeah, sure, you paid every time! But how often did I have to cover up for you? Right? Don't you remember, you boozer, Sunday before Christmas, how you were making such a racket at midnight? Like you wanted to storm the house? How I secretly let you in at the back door, and how I made you tea, and how you spat on me over and over and—

VON GRÖNINGSECK: And . . . and . . . shut the hell up. Here are six livres, you carrion. But now you have to do me one favor.

MARIANEL: Anything, anything, my precious! Tell me! Tell me! *(tries to press against him)*

VON GRÖNINGSECK *(pushes her from him)*: That's not necessary now. When a soldier has a breakfast roll to eat, he doesn't need army bread.

MARIANEL: Think about it, my precious. You're in rotten shape now, but you'll be in a better mood again someday, and then you'll be back.

VON GRÖNINGSECK: Yes, I think so too, my stupid. I didn't mean to sound so rude. Now, here is a little packet. Take it, and when I call for punch, put the little powder inside in the first glass you set on the table.

MARIANEL: Go to the devil and take your goddamn powder with you! You want *me* to poison these people for you? You think I have no conscience, you hellhound?

VON GRÖNINGSECK: Now just listen to me, Marianella! Damn it, listen to me or—it's not a poison. It's a little sleeping powder, if you want to know. And here's a great big taler.

MARIANEL: Oh, well, that's something else. Give it here. *(she grabs at the money; he sticks it back into his pocket)*

VON GRÖNINGSECK: Here is the powder. Now don't screw things up. When I leave, you'll get the taler.

MARIANEL: Why not now?

VON GRÖNINGSECK: A whore is never to be trusted.

MARIANEL *(as she leaves)*: Nor a whore's trick. If there weren't any of your sort around, there would be nothing but good girls. You're a fine one to insult! First you carve yourself a god, then you crucify him.

VON GRÖNINGSECK: Shut up and do what I tell you!

MARIANEL: It won't do you a hell of a lot of good. *(exit)*

VON GRÖNINGSECK: That's my problem! Things might get out of hand if I can't take the old lady in. *(To Evchen, who has returned, followed by her mother)* Yes, *ma chère,** that's right. That's lovely, lovely! *Le diable m'emporte,* you do look appetizing! Such sheer, light clothing! On my honor, you have grown into a beauty. So thin, everything standing out so much.

FRAU HUMBRECHT: Now, Lieutenant, how do *I* look? All right for the show?

VON GRÖNINGSECK *(without looking at her):* Superb! Superb! The gown flatters you.

FRAU HUMBRECHT: Yes, that's what you say. Thoughts are free is what you think. If only there were a mirror here!

VON GRÖNINGSECK: How divinely beautiful your disarrayed hair makes you, my darling! I can't gaze upon you enough. Ah, the floating tresses! *(kisses her and leads her, his arm around her waist, to the table. Sits next to her)*

FRAU HUMBRECHT *(observing herself during this):* You're almost right, Eva, I should have put my domino back on. Now I see; before, I couldn't. I couldn't tell by the lamp, but my coat is too dirty.

EVCHEN: I tried to tell you, but you wouldn't listen.

VON GRÖNINGSECK: You look fine, both of you. You look fine, Humbrecht, you look fine. You look fine.

FRAU HUMBRECHT: Oh well, then. As long as it's good enough for you. *(goes over to him and plays with his epaulettes)* I figured under the mask nobody can tell if my collar is dirty or not, and if I put on a fresh one, sure as anything it'd get crumpled.

VON GRÖNINGSECK: An exemplary housekeeper, by my faith! *(lets go of* Evchen's *hand, seizes* Frau Humbrecht *and sets her between his legs) Très bonne ménagère!*† Aren't you tired then, after the ball, little woman?

FRAU HUMBRECHT: Oh, who could be tired, there's always something to see! Always something new! I think I would have been able just to sit in one spot the whole night and the whole day through, not eating or drinking.

EVCHEN: Not I! I don't find any fun in just watching.

VON GRÖNINGSECK: You'd rather get in on the fun, is that it?

EVCHEN *(innocently):* Yes!

FRAU HUMBRECHT *(laughs so hard she leans forward onto the lieutenant's chest; her face is turned away from* Evchen. *He plays*

*My dear.
†What a good housewife!

with Frau Humbrecht's *necklace; she presses his hand and kisses it):* She didn't understand you. You mustn't misinterpret her naïveté. *(straightens herself)* You really are too wicked. If you only knew!

(Marianel brings in food, wine, and glasses and sets them down. Exit)

VON GRÖNINGSECK: *Allons,** let's eat! Take your places, my dears. Breakfast is served. Dig in! *(Frau Humbrecht sits down. He serves her)* Here, Madame—

FRAU HUMBRECHT: Oh, bosh! I've told you before, I don't want to be called madame, I'm just plain Frau. Go ahead, serve yourself.

EVCHEN: What can you be thinking of? How could I possibly eat all of this? *(about to return her portion to the serving dish)*

FRAU HUMBRECHT: Now stop that! Behave! What you can't eat, you can stick in your pockets. Right, Lieutenant? I mean, it's already paid for.

VON GRÖNINGSECK: Right, little woman! *(pinches her cheek and leers at* Evchen*) Ma foi,* you have the mind of an angel. Surely you know how to help yourself. *Pardieu!* The muscatel is magnificent! *(lurches)* To our health! To your future husband, Evchen!

FRAU HUMBRECHT: Oh, she's still got plenty of time. She's only eighteen years old.

VON GRÖNINGSECK: Already three years lost!

FRAU HUMBRECHT: Now really! I was nearly twenty-four when I married Herr Humbrecht, and all my girlfriends laughed at me for marrying so young.

VON GRÖNINGSECK: Gothic times! Gothic customs! *(lurches)* Now to the wedding night, Frau Humbrecht!

FRAU HUMBRECHT: Hee, hee, hee! You are trying to get me tipsy. No, no, it won't do you any good. Well then, to the honor of my dear husband; I give myself the honor—*(about to rise)*

VON GRÖNINGSECK *(restrains her):* No ceremony! We have to finish the bottle. Then we can have a nice little glass of punch on top.

FRAU HUMBRECHT: Take care and watch out! That could be a pretty mess. No, no, if you don't mind, we really should be leaving.

VON GRÖNINGSECK: Leaving? Already? Are you out of your mind, little lady? *(flings his arm around her neck)* Truly then we *would* be making a public display of ourselves. *(looks at his watch)* Only half past two! The whole neighborhood would laugh at us if we

*Let's go.

came home from a ball at only half past two. Don't even dream of it, Frau Humbrecht. I won't let you budge from here for another hour. Then we'll go right back to the ball. I still have the ticket stubs.

EVCHEN: Oh yes, Mother! Back to the ball!

FRAU HUMBRECHT: Oh well, then. I'll permit it only because I want to let you have a good time, and because the lieutenant is doing us such a great honor. Your fool of a father never lets you out of the house like this.

VON GRÖNINGSECK: Now you're making sense. When one partakes of pleasure only rarely, he should make the most of it. Besides, tonight is the last ball of the year. Come on, Evchen! Don't sip it like that. The glass must be drained. *(Evchen finishes her glass)* Well done! For that you get a kiss. *(kisses her) Holà! la maison!** *(*Marianel *opens the door)* Punch!

(Exit Marianel*)*

EVCHEN: What kind of drink exactly is punch, Mother?

FRAU HUMBRECHT: Oh . . . yes, well . . . there's some . . .

VON GRÖNINGSECK: What, Evchen? You don't know what punch is? You've never tasted it? You people live like the mendicant monks. Eighteen years old, and this is your first ball, and you don't know what punch is? Ah, nectar! A drink fit for the gods! *Le diable m'emporte, s'il n'est pas vrai!*† If I were the king of France I could not conceive of a more delicious hooch than punch. It is and will always be my favorite drink, so help me God. *Ah, le voilà.*‡ *(*Marianel *brings three bar glasses on a salver. He takes them from her one at a time. With the first that she gives him, he asks:)* Is everything there?

MARIANEL *(with a deep curtsy):* Exactly as you ordered it, sir. *(pinches him, unseen by the others, on the arm. He looks at her haughtily and gestures that she should leave. She curtsies again and leaves, biting her lip to keep from laughing)*

FRAU HUMBRECHT *(holds the glass to her nose):* Oh yes, that would finish me, by God! I'd better not have a drop of that. It smells so strong, God forgive me, that you could get drunk on the smell alone.

VON GRÖNINGSECK: Just the opposite, little woman, just the op-

*Hey! Service!
†The devil take me if it isn't true!
‡Ah, there it is!

posite! I give you my *parole d'officier,** or my *parole de maçon,*†
whichever you want, that I have been drunk two or three times in
an afternoon, and each time it was punch that restored me.

EVCHEN: Yes, your stomach is used to such things, but I'm not used
to anything strong.

VON GRÖNINGSECK: Good! So I'll capitulate: Evchen drinks as much
or as little as she wants, and I'll finish what she doesn't take as
well as my own. Mama, however, must empty her own glass. That
way everything's in proportion. *Allegro!* To arms! *(he hands each
her glass, then takes his own. He raises his glass; they drink)*

EVCHEN *(spits the drink back out):* Pfooey! Wow, does that burn!

FRAU HUMBRECHT: You rude—! Is that how one treats a gift from
the gods? *(takes a larger gulp herself)* This is delicious. Almost
like Rossoli.‡

VON GRÖNINGSECK: More or less, to be sure! I'm glad you like it,
dear lady. But one thing, Evchen, you must promise me. When we
go back to the ball, you must dance no allemand with anyone else
but me, however many quadrilles you want.

FRAU HUMBRECHT: Is that so? She can't do that. She's forgotten all
that.

VON GRÖNINGSECK: Not at all! She dances only too well, makes her
figures, turns and steps with too much *grâce,* too charming, too
captivating. I cannot see you with anyone else without secretly
becoming very jealous.

FRAU HUMBRECHT: Ooh, you do love to tease. Though she *did* take
lessons for three years with Sauveur.§

VON GRÖNINGSECK: With Sauveur! *Pardieu!* Now I am not at all
surprised. I have also been a student of his. *C'est un excellent
maître pour former une jeune personne!*‖ To his health! *(Frau
Humbrecht and he drink)* But *comment diable** * did you wind up
with Sauveur? He's always busy with counts and barons.

EVCHEN: There were three barons and a wealthy Swiss who
boarded next to us at Frau Schaffner's. They needed female part-
ners, so they invited me along.

---

*Word as an officer.
†Word as a mason.
‡A popular drink made of fruit and its blossoms.
§Anton Sauveur, Strasbourg dance instructor.
‖He is an excellent master for shaping a young person.
* *How the devil?

VON GRÖNINGSECK: Damn me, the fellows didn't have bad taste. How long ago was that?

FRAU HUMBRECHT *(yawning)*: Oh, it must have been five years or so, I think.

EVCHEN: Yes, at least that many. Maybe even six.

VON GRÖNINGSECK: That's close enough. So you were then only twelve years old, and you'd already caught the eyes of barons.

EVCHEN: Oh, Mother! I hope you're not about to go to sleep?

VON GRÖNINGSECK *(supports her with one arm around her neck; with the other hand he brings her glass to her lips)*: The rest, just a bit more, Frau Humbrecht.

FRAU HUMBRECHT *(pushes the glass away)*: Not another drop! *(he sets it aside)* I can't keep my eyes . . . open . . . any . . . long . . . *(falls asleep against the* Lieutenant's *chest)*

EVCHEN: Good God! What's wrong! *(leaps up, frightened, and tries to rouse her* mother) Mother! What's the matter with you? Can you hear me? Can you hear me? God in heaven! I hope she's not ill!

VON GRÖNINGSECK: Calm down, Evchen. It doesn't mean anything. In a quarter hour, she'll be as awake as ever. The punch did it. She's not used to it.

EVCHEN *(shakes her again)*: Mother! Mother! I think she must have fainted, or else she's dead.

VON GRÖNINGSECK: Fainted! Dead! Balderdash! Feel her pulse. She just drank a little too quickly, that's all. Come on, Evchen, help me get her onto the bed. She's really too heavy for me. *(Evchen and he carry her to the bed and lay her across it) Pardieu!* We made fun of this bedframe before, but now we're glad we've got it.

EVCHEN *(quite disturbed)*: I still don't know what's going on! If only I could get her home!

VON GRÖNINGSECK *(sits down next to* Frau Humbrecht, *draws* Evchen *to him)*: Don't be a child, *ma chère!* Nothing else is going to happen. We still have time to get back to the ball. *(gazes at her fixedly)* Do you still like me, Evchen?

EVCHEN: For heaven's sake, don't look at me like that. I can't stand it.

VON GRÖNINGSECK: Why can't you, my little fool? *(kisses her hand passionately, looking deeper and deeper into her eyes with each kiss)*

EVCHEN: That's why! I won't! *(he is about to embrace her and kiss*

her. *She struggles, breaks free, and runs into the next room)*
Mother! Mother! I am lost!
VON GRÖNINGSECK *(hurrying after her):* You shouldn't run away
from me! *(slams the door shut behind him. Pandemonium offstage. The old* Landlady *and* Marianel *enter; they behave as if
they hear nothing. By and by it grows quiet)*
LANDLADY: Clear away fast. Look—the old woman is sleeping like a
baby.
MARIANEL: If you had only let me have my way, I know who'd be
sleeping there now. *Then* we would have been able to nab something!
LANDLADY: Yeah, nab! You and the devil go nab! You just keep
dealing with officers. A year ago one from the *corps royal* lost a
trifling little ring. The bastard wanted to fleece me! He'd have had
me turn the house upside down if Christine hadn't found it again
in the mattress. You and your officers can go to hell! But I'm not
coming along—what are you sticking in the mattress? Huh? Back
to your dust mop! What are you sticking there? Can't you tell me?
MARIANEL: Shh! Shh! A snuffbox. We'll share it. It belongs to the
old one there.
LANDLADY: Really? It's not the lieutenant's?
MARIANEL: No, really, I'm sure.
LANDLADY: So go on and get out—march! The bottles can stay
there. If he asks for the bill, tell him one and a half louis d'or. *(exit)*
MARIANEL: Fine! And a half for me makes two. *(clears everything
away and tiptoes out)*
EVCHEN *(bursts in from the adjoining room and flings herself on her
mother):* Mother! Cruel Mother! Sleep, sleep forever. Your daughter is a whore! *(falls sobbing onto her* mother's *bosom. The
lieutenant paces a few times up and down the room. Finally he
stands next to her)*
VON GRÖNINGSECK: Have you taken leave of your senses,
Mademoiselle? Do you want to be a prostitute? To let the whole
world know what's happened between us?
EVCHEN *(straightens herself; her face is hidden, however, in her
handkerchief):* Go! Go, tormentor! Devil in angel's clothing!
VON GRÖNINGSECK: You've been reading novels, I presume? It
would be an eternal shame if you weren't a heroine yourself.
(paces again)

EVCHEN: Joke away, thief of my honor, joke away! Yes, I've read novels. I read them in order to learn about you monsters, to be able to protect myself from your wiles—and now look! God! God! Your sleep is not natural, Mother. Now I understand.

VON GRÖNINGSECK: For heaven's sake, pull yourself together! You certainly aren't the first.

EVCHEN: That you've ruined? I'm not . . . not the first? Oh, say that just once more . . .

VON GRÖNINGSECK: Not the first, I say, who gave in before she was married. From this moment on, you are mine. I made this oath already in the bedchamber and repeat it again here by all that is holy. On my knees I repeat it. In five months I shall be of age. I shall lead you to the altar then and proclaim you publicly to be mine.

EVCHEN: How can I trust you after what's happened? But of course I must. I'm as despicable as you—more despicable! I can't become any worse, can't sink any lower. *(wiping away her tears)* Good. Lieutenant, I shall believe you. *(stands)* Get up and hear my conditions! Five months, you said! Good! That's how long I'll choke back every emotion. No one will learn of my disgrace from my face. But!—is it really and truly in earnest, this oath of yours? Well, have you been struck dumb? Yes or no?

VON GRÖNINGSECK: Yes, yes, Evchen! As true as I'm standing here!

EVCHEN *(kisses him, but tears away as soon as he kisses her):* Listen! May these kisses be the rings that we exchange in promise of our marriage. But from now on, until the minister says, "Amen," from now on—listen to what I am saying—do not be so bold as to even kiss my finger. Else I shall hold you to be a perjurer, who sees me as a fallen woman to whom he owes no respect, whom he can play with as he wants. As soon as I sense this, I shall reveal the whole story to Father or Mother. It doesn't matter which one, right? To whomever, I'll tell everything that happened, even if they should trample me to dust! Do you understand? Why so silent, sir? Are you surprised at what I said? Now go call the coachman!

VON GRÖNINGSECK: You astonish me, Evchen! This tone!

EVCHEN: Offended virtue speaks. It must speak so. Now everything depends on you to prove that you have spoken the truth.

VON GRÖNINGSECK *(about to embrace her):* Angelic child!

EVCHEN *(draws back):* Are you insulting me, betrayer? Can you say "angel" without thinking of the fallen ones? Brought down by you!
(Exit von Gröningseck)

(The curtain falls.)

Act 2

(Living room in the Humbrechts' *house. Middle-class furnishings. A piano is off to the side.)*
(Martin Humbrecht sits, quite grumpily, in a corner, his head propped up by his hand. Frau Humbrecht is working.)

FRAU HUMBRECHT: I really don't know who you think you are, Husband! You, you grudge your daughter a little sunshine, much less any other pleasure.

HUMBRECHT: You're right, dear. You're always right.

FRAU HUMBRECHT: It's true, isn't it? Look at him sitting there, with a face like a garden spider. If we dare once every six months to sample some pleasure outside this house, right away you fly off the handle.

HUMBRECHT: You're right, dear, you're always right. I advise you, however, with the best of intentions—to shut up. I swear, I shall never again leave this house, even if everything here goes to blazes!

FRAU HUMBRECHT: Now what are you going on about? You haven't any cause to complain about me. I don't debase you, I don't waste your money, I never get out of the house—

HUMBRECHT *(laughs in her face):* Oh, you're the model of the ideal wife; everybody in town knows it. It's a shame that you're not Catholic. Why, eventually you could be canonized! Saint Frau Humbrecht, pray for us! Ha, ha, ha!

FRAU HUMBRECHT: Joke all you want. I am, and always will be, what I am.

HUMBRECHT: Who could deny it? You are, and through all eternity will be, a—

FRAU HUMBRECHT: A what? Come on, if you know anything to say, out with it! Can you show me where I have neglected you in the slightest? Aren't my eyes always everywhere, always checking?

HUMBRECHT: Oh yes, checking everything except the one thing they should be checking. You give your daughter too much freedom, no matter how many times I warn you.

FRAU HUMBRECHT: And you don't give her enough. It's a big deal if she goes *once* to a ball. Now really, where's the harm, eh? Aren't there a great many virtuous people at balls?

HUMBRECHT: It's not right for middle-class people. I've lived fifty decent years, I've never been at a ball, and I'm still alive. *(Master Humbrecht enters)*

FRAU HUMBRECHT: You're right on time, Cousin. My little girl won't have her piano lesson today, so you can help me bring my husband to his senses.

MASTER: I'm sure, Cousin, you're quite capable of doing that without my help. However *(adjusting his white collar)* may I ask if your daughter is ill?

HUMBRECHT: Not at all, Cousin! Not at all! She's just beginning to follow the latest fashion, make day out of night, and turn everything upside down.

MASTER: That would mean, then, she's still asleep?

FRAU HUMBRECHT: It's nothing to worry about, Cousin. Last night we were at the ball, Eva and I. The lieutenant from upstairs just wouldn't leave us in peace. Every Sunday during carnival season he had begged us very insistently to do him the honor. Yesterday he came again and invited us, and since it was the last ball, as he said, which decent people could attend—since on *mardi gras* only wigmakers go, as he said—he wanted to be absolutely sure not to be refused—

HUMBRECHT: And because I had just gone off on some business, they grabbed their chance and were off shaking their tails at the ball.

FRAU HUMBRECHT: Now, is there anything wrong with that, Cousin?

HUMBRECHT: There you're asking the right man! What would a cleric know of balls? He knows as much about them as about bulls. And I'll be hanged if he knows the difference between a bull and an ox!

FRAU HUMBRECHT: Don't be ridiculous. These men have been around; they hear tell of what mores are. Tell him frankly, Cousin, is there anything so sinful about going to balls?

MASTER: To answer your question, my esteemed cousin, I must distinguish first the going to balls itself from the various other conditions that go along with it or could go along with it. Considering the first point, I see nothing sinful in going to balls in itself; it's a delight and, according to the new theology, which however is at bottom also the oldest and most natural, delight is also a form of divine service—

HUMBRECHT: Cousin! Cousin! Take care that all you blackfrocks aren't thrown to the devil, once this new divine service is introduced!

MASTER: I'm only saying that delight is a type of divine service. It doesn't exclude all the other types, however, and consequently we teachers are not yet superfluous. Nonetheless, putting aside this argument, which I could better explain to you at another opportunity, that is, in clearer exegesis, I wish—with your permission, Cousin—to use the Socratic method, and thus I pose two questions to you. First, do you believe then that so many thoroughly righteous mothers, upstanding women, even women of the aristocracy, themselves would go to balls *and* take their daughters there if their consciences bothered them about it?

FRAU HUMBRECHT: Right, Cousin! Exactly!

HUMBRECHT: As far as I'm concerned, they may have a conscience as broad as the town square! But what does the aristocracy have to do with me? I have a position of my own, and everyone should stick to his own! And I never said that going to balls is fit for nobody. *My* family shouldn't be going to such things, is what I say. Let those who belong at such doings dance about. Who's to say no? For the aristocratic ladies and gentlemen, landowners and their ladies, who because of their great position don't know what to do with the time that God gave them, such doings may be very pleasant ways to kill the hours. Who would stop them? But tradesmen's wives and decent middle-class daughters should keep away from all that. They can go to weddings and guild banquets and that sort of thing if they're so eager to wear their shoes out dancing. They don't have to seek out places to put their honor and good name in jeopardy. When, however, a sugar-sweet fellow in a uniform, or a little baron—God have mercy on him—takes a middle-class girl to such places, it's ten to one that he will not bring her home in the same condition she was when she left.

FRAU HUMBRECHT: Oh, Husband! Are you crazy? You really don't believe that our daughter—

HUMBRECHT *(mimicking her):* You really don't believe—that that little brat! I only believe what I know. But if I *did* believe such a thing—*(makes two fists)* God in heaven! How I would thrash you!

MASTER: No, Cousin! Not that! You will not, I hope, fly into a rage over a matter that is so insignificant, one that remains completely within the class of those that the most stringent casuistry must consider neither good nor bad.

HUMBRECHT: Are there many such "matters" in your catechism?

MASTER: Several! And I am so convinced that going to balls should be reckoned as one of them that I will tell you—just between us—I was there myself.

HUMBRECHT *(leaping up angrily):* So that's what your church school comes collecting at our church doors twice a year for! *(as he leaves)* Adieu, Cousin! And I'll be damned before I throw another sols* in your bowl. *Adieu! (exit)*

FRAU HUMBRECHT: You did not handle that very well, Cousin! I'm afraid you've ruined things for a long time with my husband.

MASTER: Is he really in earnest?

FRAU HUMBRECHT: Oh, absolutely. He is totally of the old world. You just can't imagine what a cross he is for me to bear! Two years ago, at the beginning of winter, we just missed separating by a hair—God forgive me!—because I wanted to exchange my fur stole that he had inherited from his grandmother for a more stylish one. And only eight days earlier, when Evchen was supposed to attend a christening, he insisted with all his heart and soul that she had to wear the golden bonnet. But nobody wears them any more except at best a gardener's or a linen weaver's daughter! No, you might have admitted it, Cousin, but you shouldn't have announced it.

MASTER: As long as I need not reproach myself for having done something, I can speak of it. Of course, there are some distinctions. My superiors, for example, in order to prevent wrong-doing, must totally forbid some things, which they wouldn't if there were no danger at all. It wouldn't be wise to draw their attention to these activities. But otherwise I make little secret of the fact that I consider it rather my duty to see everything and test everything before passing judgment on it.

(Lieutenant von Gröningseck enters hastily and dashes up to Frau Humbrecht. Master Humbrecht rises)

**sols:* sou, a former French coin.

VON GRÖNINGSECK: Quite a *tête-à-tête!* Lovely! I'll tell your husband, Landlady, if you don't find a way to stop me!

FRAU HUMBRECHT: Hee, hee, hee, hee, hee! Go ahead, my husband knows all about it. He's already left.

VON GRÖNINGSECK: So! *(sings)* "The good husband, the well-behaved husband"—do you know the song? No? I must teach it to you. I'm sure I've seen this gentleman before.

FRAU HUMBRECHT: This is my cousin. He gives my Evchen piano lessons.

VON GRÖNINGSECK *(carelessly takes a pinch of snuff):* Yes, yes, Mr. Piano Teacher, yes.

MASTER: Your servant, sir! *(The Lieutenant takes Master Humbrecht's chair and sits close by Frau Humbrecht. Master Humbrecht gets another chair and sits on her other side)* With your permission, Cousin.

VON GRÖNINGSECK: No ceremony! *Pardieu!* I do believe this was *your* chair. Oh, I *do* beg your pardon, Mr. Piano Teacher!

MASTER: I am only a piano teacher to my friends, to whom I am more than happy to extend the favor. I do not have to stand for—

VON GRÖNINGSECK: As you wish, as you wish. It wasn't intentional, abbé!

FRAU HUMBRECHT: If you only knew, Lieutenant, what sort of row I've been having with my husband over the ball. Oh, you just can't imagine!

VON GRÖNINGSECK: *Comment?** Because of the ball? *C'est drôle!*†
On my honor, that's insane.

FRAU HUMBRECHT: And think of it: here's my cousin, who I thought would help me bring my husband to his senses, and instead drives him even more furious!

VON GRÖNINGSECK: I'm so sorry for you! However, Mr. Blackfrock must be used to that sort of thing.

FRAU HUMBRECHT: Everything would have been fine, you see, if he had told him the truth quite skillfully. But then in the passion of the moment he let it slip that he had been at the ball himself, and then of course my husband didn't want to hear any more. That's what did it! That alone!

VON GRÖNINGSECK: Ho, ho! The abbé himself at the ball. I really wouldn't have believed it of you. No, sir!

*What?
†That's funny!

MASTER: And why not, sir?

VON GRÖNINGSECK: Hm! Because of the coat.

MASTER: Really! Since you like to give yourself such airs, you should know that this prejudice shows you off rather badly. If you had been closer to the hub of France, or even at the intellectual courts of Germany, you would know that prelates of the first rank in no way consider themselves obligated to renounce their right to the pleasures permitted to man. If our church would only begin to think so sensibly and behave so sensibly, there would be fewer religious fanatics and consequently fewer mockers of religion!

FRAU HUMBRECHT: Oh, Cousin!

VON GRÖNINGSECK: Damn, what a sermon! *Ma foi,* you're going to get the first position of tutor that's mine to give.

MASTER: I doubt it. The father who is willing to entrust his son to me after talking to me for fifteen minutes is yet to be born.

VON GRÖNINGSECK: Why? Now you're making me curious.

MASTER: You're joking, sir.

VON GRÖNINGSECK: *Parole d'honneur!** No! I repeat, you're making me very curious about your reasons.

MASTER: To explain it all at once is impossible. In general, I can say that nowadays my educational axioms would hardly win approval.

FRAU HUMBRECHT: Oh, Cousin! You don't think as old-fashionedly as my husband.

MASTER: Quite the contrary! My thoughts are far too modern to escape prosecution.

VON GRÖNINGSECK: A little test, master. Just one example. I like to hear things like this. I think they are called "paradoxes," right?

MASTER: I would, for example, at the critical moment in which a boy becomes a young man, begins to be aware of his own feelings, and to sense the physical reasons for his existence—a moment that is a critical stumbling block for the virtue of almost all young people, a dangerous rock—

FRAU HUMBRECHT *(rising):* This is all over my head, gentlemen. I'm going to find my daughter. *(exit)*

MASTER: I would, I was about to say, treat my student in these years in a manner that was exactly the opposite of what is customary. Instead of leaving him in his ignorance to some mere chance that certainly leads astray nineteen out of twenty, I would be careful to

*Word of honor!

make him aware of the greatness, the nobility of his destiny.

VON GRÖNINGSECK: Certainly others have suggested that.

MASTER: But more! To instill in him forever a dreadful repugnance for all crimes of this type, I would imitate the Spartans, who in order to warn their youth of the perils of drunkenness showed them a few drunken slaves to laugh at. I myself would accompany my student to licentious and degenerate places. The insolent, self-seeking, vile behavior of the venal prostitutes would certainly make an imperishable mark on his tender, still uncorrupted heart, a mark that no temptation could ever erase.

VON GRÖNINGSECK: You may be right. For all that, though, the treatment seems damned drastic to me.

MASTER: To be sure, it is. But all other preventive measures can be overthrown by a glass of wine, a dissolute friend, an unfortunate moment. To be even surer, I have another prescription up my sleeve.

VON GRÖNINGSECK: Namely?

MASTER: The nearest infirmary or sanatorium for the incurably ill. The young man, when he has suitably absorbed the prior scenes and reflected on them and is then led to this living hell and sees before his very eyes the pitiful, horrible consequences of a single misstep, a single intemperance of this type—if he's not restrained forever, he has neither head nor heart.

VON GRÖNINGSECK: You're getting excited, master. I like that. I hate everything about the phlegmatic temperament. Pardon me, if my first impression of you was not a true measure of your merit. We must talk further. Give me your hand on it!

(Master Humbrecht *gives him his hand trustingly as* Frau Humbrecht *and* Evchen *enter)*

FRAU HUMBRECHT: Eh, look at that! How nice! Already such good friends?

VON GRÖNINGSECK: Now I know your cousin. Before, the clothing fooled me. Good morning, Mademoiselle Evchen.

MASTER: Are you all slept out, little cousin? (Evchen *lowers her eyes, blushes, curtsies, and sits down to work)* Such red eyes! Were you crying?

FRAU HUMBRECHT: Not at all. You know, Cousin, he who seldom rides—she's not used to staying up late, that's all.*

VON GRÖNINGSECK: I am so terribly sorry if I . . . or the ball . . .

---

*The saying goes: the person who seldom rides soon gets chafed.

EVCHEN *(interrupting):* You are very kind, Lieutenant.

FRAU HUMBRECHT: So don't be so surly! I don't know what's with her today. If I hadn't been with her every minute, if I didn't know that she had enjoyed everything fine and good, I'd wonder if some misfortune had befallen her.

VON GRÖNINGSECK: If I could only offer something for your reassurance . . . amusement, I mean . . . mademoiselle . . . it would be my pleasure . . .

EVCHEN *(with a forced smile):* I'll look forward to that, Lieutenant. I hope you keep your word.

VON GRÖNINGSECK: Absolutely! *(looks at his watch) Pardieu!* I've scarcely enough time to make the parade.

MASTER: I'll go with you. It seems that today my little cousin has no head for music.

EVCHEN: No, not today! I have a headache.

(Exeunt Lieutenant *and* Master Humbrecht)

FRAU HUMBRECHT: Oh, Child, Child! I beg you, for God's sake, not to mope around so. If your father comes back—you know how he is—and sees you so depressed, he'll start in all over again about the ball.

EVCHEN: You're right, Mother. *(with a deep sigh)* If only you hadn't fallen asleep! Then—

FRAU HUMBRECHT: Go on! Then *what?*

EVCHEN: Then you wouldn't be any more awake than I, or at least I'd seem as awake as you.

FRAU HUMBRECHT: Infant! A little sleep will do you good! Didn't you say yourself I didn't sleep long?

EVCHEN: No, not long, but longer than—

FRAU HUMBRECHT: I'm going to lose my temper! Do I have to throttle each word from your throat one at a time? *(mocking her)* "No, not long, but longer than—" Than *what?*

EVCHEN: Oh, well, than me! Isn't that right?

FRAU HUMBRECHT: Oh, what's the use? Look, Evchen, do your mother a favor and wipe that gloomy expression off your face. Your father already thinks that we went to the ball more for my sake than for yours. If he sees you so thoroughly miserable, I'll be the one he yells at again, for sure. Now Evchen, won't you be a dear for me? There isn't anything else wrong, is there?

EVCHEN: I'll do what I can.

FRAU HUMBRECHT: And good God, there's something else! Do you know where my snuffbox is?

EVCHEN: No. You mean the silver one with the gold trim?

FRAU HUMBRECHT: That's it. The one your father gave me for an engagement gift. I can't figure out what I—

EVCHEN: You had it in your hand yesterday morning. I saw it.

FRAU HUMBRECHT: Oh, God! If I've lost it! I'll go this instant and search through everything again. If I don't find it, I'll report it missing after dinner. *(exit)*

EVCHEN: Poor mother! All that fuss over a box! If only that were the biggest loss! Oh, that terrible moment, that ill-fated ball! How low I have fallen! It's my burden alone! I wanted to pull my braids out by the roots, but I was ashamed to in front of the maid doing my hair. May nobody see me, no man look at me in the eye! If the hope weren't there . . . my only hope . . . he swore it to me, twice, three times! Be still, my heart! *(frightened)* My God, I hear my father! Every word from him will be a dagger in my heart. How he thunders! By Heaven! Could he have already learned of my downfall? *(turns from the door in anguish and covers her face with her hands)*

HUMBRECHT *(to his wife, who has entered with him):* That piece of trash! That goddamned, pigheaded—! I want her out of this house this instant! Did you hear me? I said this instant! I won't eat a bit in peace as long as the little tramp is under my roof! So are you going to tell her or not? If I have to do it, I can't be sure I won't throw her down the stairs headfirst!

EVCHEN: My God! That means me!

FRAU HUMBRECHT: At least tell me why! I have to be able to give her a reason. Up to now you've never had any cause to complain about her.

HUMBRECHT: Reason! *I'm* supposed to give *you* a reason? You should be ashamed of yourself for being such a poor landlady and not keeping order in your own house. Because she's a slut! A whore! *That's* the reason!

EVCHEN *(leaping up):* I can't bear it any longer! *(falls suddenly at her* father's *feet. Humbrecht, who hadn't seen her, jumps, startled)* Father! Dearest father! Forgive me! *(falls silent and lets her head sink to the ground)*

FRAU HUMBRECHT *(grabbing her by the arm):* Eh, girl! What's the matter with you? Are you dreaming? Get up. I swear, she must have thought you were talking about *her.*

HUMBRECHT: The fool! What a fright she gave me! Falling before me like a sack of potatoes! Get up! Get up! *(helps her to her feet)* I can't stand grimaces, you know that. I had made up my mind to scold you thoroughly, but now it's just as if I hadn't a dram more bad temper in me. I believe the fright has wiped out everything. Well? Aren't you going to thank me for my leniency? This time you escaped. But if it ever happens again—thunder and lighting! Just once more and I'll break every bone in your body, so that you won't get much pleasure the third time.

EVCHEN: I swear to you, father! If I had it to do over, I wouldn't.

HUMBRECHT: Really? You wouldn't? Now that's my good girl, Evchen! That's wonderful. So you're sorry, eh? Come here and let me kiss you! What? You blush when you kiss your father? Why should you be so upset? But I forget that the mamsell* was at the ball. In the future you'll stay at home. The balls will go on very nicely without you.

EVCHEN: Mamsell!

FRAU HUMBRECHT: Don't be so hard on her! Look how she's shaking!

HUMBRECHT *(taking her hand):* Does the word bother you, Daughter? I'm glad! One must never want to be more than one is! And now, Wife! We almost didn't get to the most important thing—even if you do only know it because I have to tell you. The pretty young girl in back let a sergeant take her measurements. Her mother knows about it and lets them do as they please. The whole neighborhood is worked up over it. Now—march! Terminate her lodging. Now you understand why, right? Better the whole rear section stay empty our whole life long, abandoned to mice, rats, and owls, than harbor any more such riffraff. I wouldn't let my own daughter stay in the house one more hour if she went so far astray. *(Exit* Frau Humbrecht; *he calls after her.)* I want her packed up by sunset or I'll fling everything out the window and the both of them, mother and daughter, right after that! *(turns to* Evchen*)* You, go set the table. *(exit)*

EVCHEN: His own daughter! Those few words are my sentence of condemnation! What a treasure a clear conscience is! *(beating her breast as she exits)* But that's gone! Everything's gone! *(exit)*

---

*Here, "maid" (from *mademoiselle*).

Act 3

(Lieutenant von Gröningseck's room in the Humbrechts' *house. A bathroom off to the side) (Lieutenant von Hasenpoth stands before the mirror, whistling. von Gröningseck sits, lost in thought, in an easy chair.)*

VON HASENPOTH *(turning away from the mirror):* To hell with all those melancholy thoughts, Gröningseck! Come, the weather's beautiful. Have a cabriolet brought and we'll go to the Wasserzoll.*

VON GRÖNINGSECK: Go by yourself. I'd rather stay at home.

VON HASENPOTH: Forever and ever at home. How can you stand it? This whole summer you didn't go anywhere unless you had to with the company. I'd like to live that way too. Like a Carthusian! Really! Ten times better a bullet in the brain!

VON GRÖNINGSECK: To each his own.

VON HASENPOTH: Fine! But this moping around isn't your normal style. Only for the last four or five months . . . since the last carnival. That's it! I remember, *that's* when you began this Capuchin life. Why! Just why, that's all I want to know. Just give me a reason! Are you in love? Are you homesick?

VON GRÖNINGSECK: Homesick? Are you crazy?

VON HASENPOTH: Has to be one of them. If it's not homesickness, it must be love. And . . . when I see you in the light . . . no, it's not possible! I mean, what I don't know is *who?* In this whole, dear, long time I don't believe you've spoken to three women. Once every four weeks, for appearance' sake, you pay your respects to the marshall. And as soon as you make your obeisance you stand way off from everyone, like Nicodemus.† Elsewhere you're never

---

*A popular inn on the Ill River near Strasbourg.
†In fact, Nicodemus, a pharisee and member of the Jewish Council, visited Christ twice and helped prepare him for entombment.

seen with anyone. If I didn't know for sure that you'd had the Humbrecht girl, I'd think—

VON GRÖNINGSECK: Had? Me? Who said that?

VON HASENPOTH: Take it easy, Gröningseck, take it easy! We're speaking as friends, just between us. You don't think I'm some kind of child who can be persuaded that red is green?

VON GRÖNINGSECK: Haven't I already sworn to you several times exactly the opposite?

VON HASENPOTH *(laughs):* An excellent proof! You're crazy enough in love not to confess your conquest to me. When I could have directed the whole siege from my room!

VON GRÖNINGSECK: I have nothing to confess!

VON HASENPOTH: Your ardor indicates the opposite, and besides— to put it bluntly—how can you expect me to think she's a vestal virgin? You both sneaked away from the ball at two, and it wasn't till five that I heard the carriage pull up.

VON GRÖNINGSECK *(very serious):* Talk about something else, please!

VON HASENPOTH: And the sleeping powder that I delivered to you. If you didn't use it, why haven't I gotten it back?

VON GRÖNINGSECK: Because . . . because I . . . misplaced . . . lost . . . oh, I threw it to hell. Now stop it, Hasenpoth, not one word more if we're to remain friends!

VON HASENPOTH: I believe you would break a lance for her, play Don Quixote for her.

VON GRÖNINGSECK: Possibly.

VON HASENPOTH: But not with me? Your countryman? Your *compagnon de débauche?** Hear me, brother! I certainly hope that you have not pushed foolishness to its limits and really fallen in love with the girl. May the devil tear me apart, that would be against all *esprit de corps.* I wonder if that's why you're spending so much time with the blackfrock, the cousin from the house. Well? Good! So you don't lack the means to have your fill of her soon. You live under the same roof—or if that's not convenient, should I find you two a time and a place? I am full of ideas.

VON GRÖNINGSECK: Like Satan! I know!

VON HASENPOTH: At least you've put it to the test. You would never in your life have thought of the sleeping powder.

---

*Companion in debauchery.

VON GRÖNINGSECK: Powder! Powder! That damned powder! I wish I'd never seen it, or you, or this house, or anything! I wish it had turned to poison in my pocket and that I'd died from it as soon as I touched it!

VON HASENPOTH: What the hell kind of talk is that? Are you sorry you did it? It's because of it you were able to—

VON GRÖNINGSECK: Yes! Yes! Devil take you! I followed your accursed teachings to the letter! I have—if you want to know—desecrated an angel and become a monster.

VON HASENPOTH: A prank! A prank! Little brother! A childish prank! Priest's prattle! You did what you set out to do. Well and good! You ought to be pleased with yourself.

VON GRÖNINGSECK: If she'd been one of the run-of-the-mill lot, who wouldn't be good for anything if we didn't need them for our games—yes! Then I'd be happy. But she's not like that. You should have seen her, should have heard her, at the instant, the critical instant that follows the pleasure, when the greatest beauty disgusts us. You should have seen her. How mighty in her weakness! How great her virtue, even after I had taught her what depravity was! And I, how small! How—oh, I can't bear to think of it!

VON HASENPOTH: Can grimaces make you so tenderhearted? You poor simpleton!

VON GRÖNINGSECK: Grimaces! You're saying I can't tell grimaces from true expressions? The distempered gravediggers, the embellished, varnished dolls that you see stinking everywhere around here—*there* one finds grimaces! But not in a simple nature!

VON HASENPOTH: Simple or not simple! I say a woman's a woman, and in this matter, even the inexperienced ones give us food for thought. I've met few women who didn't passionately want to be taken by storm, and not a one that didn't cry a few crocodile tears after the overthrow! It's born into them!

VON GRÖNINGSECK *(with smoldering rage):* You paragon among libertines! You can thank my guilty conscience that I listen to you so indulgently. I'm a coward, a poltroon ... but I still can't guarantee I'll listen to much more of your talk! I may no longer be enough at peace to be deliberately valiant, but rage may make me foolhardy. Do you understand?

VON HASENPOTH: Better than you understand *me*. I assure you, I was speaking of course only of the women whom I—

VON GRÖNINGSECK: Ha! Of the frivolous ones, fifty of which on the subtlest scales of conscience wouldn't weigh an ounce. But I beg to remind you, Lieutenant. . . .

VON HASENPOTH: If we're speaking seriously, you don't need to be so formal! It sounds so strange to me—

VON GRÖNINGSECK: Let it be! But mark this, Hasenpoth! We shall never be at ease with one another again if you fail to do what I expect. To a sensible woman, of course, it matters very little what you and the likes of you or others think of her. Your praise is a stigma. In your disapproval lies inner greatness. But it matters to *me* what you say of the girl whose name you earlier let fall from your unwashed lips. Not a word! Just listen to me. And just so that there's no further misunderstanding, you should know—

VON HASENPOTH: Someone's coming.

VON GRÖNINGSECK *(looking around):* The master! I met him out walking. Don't you breathe a word of this! He doesn't know anything about it. *(*Master Humbrecht *enters)* Bravo! Master Humbrecht, how wonderful! You don't forget me when you visit your relatives.

MASTER: Certainly not, you know that. When I haven't seen you in a few days, I feel something's missing.

VON GRÖNINGSECK *(shaking his hand):* I'm glad for that. How are things with the family?

MASTER: You live here in the house and ask me that?

VON HASENPOTH: Good point! To inquire of an outsider about the people in your own house may be all right in Paris or London, but here? If the lieutenant weren't such a night owl, out trying all manner of things, he'd go look for himself and—

VON GRÖNINGSECK: And! Perhaps I have my reasons? Yes, Master Humbrecht! I ask you because as their cousin you already have their trust and access. As good as my landlord may be at heart, he and I are not good for each other. He has his own whims, as well you know . . . and I can be rather hot-tempered. In the long run it wouldn't be good.

MASTER: So you should wait till he's not home. My cousin and her daughter—

VON GRÖNINGSECK: —have my best wishes, master, Evchen especially, and that's exactly why I don't want to get them in trouble. Since the carnival I have been with them some four or five times, and unfortunately once or twice he wasn't there, and— ugh! Was there ever a row!

MASTER *(laughs):* He just can't forgive your escorting his women to the ball. As he said to me—

VON GRÖNINGSECK: Have you seen your little cousin?

MASTER: Not for two whole weeks, I think. She sits in her room constantly. Melancholy eats at her. I can't make head or tail of it. Asking, praying—everything's in vain! It makes her father even more intolerant.

VON GRÖNINGSECK: Merciful God! I! I!

MASTER: Sympathize with her? Oh, you do have a kind heart.

VON GRÖNINGSECK: That's it, Master Humbrecht! Yes! You took the words right out of my mouth. Kind! Yes, that's my heart, all right. So full of—

VON HASENPOTH *(who, during this, has been whistling. To von Gröningseck):* Don't let the cat out of the bag! *(to Master Humbrecht)* Has she been like this for long?

MASTER: Well, I can't fix the time exactly. It came in stages. Unfortunately, it gets worse every day. Her favorite book is Young's *Night Thoughts* in the French translation.

VON HASENPOTH: May God have mercy on her! If I had to read a single page of that, I'd be as melancholy as an Englishman and hang myself by my garter.

VON GRÖNINGSECK *(scornfully):* You! But my dear Master! As much beauty as Young may have for a cheerful, tranquil soul, at peace with herself and the world around her—you would know this better than I—this reading is hardly appropriate for a discontented, world-weary, lifeless heart, without which melancholy could not occur. Shouldn't you as a friend—

MASTER: Take it away? I tried that already, because I happen to think exactly as you do on the matter. But she wailed for so long that she was going to die from grief and oppression—in short, I was happy to give it back.

VON GRÖNINGSECK: God! God! Is there no solution! I'm sorry for her from the bottom of my soul, the dear child! What if—ah, what good will it do? Most things like this take time . . . still . . . it might be tried! At least it's a courtesy that can't offend her even if it can't help her. As soon as you see her *alone* again, Master, would you tell her for me that I am very concerned for her well-being and have often asked about it. Asked *you* about it, and that I hope she will again be cheerful and lively, and the sooner the better. She can absolutely—*(stops short)*—Oh, well, it sounds like an empty compliment, but it comes truly from the heart. She can depend on me absolutely to be always at her service, now or in the future. Tell her that, would you, Master? Word for word! And better a little more than a little less!

MASTER: Gladly, Lieutenant! I thank you for your interest, but before long you will—

VON HASENPOTH: Put crazy ideas in your head! Not at all, Master! You judge him wrongly: his heart is colder than ice. But nonetheless he is so soft that if he sees somebody suffering or only hears about it—well, I still don't know how he could let himself become a soldier. And then if it's a woman we're talking about—

VON GRÖNINGSECK: Good God! You pompous ass, will you never shut up! Don't forget, Master. Tell her as a courtesy, if for no other reason.

MAJOR LINDSTHAL *(enters):* Furlough! Furlough! Von Gröningseck! Your furlough papers have arrived. I've got them here.

VON HASENPOTH: Furlough! You asked for a furlough?

MASTER: You're going to leave us?

VON GRÖNINGSECK: Oh, Major, you are doubly welcome! *(To Master Humbrecht)* I'm only going home for a short time.

VON HASENPOTH: When did you ask for that? Damn! A furlough! And I didn't know a thing about it.

VON GRÖNINGSECK: A capital offense, really! I asked the inspector himself for it at the general review.

MAJOR: And I also wrote to the secretary and can say, without flattering myself too much, that I have the *congé,** properly signed, in my pocket. *Preuve de cela!*† Here it is! *(hands the papers to* von Gröningseck)

VON GRÖNINGSECK: Thank you for your act of friendship.

MAJOR: If it's an act of friendship, as I hope, and as I hope you take it, then no thanks is necessary. Thanks are for alms.

VON GRÖNINGSECK: Your double graciousness puts me to shame.

MAJOR: Paperla, paperla, pap! Another stupid word that I've never been able to tolerate: shame! A low-down card, when you tell him to his face he is a cad, *he* is put to shame, but never an honorable man.

MASTER *(aside to* von Gröningseck): A singular man! His mood pleases me.

*Furlough
†Proof!

VON HASENPOTH: The best or the craziest man in the whole regiment, as you wish.

MAJOR: Rid yourselves of such tasteless words, gentlemen! It will trouble you little now, but once a bad habit's established, it's damnably hard to break. Apropos! Today I witnessed a great joke! In the *auberge** where I eat, and devil take me, I wouldn't take a thousand gold pieces not to have seen it. Perhaps you already know the story, gentlemen? *(von Gröningseck and* von Hasenpoth *look at one another and shake their heads)* No? That surprises me. It's spreading like wildfire from mouth to mouth. So much the better! Now you'll hear the plain unvarnished truth, for I saw the whole thing myself, and may the devil tear me apart alive if I change a word of it! Yesterday afternoon, while I was drinking my glass of liqueur—to aid digestion—at the Spiegel† I saw two officers through the window that faces the courtyard. One was from Lyon and the other from Anhalt, and they were playing a game of piquet. It was razor-sharp, I can assure you. At stake were three pounds, and all honor cards were paid for. As it's my favorite game, I went out and watched things for a while. I sat behind the officer from Anhalt who was already losing terribly. In my whole life I've never seen such poor luck. Every moment he went down pique and repique, and God knows, his little talers were running away. Damn it, it was a pleasure to see. Meanwhile Lieutenant Wallroth from Salis stood behind the other one, facing me. He watched three or four plays, going first red, then white in the face. I thought he was *moitié*‡ with my man, and the loss bothered him. All of a sudden—God only knows how he caught on so fast!—he leaped on the pile of money that lay between them and pushed everything, big and small, to the officer from Anhalt, saying: "Sir, this money is yours! It's not right; you've been the dupe in this game. Three times this man has kept the ace up his sleeve. I've seen him do it myself." Well, before he'd even finished talking, just listen, just listen! The officer from Lyon gave him such a smack in the face that the whole room rocked. They grabbed for their swords, but they were stopped by Osterreid and his men. We all just stood there, thunderstruck. The *chevalier de*

---

*Tavern.
†A cafe in Strasbourg.
‡Gone halves with.

*fortune** finally slipped out without our being aware of it, and a bit later the honest Swiss did too. "A felicitous *retour!*"† I thought to myself, for certainly somebody would have been set on his ass. But *pardieu,* no! Wallroth went to the commandant, reported the whole thing, and the crooked officer is stuck in *pontcouvert.*‡ Dismissed and kicked out of his regiment in shame and degradation—it's the least that'll happen to him.

VON GRÖNINGSECK: The blackguard deserved it, too! And Wallroth?

MAJOR: He will *bon gré, mal gré*§ have to quit too.

MASTER: But why, Major? Didn't he behave as any decent man would?

MAJOR: Decent and not decent! *You* don't understand. A man of honor wouldn't have run to the commandant, but would have just quietly asked to meet his man somewhere alone. Now I'm just reporting what happened. Today at noon Wallroth arrived at the *auberge* for lunch. As usual thirteen or fourteen of us were already there. As Wallroth entered the room, his neighbor turned his— Wallroth's—plate over. Wallroth sat down, as if he didn't understand, and turned it right side up. Then one after another stood, just as if a signal had been given, and left for sanctuary. Finally I left, too. You should have seen the face he made. I'd like to have a picture of it. Then you could see how stupid one looks when one is truly ashamed.

VON GRÖNINGSECK: I feel sorry for the poor devil.

MAJOR: Me too. However! You do understand, sir, why he has to quit? Before, he'd have only to tangle with one man. Now he has fourteen against him. If he wanted to stay, he'd have to duel with them all.

VON HASENPOTH: Naturally! They had all insulted him.

MASTER: But . . . dueling is forbidden.

MAJOR: Forbidden! Pah! The ban doesn't matter to us! Or to any soldier!

MASTER: You'll permit me, Major! Are you not also a citizen of the state, a subject of the king, as much as any other? And didn't you swear to our king, at his coronation, to give no quarter to any dueller, without exception?

*Knight of fortune.
†Return.
‡Confinement.
§ Whether he likes it or not.

MAJOR: That may well be true, Master. I have faith in every honest officer that he will not intentionally offend the king or go against his command. But do we want then to let every scoundrel ride roughshod over us? We cannot endure these daily insults silently, even at meals, as you see with Wallroth—

MASTER: Must you break the law?

VON GRÖNINGSECK: There's no other way, my dear Master! Does that surprise you? At one time I would have agreed with you. We other epaulettes have only two paths once we are insulted, with or without cause—we risk our lives or our honor!

MASTER: That is a contradiction. In order not to be considered dishonorable, a law-abiding man must break the law and place his head on the executioner's scaffold. Unbelievable!

MAJOR: Not unbelievable at all! Not at all! Better to lose one's life than one's honor. The scaffold does not dishonor a man. Only crime can do that, and a crime that one is forced to commit is not a crime. If I'd been in Wallroth's place, I'd have dueled before I let that insult go by. Better to fight with the whole garrison—one after another, of course. If he still demands satisfaction from me, he'd have it today, even if a thousand scaffolds or a thousand gallows stood nearby. If you want to eliminate all contradictions, Master, or make all the crooked straight, go ahead! You have my blessing. *A l'honneur,** gentlemen! Before you go, Gröningseck, will I see you again?

VON GRÖNINGSECK: Of course.

MAJOR *(as he leaves):* Without saying farewell then—(von Gröningseck *accompanies him to the door*)

MASTER: The major speaks—

VON HASENPOTH: As becomes a soldier, and you as becomes a man of your profession. Each in his own way may be right.

VON GRÖNINGSECK *(returns):* Yes, Master, quite so! You don't know what a trial it is for us to remain honorable, how carefully, how circumspectly we must measure every step. But *(in flattering tones)* the learned argument has not caused you to forget my instructions?

MASTER: Certainly not! To remove any doubt, I'll leave now and find an immediate opportunity to speak to my little cousin.

VON GRÖNINGSECK: Do that and I'll be forever in your debt. I only believe I have the right to ask this kindness of you because I know

*To honor.

that I would do the same for you. *(grips the* Master's *hand. Exit* Master)

VON HASENPOTH: Hellfire and damnation! Gröningseck! You've never conducted yourself so stupidly. Anyone could read the whole secret in your eyes. If the master were to the slightest degree a mistrustful—

VON GRÖNINGSECK: Oh no, he's far too good-hearted.

VON HASENPOTH: And the instructions you gave him!

VON GRÖNINGSECK: I made them very ambiguous. With great pains, I assure you. But if he repeats them exactly as I gave them to him, it will have a good effect. Evchen will understand every word, and perhaps she will be comforted. For I don't know any sure way to send her a letter.

VON HASENPOTH: You mean you've never written to her?

VON GRÖNINGSECK: No. Since I've been in the house, I haven't spoken to her for a moment without witnesses. So I have to seize any opportunity I can.

VON HASENPOTH: So tell me, what really went on between you two? As far as I can see, her melancholy has some physical cause.

VON GRÖNINGSECK: Oh, that it has, to be sure! She's pregnant. I've been around too much to be able to deny it. But half a *confidence* is good for nothing. She's pregnant by me. Do you know what that means? By *me* she's pregnant, so you can—I should hope—figure out what I have to do with her, and what I will do, what I must do. I shall marry her.

VON HASENPOTH: You?

VON GRÖNINGSECK: I! That's the least I can do for her.

VON HASENPOTH: Lieutenant von Gröningseck and the Humbrecht girl! Impossible!

VON GRÖNINGSECK: Why, if I may ask? Why? Why impossible?

VON HASENPOTH: To begin with, as a lieutenant—

VON GRÖNINGSECK: I can resign, so where's the impossibility? It will not be difficult to have her as my wife. I've squandered a lot, but I've also saved some. I'm going to take control of the rest of my possessions; that's why I'm taking the furlough. I'm now of age and can take control at any time. As soon as this is in order, I'll come back and ask for my Evchen. When I take off the blue coat for good, she'll be mine. I know it.

VON HASENPOTH: You want to give up everything then?

VON GRÖNINGSECK: Everything! Everything! Rather than drag the pains of hell along with me! But one more thing! Mark this, Lieutenant, mark this. *(takes him by the hand)* You are the only one to whom I have opened my heart. Not a word of this has crossed my lips before. Your plans pushed me into this abyss. I don't reproach you. You misjudged the angel. I did too! And I should have known her better. I alone! Not you! Now you must also help me wriggle out of this again. I don't believe I am trusting too much to your virtue. *But* if I am deceiving myself, and even a suspicion of what I have told you comes to light before the proper time—then, Hasenpoth *(lets go of his hand and recoils)* you or I will go to the devil in revenge! Now let me go! I must catch my breath and make preparations for the trip. We'll talk later. *(goes off into the bath)*

VON HASENPOTH: If you, with all your inflated ideas of virtue, take her as your wife—then let Satan make me run the gauntlet of his whole army of devils, back and forth, twenty-four times. No, Herr von Gröningseck! I must first sift things out. *(as he leaves)* I'll shuffle these cards myself. Better than that dummy at the Spiegel. Just wait. *(exit)*

Act 4

(Evchen's bedroom. At the right is a door. Opposite the door are windows facing the street.)
(As the curtain rises, Frau Humbrecht *is closing the windows.* Evchen *is reading)*

FRAU HUMBRECHT: Still I see and hear nothing of him.

EVCHEN: He's hardly likely to come this late, Mother! Go to bed! The gates have already been shut for a long time.

FRAU HUMBRECHT: Who knows? Couldn't he get in through the servants' passage? It hasn't yet struck eleven.

EVCHEN *(sighing):* I hadn't thought of that.

FRAU HUMBRECHT: Again a sigh! Didn't you promise me to stop all this eternal moaning and groaning? Be a man of your word!

EVCHEN: Oh, if only I were a man!

FRAU HUMBRECHT: Why?

EVCHEN: I'd set off straightaway for America and join their fight for freedom.

FRAU HUMBRECHT: And leave your father and mother back here alone? Pfui, Evchen! I know why you're talking this way. You don't love us anymore.

EVCHEN: How can you think that, Mother!

FRAU HUMBRECHT: How? Because you no longer trust your parents. Where there is no trust, there can be no love.

EVCHEN *(agitated):* Mother!

FRAU HUMBRECHT: Nothing else. I'm sorry I have to tell you this. Before, if you hurt your little finger, you'd come running to me to complain about it. Now—may God forgive you!—you get goose bumps if you just catch sight of one of us.

EVCHEN: It's not true! You do me the greatest injustice in the world, Mother, when you say that! I love you just as much as ever . . . but . . .

FRAU HUMBRECHT: Well?

EVCHEN *(timidly):* But . . . there are things that one cannot reveal to anyone.

FRAU HUMBRECHT: Why not?

EVCHEN: Because they aren't yet ready. Because one can't admit them even to oneself.

FRAU HUMBRECHT: Nothing but mystery! If your father heard an answer like that he'd be furious. You know he can't stand keeping things secret. Well, neither can I. Yesterday, before he rode off, I thought he was going to go raving mad. When he'd set you so sweetly on his lap, talked to you so sweetly, pressed you to his heart, and squeezed you.

EVCHEN: And pushed me off again, so that I staggered off to bed.

FRAU HUMBRECHT: That was your own stubborn fault. It hurt him; I could see it in his eyes. But on the stairs he swore that if you were still hanging your head so low and wouldn't tell him why, then he would no longer recognize you as his child. He said: "I will not let myself be dragged about anymore by her whims like a calf on a rope."

EVCHEN: As true as God lives, Mother, it's no whim! Would that it were! I cannot admit to myself the source of my sorrow. But to tell the truth, Mother, the vehemence with which you've tried to discover it, by reading it in my eyes or by pressing it out of me with threats or caresses, has contributed greatly to my melancholy, or headhanging, as you call it. You mean well, I know you do. I can tell, and I suffer doubly because of it, because right now I can't thank you for your tenderness. Just try this, Mother! Let me linger a while in my dreaming. Act as if you didn't notice anything at all. Leave me to myself, and tell Father to do the same. Only for a little while! Perhaps everything will clear up. It *must* clear up, and then I shall be your daughter again, or—

FRAU HUMBRECHT: Or?

EVCHEN: A child of death.

FRAU HUMBRECHT: Another thrust to the heart! Oh, Evchen! Evchen! You're going to send me to an early grave!

EVCHEN: No, Mother! No! Not you! More likely me, if you don't give me any peace. Just try what I ask, I beg you. Everything will turn out all right. *(flings her arms around her mother's neck)* Here, hanging around your neck, I implore you—don't block your daughter from the one path that can save her!

FRAU HUMBRECHT *(extricates herself):* Your father! I hear him.

EVCHEN: Promise me!

FRAU HUMBRECHT *(taking a lamp from the table, turns toward her husband):* What else can I do? I have no choice.

HUMBRECHT *(enters, wearing boots and spurs):* What the hell are you sitting up here for, woman! Letting the house below go unattended!

FRAU HUMBRECHT: I only came up this minute to see how she was doing.

HUMBRECHT: Delightful! Now the mother has to go to the daughter! Couldn't she just as easily have come to you? And she's standing there as if she'd lost the grace of God! Can't even say "Good evening" to her father!

EVCHEN *(timidly):* Good evening, Father.

HUMBRECHT *(scornfully, mimics her):* Good evening, my dearest Daughter!

FRAU HUMBRECHT: You're always snapping at her. No wonder she's afraid of you.

HUMBRECHT: Afraid? Of me? Balderdash! Aren't I her father? Well, Evchen, aren't I? Do I have to weigh each word before I say it when I'm talking to my own child? I'll be damned before I do anything like that!

FRAU HUMBRECHT: Idiot! Who said anything like that? Only your tone—

HUMBRECHT: My tone! My tone! I admit it's not one of the sugar-sweet, butter-smeared types that our silver-tongued gentlemen use to squawk their compliments! But I assume my daughter after seventeen or eighteen years would have gotten used to it! By all that's holy, I am hardly a man-eater! Come here, Evchen, come! Have you been a good girl? Have you confessed to your mother? That's it! You have!

EVCHEN *(agitated):* Dearest Father!

FRAU HUMBRECHT: Yes, yes, she has! Now leave her in peace. You'll hear all about it later.

HUMBRECHT: That's wonderful! That's right! *(kisses her)* Now you are doubly dear to me. Was it worth all the trouble, though? All the moping about?

FRAU HUMBRECHT: You'll hear all about it later, I said.

HUMBRECHT: I should be very angry that you didn't do me the courtesy. Only yesterday I thought I'd have to use sorcery to get it out. Then, no doubt, my tone was to blame. Will you be my pretty and lively Evchen again?

EVCHEN: As much as I can.

HUMBRECHT: Back into society, going to church? Not always sitting in your stall?

FRAU HUMBRECHT: Pooh! What questions! Things will work out: one after another. It's time now to go to bed. It's already struck twelve. Come on, Husband! *(pulls on his sleeve)* Good night, Evchen.

HUMBRECHT: *Busoir, busoir!** Tonight I'm going to saw wood, Wife! *(breaks free, turns, and takes Evchen's hand)* May God forgive you all the sleepless nights that you have given us for some time! I know He has counted all my sighs and all your mother's tears. May He not count them against you, my child. None of them! Otherwise they'd start all over again. *(Evchen embraces him, crying. She kisses him)* Now, sleep well! *(Exeunt parents)*

EVCHEN *(looking after him):* Poor man! Good, unfortunate father! *(sighs deeply)* I fear, I fear you still have sleepless nights ahead! Your wrath terrifies me, but—God knows!—not so much as your love! *(sits down and reads for a while)* No use! It's no use. I read and read, but when I close the book *(slams it shut)* I can't remember a word of what I read. *(lays the book aside. Paces excitedly a few times back and forth)* Gröningseck! Gröningseck! What you have to answer for!

VON GRÖNINGSECK *(who meanwhile has slunk in. He is fully dressed, but without hat or sword. He places his lantern on the table and throws himself at her feet):* I know, my dearest, my most precious! I want to answer for everything, make everything good.

EVCHEN *(shrinks back):* How? You dare . . . at midnight? What do you want? What are your intentions?

VON GRÖNINGSECK: The purest, the most virtuous that ever a man had. To give you back your peace of mind.

EVCHEN: Can you? Can you make things that happened unhappen? Or do you intend to swear falsely before God and deceive me again?

VON GRÖNINGSECK: No Evchen! Truly, no! The latter I would not, the former I cannot. And nonetheless I wish I could. With my blood I would buy back the unfortunate moment when I madly—

*Bonsoir (good evening).

EVCHEN: It's burned deep enough in my soul. You don't need to remind me of it. Or are you so satanic as to be both seducer and accuser?

VON GRÖNINGSECK *(leaps up):* For the love of heaven, what a horrible monster you take me for! I came here—

EVCHEN: At a time, at an hour, at which you would not have come if you had the slightest respect for me.

VON GRÖNINGSECK: Forgive me! Evchen! I swear to you, just the opposite! I know and respect your delicacy, and I hesitated long before I decided on this untimely visit. I had to take the risk! I owed it to you and me to speak to you alone, once more, before I leave here.

EVCHEN: You're leaving?

VON GRÖNINGSECK: As soon as possible, in order to return in good time and ask you properly for your hand.

EVCHEN: Are you serious, Gröningseck? Is this your heart speaking? I seem to recall you swore this to me before.

VON GRÖNINGSECK: And repeat it here with all solemnity! As soon as I realized that you were not the type I had mistaken you for in my recklessness, my first instinct was to make all the amends in my power to your offended virtue! And it shall remain, when all other instincts cease with my last breath. May you find some comfort in this promise. I shall not go back on my word. But you, Evchen! You have not kept your word to me.

EVCHEN: What do you mean?

VON GRÖNINGSECK: Didn't you promise me to control your features? That nobody would notice anything?

EVCHEN: It's true, I promised to try very hard. I did too, and—

VON GRÖNINGSECK: And so I never came into the room when you didn't blush all over! Was it anger, contempt, or loathing?

EVCHEN: None of them, Gröningseck! I loved you from the moment I met you. Now I can say it to you. Otherwise you would not have found me to be so weak. You cannot hate me for having the hope of becoming yours. But I have not yet learned to stifle the little voice of conscience that nagged me. If I could, I would blush doubly for myself.

VON GRÖNINGSECK: Divine child! *(grasps her hand and presses it to his lips)*

EVCHEN *(pulls it quickly back):* I thought you had only *one* word. Is it oblivion?

VON GRÖNINGSECK: Oblivion! Outpouring of the soul! Call it what you will! I must seal my oath of eternal fidelity with a kiss on your hand. *(is about to kiss her hand with force; she pushes him away)*

EVCHEN: No, Lieutenant! That's just affectation. A kiss on the hand is nothing, I know, and yet it can lead to anything. If you can't keep your word in trivialities, how can I trust you in more serious concerns? At least I shall spare you one perjury. Those who have been burned learn to be careful with fire. When do you plan to return here?

VON GRÖNINGSECK: Two months will more than do.

EVCHEN: Two months! My heart will not always be quiet in that time. But there's no other way. I must put up with it. I shall not order you to hurry; if your heart does not command you to, I shall be lost anyway.

VON GRÖNINGSECK: I shall certainly make haste.

EVCHEN: Gröningseck! Yes, I believe you. I trust your integrity. But who can guarantee me the future? No one! Not even you! None of us has read his fate in the Book of Providence. An inner voice, which I try in vain to still, tells me that mine is written in blood!

VON GRÖNINGSECK: Evchen! How can that come to pass?

EVCHEN: How? In the easiest, simplest way possible. If you don't keep your word.

VON GRÖNINGSECK: That is impossible.

EVCHEN: Time will tell. Meanwhile, suppose—hear me out—that you don't keep your word, that you abandon me to my fate, to the whole burden of scandal that lies in wait, the wrath of my family, the fury of my father. Do you believe that I shall wait for all this? No! I would seek out the most horrible wilderness, far away from everyone who has a human appearance. I would hide myself in the thickest shrubs and only drink the rain of heaven, in order never to see my face in the brook, the reflection of an immoral being. If heaven should work a miracle and preserve me and the wretched creature—an orphan even before it has a father—I would, as soon as it began to stammer, instead of repeating "Father" or "Mother" in its ear, say the dreadful words "whore" and "perjurer," until it repeated them clearly. Then in a fit of rage at this insult, I would be driven to put an end to my misery and its. Wouldn't that be bloody, Gröningseck?

VON GRÖNINGSECK: Only too much. My hair stands on end. I am a soldier. I was in the field at a very young age. I have witnessed many frightening scenes. But never such a—

EVCHEN: You have only to order and I shall carry it out!

VON GRÖNINGSECK: May God protect you! I shudder at the very thought! For God's sake, Evchen! Give up all this melancholy preoccupation! Put it out of your mind! Trust yourself to me, to my word of honor, to what remains of my feeling and virtue. If there's even a spark left, you will blow it into a flame.

EVCHEN: Good, Gröningseck! So be it! I promise you.

VON GRÖNINGSECK: Do you also promise me to maintain your composure during this time?

EVCHEN *(meditatively):* I wouldn't like to promise more than I can do.

VON GRÖNINGSECK: You can do it, darling! As soon as you believe in me, that I can be an honorable man.

EVCHEN: If I don't want to betray myself and make my parents suspicious, then I shall have to do so. You can't believe how close they are to guessing, how much they have plagued me! More than once the fatal secret has trembled on my lips. Only fear—

VON GRÖNINGSECK: Maintain your silence. I implore you, I tremble when I think of your father. Use every power, summon up every bit of cheerfulness, so as not to arouse suspicions. No one has an idea—

EVCHEN: I trust the master least of all. His eagle eyes have rattled me more than once. The message you gave him yesterday haunted his mind. I saw it, so I pretended I wasn't the least bit concerned.

VON GRÖNINGSECK: Could he be base enough to harm you?

EVCHEN: Oh, no! He never intends me any harm. Perhaps only too much good. As far as I can tell, he has secret designs on me. My mother may encourage him. Clerics are accustomed to choosing their wives while they're still probationers. When in ten or fifteen years they get a village parsonage, they don't want to take long looking for a wife.

VON GRÖNINGSECK: By that time perhaps we could offer him our daughter.

EVCHEN: Take care that she is not ashamed of her mother. Now go! The neighbors aren't used to seeing my light on for so long.

VON GRÖNINGSECK: Is Evchen also concerned?

EVCHEN: When it's not right here *(pointing to her heart),* when it rebukes us, then one can be afraid of his own shadow. Now go, I say! Tomorrow you can see me again with my mother. You will say a proper farewell to her.

VON GRÖNINGSECK: See you! But not speak!

EVCHEN: I will understand every look. *(she goes to the door)* Two months, you said?

VON GRÖNINGSECK: Two months at most! I swear to you again by the moon and all the stars that shine in the heavens. My last look, when I board the carriage tomorrow, will swear it to you again. Only trust me, my darling! *(presses* Evchen's *hand and exits)*

EVCHEN *(opens the door halfway, sticks her head out, and calls in a muffled voice):* Gröningseck! One more thing! *(He returns. She kisses him)* I won't be able to do that tomorrow. *(Exit* Gröningseck. Evchen *locks the door tightly after him)*

(The curtain falls.)

Act 5

(The room of the second act. Daybreak.)
(Evchen stands before the mirror and puts on a cap. Lissel, *her maid, enters)*

LISSEL: Hey! Heavens! Where are you going so early, Miss Evchen? The fog stinks of brimstone.

EVCHEN: That doesn't matter. That's not to be avoided around Michaelmas. I just want to slip out somewhere quickly. Lissel! Run and get me your cotton cloak. Hurry! Run!

LISSEL: What are you going to do with it?

EVCHEN: What do you think? Put it on! You'll get it back again. In the meantime you have my taffeta one. Go ahead, wear it until I come back. So go! I must leave now before people are up.

LISSEL: Why? Do you have an appointment?

EVCHEN: Of course! Don't keep me waiting any more! Go! *(Exit Lissel)* Where shall I go? I don't know myself. As far as my feet shall carry me. Gröningseck, Gröningseck! Your defiances should cause you pain! The letter you wrote me! Do I still have it with me? *(searches in her pocket and pulls it out)* Yes! *(reads it through once)* To send Hasenpoth with such a letter, portraying me as an out-and-out whore! His mocking of the place where we got better acquainted. I don't understand at all. I don't want to understand! *(puts the letter away again)* All things considered— oh, I must fly! *(catches sight of the portrait of her parents)* Ha! You dears, are you there too? Here on my knees I thank you for all the love and kindness you have shown me. *(crying)* I am doing a poor job of paying you back. Don't curse me! Just don't curse me!

LISSEL *(returns.* Evchen *leaps up):* I hear your father already up and about in their room.

EVCHEN: Haste, then! For God's sake, hurry! Throw it over me, so

I'm not recognized so easily. Now the cape over that. *(as she leaves, she turns around once more)* The cloak, Lissel! Keep it until I come back. Do you hear? *(from the other side of the door)* Don't give it up till I come back! *(exits)*

LISSEL *(straightening up the room):* Till! Till! God only knows what's going on with her. Something's got to be wrong. I've never seen her so agitated. What if something terrible's happened to her? Such a good, decent girl! It would break my heart. *(about to leave with* Evchen's *cloak.* Master Humbrecht *bursts in hastily)*

MASTER: Has Herr Humbrecht already left, Miss?

LISSEL: Gone! Hardly. He's only just got up.

MASTER: So much the better. I didn't miss him. Tell him I have something urgent to discuss with him and that he should come here immediately.

LISSEL: Right away, Master Humbrecht. *(exit)*

MASTER: I would give something to be outside this house again. I'm risking a lot. Nonetheless, if it's to prevent a great misfortune . . . if it *is,* as I am entitled to guess, then it's better that I break the news to my cousin gradually, rather than that he hears it from strangers, or finds out for himself. He wouldn't know how to contain his wrath.

HUMBRECHT *(in nightshirt, nightcap, and worn-out shoes):* Good morning, Cousin! Where the hell have you come from?

MASTER: Straight from home. I left especially early in order not to miss you.

HUMBRECHT: It must be a matter of great importance.

MASTER: I wish it were not so. You are a man—?

HUMBRECHT: At least I've proved it to my wife.

MASTER: No jokes, if you please. You are a man of reason?

HUMBRECHT: I have as much common sense as it takes to run my house.

MASTER: Good! Pull yourself together, Cousin, and listen to what I have to tell you! I am personally concerned . . . perhaps I am mistaken . . . but it is nonetheless my duty—

HUMBRECHT: Not so much preamble, Master! Get to the point.

MASTER: First you must give me your word as an honorable man that you will hear me out quite patiently, and not move from the spot before I am finished.

HUMBRECHT: What the hell kind of sermon is this going to be? As far as I'm concerned, you have my word. Here's my hand on it.

MASTER: Now to the point! Were you at St. Clausen's Church yesterday, Cousin?

HUMBRECHT: No, I wasn't. But my family was. I wouldn't tolerate anything else.

MASTER: It was a catechism sermon.

HUMBRECHT: That could be.

MASTER: The text was the Ten Commandments.

HUMBRECHT: So, what else? I still don't see any rhyme or reason to this.

MASTER: Have patience! The minister lingered especially on the seventh commandment.

HUMBRECHT: The seventh? Wait a minute, which one is that? Thou shalt . . . thou shalt . . . thou shalt not commit adultery. Right?

MASTER: Exactly. And in addition, as you know, four times a year the minister reads from the pulpit the decrees of our king against dueling, burglary, and infanticide.

HUMBRECHT: I knew that before I was old enough to button my clothes. What's your point?

MASTER: Now you shall hear it. In addition, you know—

HUMBRECHT: I know! I know! That I'm about to go crazy and leave you standing here if you don't get on with it.

MASTER: You promised me earlier not to go off half-cocked. You must keep your word. I was about to say, you know that the women's pews are exactly across from the organ, at least in part—

HUMBRECHT: Yes! And that you young men almost go blind during the divine service from gawking at the young girls! I know that too! Many a time I've worried about it. I'd like to be a preacher just once, for twenty-four hours. I'd have the sexton drive you and your spyglasses out of the temple!

MASTER: If you don't choose to listen, Cousin—

HUMBRECHT: Yes, yes, I'm listening.

MASTER: I was standing by the organ, and could thus look my little cousin directly in the face.

HUMBRECHT: My Evchen?

MASTER: Yes. By chance, I was looking at her rather steadily during the sermon, exactly at the part that I have already mentioned. She blushed fire red, then instantly went deathly pale, like a linen cloth. Then she cast her eyes doward and sat through the rest of the sermon absolutely rigidly. Finally, when the ordinance against infanticide was read, she fainted dead away.

HUMBRECHT: So? Then she was carried out of the church into fresh air, and then she came to, and now she's as good as new.

MASTER: It is however—I'm sorry I have to say this—a matter for concern.

HUMBRECHT: Concern! I see nothing to be concerned about. When a young innocent thing has her ears filled with such trash as adultery, whoring, and fornication, and when a few tasteless louts are staring her straight in the eye as she listens—I see no cause for concern if she becomes dizzy, and red and white from annoyance.

MASTER: But the fainting! Right at that point!

HUMBRECHT *(removes his nightcap deferentially)*: Don't take this the wrong way, Cousin. One can see that you've been a student. You learned men always want to see more than other people. But you do it like all bleary-eyeds: when you face the sun you see everything double and nothing clearly. The devil take it! Can people order up faints and tell them when to come?

FRAU HUMBRECHT *(comes running in)*: You're shouting so loud, Husband, that people are gathering outside the door.

HUMBRECHT: I've got reason to be boiling over. This liberal arts fellow comes to me first thing in the morning and growls an earful about some blushing and fainting by our Evchen yesterday, and I think he's trying to make something of it.

FRAU HUMBRECHT *(turns up her nose and shrugs her shoulders)*: What's to make of it? She didn't feel well. I don't know what else you can make of it.

MASTER: Actually, I came here to speak with your husband alone— however, as long as you're here! I know you are aware of my interest in your daughter. You have even encouraged me . . . *(stammering)* but . . . as your husband doesn't want to trust my skill in observation . . . I want . . . I must . . . *(opens his purse and looks for something)*

FRAU HUMBRECHT: My God! What kind of observation? Martin!

HUMBRECHT: How would I know? If I read him right, he thinks we're calves' heads, with no eyes, and our Evchen—at least a whore.

MASTER *(dismayed)*: Cousin!

FRAU HUMBRECHT: What! My Evchen? Master! Do you know what you are saying? Eh! Just what I expected! I'd pledge on my own life that my daughter is honorable. No decent man shall deny it, not even you, Master! But I shall no longer call you cousin. *(places her hands on her hips)* Is this the thanks for all the love and care that we—that my husband has shown you? After he paid for your singing lessons and made you so comfortable when you entered the seminary so that you could be so insolent now? The little piano you taught Evchen—is that your whole thanks for that master's ring on your finger? If we hadn't been there, you certainly wouldn't have been able to graduate. Not on your stipendium alone. How long have you been so greedy, eh?

HUMBRECHT *(grabbing her):* Woman! Woman! You're making six times more noise than I did.

FRAU HUMBRECHT *(breaking free):* Haven't I the right? Anyone who casts slurs on Evchen's honor wounds me.

MASTER: Cousin, for God's sake! I'll say good-bye. *(about to leave)*

HUMBRECHT: Was that all that you wanted to tell me?

MASTER: No! But *(indicating Frau Humbrecht)* as long as she's here, I'll stay silent.

HUMBRECHT: Dearest! Leave us alone for a bit. Come! *(takes her by the arm)* Just a little while!

FRAU HUMBRECHT: Ten horses wouldn't drag me away from here! I'm not moving! I want to hear everything he has to say about my Evchen.

MASTER: I don't want to say anything against her, Cousin, I swear to you. You know that I am interested in her. It is precisely because of this that I believed myself obligated to report to you one thing and another that you don't yet know ... perhaps couldn't know. Now I don't believe it myself. I do, however, owe you a great deal for all the kindnesses you just this moment threw in my face so bitterly. I am thus obligated to tell you, and it is your duty to verify it. This note was sent to me last night. Read it yourself. I wouldn't have taken any notice of it, if it weren't for what happened in church. *(gives the* Humbrechts *the note and keeps the envelope, stuffing it finally in his purse)*

HUMBRECHT: Maybe the devil can read this scrawl, but to me it looks like hen's scratchings. *(hands it back)*

MASTER: Give it here. I'll read it aloud, word for word. Just see, however, that you don't blame me again for it.

FRAU HUMBRECHT *(stamping her foot):* Well, read it, read it!

MASTER *(reads, pointing to the words with his finger. Humbrecht to one side, his wife on the other):*

"Dear Sir:

You are a Humbrecht and may have more sense than all the others in your family who bear that name. So ask Evchen Humbrecht, your little cousin, if she is really stupid enough to believe that I would really marry her. If she thinks back and remembers the place where we made our acquaintanceship, she will certainly not be able to demand anything of me. If her father doesn't fork over one hundred talers to place her child in a foundling home, then if need be, I'll find a way. It concerns you as well.

von Gröningseck

P.S. This letter requires no answer. None would reach me."

(Master Humbrecht *glances sideways at the others, holding the paper in his hand*)

HUMBRECHT: Gröningseck! That was that Bavarian officer who lodged with us.

MASTER: The very one! Who took Evchen to the ball—

FRAU HUMBRECHT (*rips the letter out of his hand*): Yes, that's the one! But whoever wrote this infamous forgery here, *him* I don't know. (*as she speaks, she tears the letter into a thousand pieces and stamps on it*) If I knew, I'd scratch his eyes out.

HUMBRECHT: Woman! What do you know of this? Call the girl down here. Now I'm angry that we can't give her the letter to read herself. (*about to gather up the pieces*) You are damned quick, woman!

FRAU HUMBRECHT: Read! What for? So it can kill her, or God knows what else? Isn't it a scandal and a mockery that such an old ass like yourself can go on so about this childish prattle? All right, if I hadn't been constantly with her—but I was!

HUMBRECHT (*imperiously*): Get her! Or I will! (*Frau Humbrecht makes a face like a donkey's at* Master Humbrecht *and exits*) Cousin! (*clapping him on the shoulder*) Just between us! I didn't want to say so in front of my wife, but . . . if it's true, what you've read to me, if that creature doesn't clear out of this house I'll break every bone in her body and her bastard's too.

MASTER (*gravely*): Cousin! If you have only a glimmer of religion in you, get hold of yourself! I didn't come here to be eyewitness to a crime. Besides, it's not yet over. If Gröningseck was my friend, as he often maintained, the tone of this letter is a mystery to me.

Taking into consideration the other circumstances, however, the matter deserves further investigation. Though, as I said, so that you don't make a mistake . . . perhaps it is also—

JAILER *(enters):* Be you Mester Humbresh, the butcher?

HUMBRECHT: I am.

JAILER: Mester Proshecuter sent me wid da box here. You should look at it to see if you recognize it.

HUMBRECHT: I recognize you at least. Aren't you Hans Adam, the beadle from Goat Alley?

JAILER: Yeah, right! But we's called jailers, not beadles.

HUMBRECHT: To hell with the title! I ask you, are you the same one who thrashed a poor child of five to death last spring in front of baker Michael's door? Claiming privilege of profession?:

JAILER: Hey! What's to cry about? It's more, I think, a blow went the wrong way.

HUMBRECHT: Wait, you scoundrel! I've plenty more to charge you with. If you're a beast, go off in the forest with the other wild animals! *(picks up a switch and thrashes him soundly)* Now go, blackguard! I've carried this grudge against you a long time, and now I have you in my forceps.

JAILER *(who, during the thrashing, drops the box):* Okay, okay! Ya won't ged off free for the thrashin'! *(rubs his back)*

HUMBRECHT: Get off free? Didn't you kill the child and get off free? Nobody made a peep, you tyrant! Hang on, I'll rub your back even better if you haven't had enough yet—

JAILER *(running out):* Okay, okay! I got yer point! *(exit)*

HUMBRECHT *(throws the cane into a corner):* He sure came at the right time! Damn it all! To thrash a child of five so long that it died of convulsions? And why? Because it begged a crust of bread, so it wouldn't have to steal one. Thunder and lightning! I should have thrashed the dog even harder.

MASTER: But consider, Cousin, the matter might have been badly explained to you.

HUMBRECHT: No! Let it cost me a few hundred guilders. I'll pay it gladly! I've vented my anger on that scoundrel!

MASTER: And insulted his authority.

HUMBRECHT: Authority! Authority! I have the greatest possible respect for my authority. But the beast doesn't have so much for his. Didn't he and his partner attack a poor journeyman in the

same straits in the most vicious manner possible? Kicking him in
the genitals till he gave up the ghost three hours later? And that's
supposed to be order, eh?

MASTER: They will soon be avenged! Cousin, Cousin! Be careful!

HUMBRECHT: Why? I tell the truth and shame the devil!

FRAU HUMBRECHT *(dashes in, tearing her hair):* Martin! Martin!
Oh, my God! Evchen is nowhere to be found.

HUMBRECHT: What? Not to be found? Oh, now I believe it all! Did
you really look for her? In her room? In the kitchen?

FRAU HUMBRECHT: Everywhere! Everywhere! I was even down in the
slaughterhouse. I'm out of breath. Merciful God, what could it
mean?

MASTER: Has nobody seen her, then? Yesterday she was—

FRAU HUMBRECHT: Ah! I was up with her very late.

MASTER: And this morning?

FRAU HUMBRECHT: I thought she was still asleep, as usual. But
according to her maid, she left the house quite excitedly first thing
this morning. I hope she hasn't thrown herself in the river! These
past few weeks she's been so melancholy—

HUMBRECHT: The devil take melancholy! I feel like I've been kicked
in the head by an ox. Check with all her friends right away. See
whether or not she's there. I will dash over to your sister's myself.
(She is about to go; he runs past her, calling:) Just a minute, I
want to talk to the maid myself. I'll be back in a moment, Cousin!
(exit)

FRAU HUMBRECHT *(on her way back, trips over the box. Gawks at
it and picks it up):* My God! My snuffbox, that I advertised for?
How did it get here?

MASTER: A jailer brought it, from the police. Your husband, who
said he'd harbored a long animosity toward the man, thrashed
him. He dropped the box from fright and ran off.

FRAU HUMBRECHT: Everything's coming at once! *(pockets the
snuffbox)* Who would have thought it, Cousin! (Master
Humbrecht *shrugs)* But still I cannot believe, cannot believe it. She
was always so gentle and pious, like a lamb! You know yourself
how many hundreds of times I've said she must be a minister's
wife. I never let her out of my sight. She never spoke to that
goddamned lieutenant—God be gracious to me—without my
being there.

MASTER: In his letter, though, he mentions a rendezvous—

FRAU HUMBRECHT: Well, he didn't have one with her and couldn't have had one, any more than with me.

HUMBRECHT *(returns):* It's all over! She's not there either.

FRAU HUMBRECHT: Merciful God! I'm a dead woman!

HUMBRECHT: Now we can only fall at our cousin's feet and beg him to forgive our insults.

MASTER: Don't worry, I let it go in one ear and out the other. *(glances at his watch)* Now I must go; as soon as my duties permit, I'll be back. Now don't get too excited! Everything may still turn out all right. Good-bye. *(exit)*

HUMBRECHT *(throws himself on a chair):* This has been quite a morning! *(His wife wrings her hands and cries)* This could stop one's heart! Thank God I have nothing to reproach myself for. I've preached to you often enough of virtue and order! I've read you sermons often enough, woman, when you gave her too much freedom! Well, now you have it!

FRAU HUMBRECHT *(imploringly):* For the love of heaven, Martin! Dear Martin, no reproaches! Not now when I'm ready to die this instant! I did my duty as much as you!

HUMBRECHT: Well, bully for you! That may be a great comfort, but not for a father's heart! *(Smites his forehead. The door opens. The* public prosecutor *enters, accompanied by two jailers.* Humbrecht *jumps at the sound)*

HUMBRECHT: Who are you, sirs? What do you want here? Whom are you looking for?

PROSECUTOR: Take it easy, my friend! You're not going to thrash me as you did that honorable fellow there.

HUMBRECHT: *Him,* an honorable fellow? He may be a blackguard, a tyrant, but not a—

FRAU HUMBRECHT: Be quiet, Martin! The public prosecutor!

JAILER: There, you heard it yourself, Mester Proshecuter! There, you heard it, and there's his cane.

PROSECUTOR: Be quiet! You'll get your compensation.

HUMBRECHT: So you are the pubic prosecutor?

PROSECUTOR: I am he. I sent earlier—

HUMBRECHT: Oh, Mr. Prosecutor! Forgive me. You cannot think badly of an honest townsman if he has the honor not to know you. I would think it's always a good sign if one doesn't have much to do with our highly commendable police force.

PROSECUTOR: No ceremony, my friend. It doesn't suit you.

HUMBRECHT: I am Martin Humbrecht, butcher and decent townsman through and through, and for the money that I have to turn over to the city, even the town council addresses me as "sir."

PROSECUTOR: I understand, Herr Humbrecht. We shan't argue over protocol. I sent a man to you earlier. He is in the service of the police, if you don't already know, and anyone who attacks him attacks the entire profession—but that will come to a hearing at some other time. Now I only stopped by to learn if you recognize as yours a certain box that the gentleman showed you?

HUMBRECHT: I don't know anything about any box. Did he show me a box? I must have been blind.

JAILER: Yeah! From anger! My back can tell ya.

FRAU HUMBRECHT: Yes, Martin, this is it. It was lying there on the floor. *(about to hand it to him)*

HUMBRECHT: That? But that's yours. How did our most esteemed police come by it?

FRAU HUMBRECHT: I lost it.

PROSECUTOR: At least that's what you claimed when you reported it missing.

FRAU HUMBRECHT: And your man there presumably found it? Here's the tip I promised. *(searches in her pocket)*

PROSECUTOR: No, not he, Frau Humbrecht. I did, and you can put away the tip. I am, of course, not obligated to say how I brought the matter to light. But so that you don't take me for some kind of sorcerer, I shall reveal how it all happened. My position carries with it the responsibility of having my eyes and ears everywhere. I heard about this very box's being reported, and I noted down the description as I generally do. Then some days ago we recovered the box—among other things—from a low-class woman who was trying to cross the Rhine. So I sent for the crier and took his statement as to whom it belonged, *ad protocollum.** Still, it was necessary that you verify it. That has now been done, and now I must ask for it back again.

FRAU HUMBRECHT: Why? It's mine, isn't it?

PROSECUTOR: Of course it was! Now, however, it belongs to the corpus delicti and must remain in the hands of justice as evidence until the verdict. If you then want to pay the expenses pro rata, you can get it back again. *(Frau Humbrecht gives him back the*

*According to protocol.

box) Meanwhile I can tell you—just between us—you didn't lose the box, it was stolen. The woman admitted everything.

HUMBRECHT: Stolen! Where? By whom?

PROSECUTOR: In a certain house where your respectable wife probably would rather not have been.

HUMBRECHT: Every minute something new! Woman, do you want to tell me about this? Come on! Where did you and your snuffbox part company?

FRAU HUMBRECHT: No matter what you do to me, I can't say anything except that I must have lost it at the ball.

PROSECUTOR: You would do better to speak out, Frau Humbrecht. Your dearest will find out soon enough. In the Yellow Cross—remember now?

HUMBRECHT: In that whorehouse? Why?

PROSECUTOR: Bah! You can assume she didn't go there for breakfast.

FRAU HUMBRECHT *(dismayed):* Breakfast! Yes, we did have breakfast. Where, I don't know . . . but the lieutenant assured me we were in an honest house.

PROSECUTOR: And gave you, in all *honnêteté,** a sleeping powder.

HUMBRECHT *(gnashing his teeth):* By Beelzebub and his living grandmother! You beast! I could wring your neck! *(lunges at her; the* prosecutor *steps between them)* Now at last my eyes are wide open. This was all dreamed up by the devil! That damned ball! Beast! Damned, accursed beast! You made your daughter a whore!

FRAU HUMBRECHT *(choking):* I! Almighty God knows that I am as innocent as a child in the womb—

LISSEL *(bursts into the room):* I can't find her anywhere. *(she catches sight of the prosecutor, becomes confused, and is about to run away. Suddenly she runs up to* Humbrecht *and falls to her knees before him, sobbing)* Ah, my esteemed, beloved master! I beg you for God's sake . . . I will confess everything gladly, tell everything. Only don't send me to the workhouse.

HUMBRECHT *(takes a step toward her):* To the gallows with you!

LISSEL: Ah, dear heaven above! Consider, sir, how very young I am.

HUMBRECHT: What's wrong with you? Did *your* mother take you to a whorehouse?

LISSEL: Oh, never! She's not so ungodly.

*Propriety.

HUMBRECHT: Listen to her, Frau Humbrecht, listen to her! A lovely little song! I'll sing it to you often.

(Frau Humbrecht *clasps her hands to her head, is about to speak, cannot, and exits*)

PROSECUTOR (*who up to now has been speaking privately with the* jailers, *to* Lissel): Admit everything now that you know about the case or my men here will take you to a place where we will find ways to make you talk.

LISSEL: Ah, my most gracious, most respected Mr. Prosecutor, I don't know anything at all, except that she pinned up her braids first thing in the morning, put on a cap, and left. She gave me her cloak, her taffeta one, and said I should keep it myself until she came back. She told me that three times in exactly those words, and that I had to give her my cotton one, then she was about to leave, and then she turned around at the door again and said: "Lissel! Until I return." May I be struck dead if I'm not telling the truth! Now have mercy on me, most gracious Mr. Prosecutor! I don't know anything else, except that I put the cloak in my trunk, as she told me to. As God is my witness, I didn't steal it. If you torture me, I won't know any other words to say.

PROSECUTOR: Who is this "she" then?

LISSEL: Who? Why, our young miss! Miss Evchen!

HUMBRECHT: Your miss and the devil's! The whore, Mr. Prosecutor, smelled trouble and left this morning. (*agitated*) If only the devil doesn't press her so hard that she—that would be a fine trip to heaven!

PROSECUTOR: We must prevent that! Men, you know your duty! (Jailers *are about to leave*) Halt! Something else! What does your cotton cloak look like?

LISSEL: Brown, with red and green stripes and yellow flowers.

PROSECUTOR: Got it.

JAILER (*to the other*): Praise God, now we can pick up a few groschen!

SECOND JAILER: So tell me what we're looking for again, Mr. Smarts.

JAILER: Go to hell! You think I don't know! A cap, a brown coat, and . . . and . . . oh, shoot, I know it all. I can see her already.

(*Exeunt jailers.*)

PROSECUTOR (*meanwhile, to* Humbrecht): Herr Humbrecht! You are a wild, hotheaded man! Control yourself and forget about breaking any necks. Take this as a warning! *(as he leaves)* You, young girl, I advise to stay honest. This house has corrupted you. *(Exit* Lissel *with him.* Humbrecht *falls, as if struck, onto a chair, his hands on the table, his head on them)*

(The curtain falls.)

Act 6

(Frau Marthan's room. In the background, a pitiful bed, no curtains.)
(Frau Marthan is ironing. She lays each piece, as she finishes it, in a basket. Evchen is sitting on the bed holding her child, who is crying.)

EVCHEN: Poor, poor baby! No, I can't bear it any longer. *(places it on the bed)* Oh, dear Frau Marthan! I beg you, for God's sake, just one solitary half slice of bread. Just a quarter. Please give it to me and a few spoons of milk, so I can make a bit of mush.

FRAU MARTHAN: And get it from where without stealing it? If you stand me on my head, not a penny will fall out of my pockets. You know yourself that I scraped together my last few pennies today to buy the little baby some army bread.

EVCHEN: Savior of the world! He's going to starve to death!

FRAU MARTHAN: Give him something to drink.

EVCHEN: If only I could! But it's all dried up. Not a drop more to be pressed out. My anguish has absorbed it all. *(goes away from the bed)* I can't face my misery. If I do, I'll go crazy.

FRAU MARTHAN: Take care and beware! You'll wind up in an asylum. You know something, Miss?

EVCHEN: Are you speaking to me, Frau Marthan?

FRAU MARTHAN: Who else? Shouldn't I call you "Miss"?* Curious! So many highborn and lowborn women go about in the city, with already three, four or so little doll babies boarded out, but they'll scratch somebody's eyes out, or hang a slander suit around his neck if he didn't call them miss! I believe though, God forgive me,

---

*The word translated by "Miss" is *Jungfer* (virgin, maiden).

that you are not like other people. What's happened has happened. Weeping and wailing won't change anything, and a child, I think, is always better than a calf. If you can't get a job right away as a housemaid, I'll recommend you as a wet nurse.

EVCHEN: If I only had milk for the wretch!

FRAU MARTHAN: How is it possible? Where could it come from? For the five weeks that you've been with me, God forgive me, you've cried a gallon of tears. And you still don't eat or drink anything. I don't want to think that it's not good enough for you. Who won't take the least, doesn't deserve the best, right? That bowl of meat soup I left out the evening before last because I had to go do some washing for my wages, why didn't you heat it up and eat it? God knows, I deprived my own mouth of it for you! Such a good, strong soup! Fit for a prince! A whole pound of the best beef, and two calves' feet! But no, you let it spoil there. Now I'll have to feed it to the cat. Isn't it a sin? Doesn't it look like you're trying to kill yourself? Can you take the responsibility for that? *(goes out to get a hot iron)*

EVCHEN: Ha! To take responsibility, that's the issue! Were it not for that, for fear of eternally, eternally . . . my mortal frame would have been long gone. *(Frau Marthan returns)* You are absolutely right, Frau Marthan! Absolutely right! But think of my position. Think of the poor little wretch here, abandoned by God and the world—

FRAU MARTHAN: Don't say that! Ever, ever! You're sinning again. God has never abandoned anybody, and He's not going to begin with you and your child. I'll gladly do anything I can. Like I said, as soon as the councilor's wife has her baby I'll bring you to her as the wet nurse. I have some influence with her, that I'm sure of.

(The child cries again)

EVCHEN *(runs to the bed)*: Merciful God! It's going to cry itself to death from hunger. *(Takes the child in her arms and rocks it)*

FRAU MARTHAN: There! That's right! Try to quiet it a bit. As soon as I'm finished with the wash I'll return it, and maybe I'll pick up a few groschen. But stop moping around so. You might be a plaything for the wicked one, from whom God preserve us. Take a prayer book and read it well—say yes, you can. In the little cupboard you'll find *The Way to Heaven and the Way to Hell.**

*Although the title is Wagner's, books with similar names abounded in the devotional literature of the day.

It's really beautiful, I tell you. During his final illness my sainted husband learned it almost by heart. Where did you work last before you got in trouble? I always say it's not right for an employer to throw a poor servant in unfortunate circumstances out of the house. We are all sinners. Bigger misfortune's likely to happen and then the master or mistress also has that on his conscience. So where'd you work last?

EVCHEN: Where? *(agitated)* At . . . at . . . you wouldn't know them.

FRAU MARTHAN: Who knows? So tell me! I won't tell anyone.

EVCHEN: At . . . at butcher Humbrecht's.

FRAU MARTHAN: Where? What! At Humbrecht the butcher's? Lord, and you never said anything. You must know his daughter then, right?

EVCHEN: Only too well, unfortunately.

FRAU MARTHAN: Yes, it's very unfortunate! Sure, one should never judge, but—there must not have been one drop of good blood in her, else she wouldn't have done what she did! Yesterday with the other washerwomen I heard a long-winded tale about her. If a hussy lets herself be led so far astray that she goes to whorehouses—

EVCHEN: What are you saying! God! Had she been in a whorehouse?

FRAU MARTHAN: Yeah, yeah! She couldn't have said it to your face. With an officer she went there. And her mother with her, that's the best part! The whole city's talking about it. They even told me the name of the house, but I've forgotten it. And so she and the officer gave her mother something to drink that put the old lady right to sleep. *Why* they did it is easy to imagine. And then supposedly the wastrel promised to marry her. But you know how men are! Another town, another girl! So he dumped her and she threw herself in the river. Early yesterday they found her in the Wantzenau.*

EVCHEN: Drowned! Ha! If it were only true!

FRAU MARTHAN: Unfortunately, it is. Only too true, as I said. I wish it weren't.

EVCHEN: Why? At least now she's out of her misery.

FRAU MARTHAN: You talk as if . . . well, I don't know what. "Out of

*The rumor, evidently, is that Evchen threw herself into the Ill River and that her body washed up at Wantzenau, an area northeast of Strasbourg near the Ill's confluence with the Rhine.

her misery"—yeah, and that's that! Just think of the disgrace when they bring her in today or tomorrow. I'll oblige her and go; she's supposed to be a very pretty girl. Who knows? Who knows? Maybe our gracious magistrate will let her body be dragged about through the city as an example to others. Like the man who killed his mother and hanged himself a year or so ago.

EVCHEN: Killed his mother! Are there people who kill their mothers?

FRAU MARTHAN: Are there people who—what a question! You never heard of the fellow, then? Oh, what was his name? Who wanted to slice his mother's throat—

EVCHEN: Yes, yes! I remember now. His mother was a whore, and he a bastard, conceived in a whorehouse. Somebody threw that at him when they were drinking, so he gave his mother the reward she deserved. I remember it very well.

FRAU MARTHAN: Not on your life! You've got it all wrong. He wanted her money.

EVCHEN: Right! Right! He was hungry and thirsty. He wanted to buy himself a roll and a glass of beer. His mother wouldn't give him any, so he tried to tear it out of her body. And then they gave him what for!

FRAU MARTHAN: Are you crazy? Soon I'll be afraid to be alone with you. Better I should tell you what happened. He was a bad lot from childhood on; he squandered most of his mother's money. She was a thoroughly honest woman; I did her wash for ten years until Anne Mey nipped me. How that happened I'll tell you another time. It was a matter of some tattered old muslin neckpiece that swam away from me in the rinsing. Anyway, he joined the imperial troops, then went over—imagine!—to the Prussians. But he deserted them too and came home again and gave his mother trouble for so long, she finally had to have the magistrate ban him from the house. More than once he had beaten her like a dog. So everything was going well for a few weeks, and then he came around again early one morning, begging to be taken back, promising to be good and upstanding. His mother, who wouldn't let herself dream that anything could be wrong, began to cry bitterly, groped about in her pocket, and gave him a whole little taler. That's a lot of money; I don't earn that much in four days sometimes. Then he sent the maid away—I don't remember now what he used as a pretext—and as soon as he was alone with his

mother, he leaped at her throat with a razor. She fought for her
life, as you can imagine, screamed as much as she could scream,
and got two cuts on her hand and one—though not serious—in
the throat. Then all the people in the house ran about and
reported the whole thing, which was the least they could do. And
you see, what really clinched it for him was that he had tied the
razor with twine so that it wouldn't snap shut. So he was trapped,
and he admitted everything, and the verdict was guaranteed and
his fate sealed. But two days before the sentence could be carried
out he let himself be deceived again by Satan—God be with us—
and hanged himself in the prison. Then he was dragged through
the city, as I said. His cousin, the alderman, a stinking-rich fellow
who lives there on the long street, offered a thousand talers for
the body to be brought to him so he could bury it secretly. Instead
he had to watch the show himself when his cousin was dragged
along the road. The head bounced on the cobblestones so nobody
could see. It was horrible, as I said. But that's what such people
deserve. Why don't they pray? *(with a very significant look)* I fear
it might not go any better with your former mamsell. She killed
her mother as much as—

EVCHEN *(who sits as if senseless on the bed during this narrative,
only staring at her* child, *suddenly sits upright)*: Killed her
mother! I killed my mother!

FRAU MARTHAN: You! Who said anything about you? I was talking
about your former mistress. Humbrecht's daughter.

EVCHEN: Oh, did she kill her mother, then?

FRAU MARTHAN: Well, she did and she didn't. Of course, she didn't
slice her mother's throat, but she might as well have used the
knife. If she'd behaved herself from the beginning, her mother
wouldn't have died of shame.

EVCHEN: My mother! Dead! And I did it! *(sinks to her knees, then
falls to the ground.* Frau Marthan *rushes to help her.)*

FRAU MARTHAN: Merciful God! What is this! You're scaring me to
death. *(sets her down again on the bed)* Who said anything about
you or *your* mother? Soon I'll have the pleasure of taking you to
the asylum, if you give me a fright like that again. God knows I'm
spooked! How often do I have to tell you I'm talking about
Humbrecht's daughter and not *you*? *Her* mother was buried
yesterday, not *yours*. I don't know your mother or even where you
come from. Her father, the butcher, has promised one hundred

talers to anyone who brings him news about his daughter. A princely sum! And now the fishermen who found her will get it.

EVCHEN *(stops short, thinks a bit):* Would you like to get the money, Frau Marthan? It would help out quite a bit, wouldn't it? A hundred talers! That's rather chintzy. Why not five or six hundred? Now I can contribute something to your welfare, Frau Marthan! I still say it's chintzy, though. And I've a right to! I'm no—

FRAU MARTHAN: Again with this "I"?

EVCHEN: Yes! Yes! I! I'm the one who killed her mother, who doesn't have a drop of good blood in her, who wallowed in the whorehouse, who let herself be seduced by a villain, who has here a nursing child that's hardly born and is already fatherless and motherless—for if I were really a mother, I'd be able to feed it, and I can't. I am the ... the ... I'm the only daughter of the Humbrechts, the one that you said drowned herself. You see, it's a lie. I wish that all I said was also a lie, but unfortunately it's all too true. What makes me happy is that now I know a way to repay you, at least in part, for all the trouble I've caused you. Go to my father immediately, Frau Marthan. Just say that I, Eva, sent you, and that he should pay you the hundred talers. It won't make him very happy, but—go, Frau Marthan! Go!

FRAU MARTHAN: Ah, dear God above! No! I don't deserve this from you. So good and so unfortunate—forgive me for all I said. You must have been seduced ... else you would never have—

EVCHEN: I was. I was seduced, deceived, when I least expected it. You told the tale yourself, except for the part about my drowning. It's all true, everything! But I must tell you that I didn't know we were in that kind of house, and I really didn't know anything about the sleeping powder. These two things that I have just learned from you show me the whole black soul of the villain who brought me so low. I always had at least a shadow of hope. Now that's gone, and everything with it. Now I can't do anything but—' *(stiffens, looks at her* child *compassionately)*

FRAU MARTHAN: Oh, you can be happy again. Perhaps he'll come back when you don't suspect it.

EVCHEN: Back! He was supposed to come back! Frau Marthan, I'm only a woman, but if he came back and stood before me ... I'd shove this letter you see here *(pulls it out of her pocket)* under his nose with one hand, and with the other I'd shove a knife through his heart. He deserves it! Before, I really didn't understand this *(indicates the letter and puts it away again)* at all. You've finally opened my eyes. Now go, Frau Marthan, go! I beg you.

FRAU MARTHAN: A hundred talers would of course be a lovely stake—in my whole life I've never had so much at one time—but I'm afraid to leave you alone right now.

EVCHEN: Why, dear? Do I look perhaps a bit overheated, a bit angry? That's only when I am thinking of the faithless cur. But it will pass. Only a fleeting moment. Now I'm quite calm again . . . just a little weak. Now, go tell my father I'm still alive and that tomorrow he'll hear more from me. If he gives you money, bring me back something for the child. He can hardly cry any more, he's so weak. Go! Go! Every moment is dear to me.

FRAU MARTHAN: Well then, for the child's sake, I'll leave now, but in less than no time at all I'll be back again and bring him back some sugar.

EVCHEN: Yes, do that, Frau Marthan. Come back soon, or it could be too late.

FRAU MARTHAN: Too late?

EVCHEN: It's already getting so dark. *(Exit Frau Marthan)* I can hardly see! It's already been so long. I was afraid I'd never get her off my back. Yes! Now what did I want? Why did I send her away? I think the little bit of reason I had left has now fled me. *(The child cries again)* Are you singing? Singing? Singing our swan song? Sing, little Gröningseck! That's your father's name! *(Picks the child up from the bed and presses it to her)* An evil father! Who doesn't want to be anything to you and me, anything at all! And who so often swore to be everything to me. Ha! He even swore it in the whorehouse! *(to the child)* Crying? Still crying? Let me cry, *I'm* the whore, the murderess of her mother. You're nothing! A little bastard, nothing else. *(doggedly)* But you'll never be what I am, never endure what I have to endure. *(picks up a pin and stabs the child in the head. The child cries out dreadfully; to drown it out she sings, at first very loudly, then more and more softly)*

Hey, little doll!
Sleep, baby, sleep!
Sleep for eternity.
Ha, ha, ha, ha, ha! *(rocks the child in her arms)*
Your father was an evil man.
He made your mother a whore.
Hey, little doll!
Sleep, baby, sleep!

Sleep for eternity!

Ha, ha, ha, ha, ha!

Are you sleeping, my darling, are you sleeping? How gently! Soon I'll envy you, bastard. Only angels sleep like this! How much my little song can do! I wish someone would sing me to sleep that way. Ha! A drop of blood! I must kiss it away. Another one! That too! (*kisses the* child *on the wound*) What is this? Sweet! Very sweet! But a bitter aftertaste. Ha, now I see it. The blood of my own child! And I'm drinking it? (*Throws the* child *on the bed*) Sleep there, Gröningseck, sleep! Sleep for eternity. Soon I'll sleep, too. Hardly so peacefully as you sleep, but sleep is sleep all the same. (*Offstage, sound of* people *approaching*) God! Who's coming? (*she covers the* child, *sits next to it, and, as she sees* Humbrecht *enter, buries her head in the pillows*)

HUMBRECHT: Where? Where is she? My Evchen? My daughter, my own daughter? (*sees her on the bed*) Ha! Are you there, whore, are you there? Here, old lady! Your money. (*throws down a sack.* Frau Marthan *picks it up and lays it aside*) Still hanging your head? You have no cause, Evchen. I forgive you everything. Everything! (*shakes her*) Come, I say, come! We'll have a post-ball celebration. I almost feel like making the sign of the cross over such a rotten carcass. If your father quarrels, you run away; if he gives you a good word, you're deaf. (*shakes her more strongly*) Are you going to talk? Or do I have to beat your brains out!

FRAU MARTHAN: You act as if you had an ox before you. It would be no wonder if she fell into a fit! Can't you speak decently?

HUMBRECHT: You're right, old woman. Absolutely right! Wait! How is this? (*kneels before his daughter*) Dearest, best Evchen! Have pity on your humbled father! Don't insult him again. Be merciful to him! See, he is on his knees before you, pleading with you. You brought your mother to an early grave. Be so good, I beg of you, as to give me the last blow as well. Me, your father—

EVCHEN (*who, during this last speech has been slowly rising, catches sight of her* child, *comes to her senses, and falls face down on the bed again*): There! There he is!

FRAU MARTHAN (*brings a lighted lamp, sets it on the table, goes to the bed, and uncovers the* child. *Just as quickly, she covers him up again*): Oh, dear God above! What do I see! I must go report it at once! Else I'll be lost. I am sorry for her, but— (*she runs off*)

HUMBRECHT *(leaps up):* There! What is that! A child! Ha! How it smiles! Your child, Evchen? It shall be mine. My bastard, mine alone. Whoever says that he's yours, Evchen, I'll wring his neck.

MASTER *(enters):* I almost couldn't find the house. So, Cousin! This is wonderful! I see you took my advice and forgave your daughter.

HUMBRECHT: I would have done it without you, Cousin! A father is always a father, and often the most so when he seems the least so.

MASTER: Right now I am doubly glad to find you so resolved. You'll soon learn why. But now I must ask my little cousin to listen to me. It concerns her the most.

EVCHEN: Me? In this whole world, nothing concerns me any more, Master. I swear it.

HUMBRECHT: Don't swear, don't swear about anything, my daughter. Look! I swore to rip off your arms and legs, too, and now, swearing or no swearing, I'm very happy that I didn't do it.

MASTER: I think so too. Circumstances can change quite a bit. Now, just listen! You love Gröningseck, little cousin?

EVCHEN: Yes, as I love Satan! I was on guard against them both and let them both lead me on.

MASTER: You loved him once though, or else you wouldn't—

EVCHEN: Yes, but I didn't know then he'd turn me into a whore and the murderess of my mother, into—

MASTER: None of that was his intention, let alone his fault.

EVCHEN: So! Are you suddenly his advocate? How long will you be so? Here. *(indicating the* child)

MASTER: I am not alone as his advocate. I mean . . . I mean . . . in your own heart, you will find another. To be brief, Gröningseck loves you as tenderly as before. A nearly fatal illness kept him from returning to you at the appointed time. *(turns to* HUMBRECHT*)* He had no idea, Cousin, of the letter I read you. I showed him the envelope and he recognized it as Lieutenant Hasenpoth's handwriting and seal. He showed me other letters from Hasenpoth, which were filled with untruths about Evchen. He smelled a rat and set out for here, though barely half-recovered. An hour ago, he stopped by the Raven and had me summoned. We saw you run past in the greatest hurry, guessed the cause, and followed you at a distance. Would you like to speak to him yourself?

HUMBRECHT: If he wants to marry her and restore her lost honor, yes! Otherwise, if he's fond of his nose and ears, he'd better not show his face to me.

MASTER: He wants to marry her.

EVCHEN: And if he wanted to ten times, I'd rather face the executioner.

MASTER: But he is innocent! He can prove it to you.

EVCHEN: So much the worse! That means all the blame lies on me. *(rises from the bed)* This letter here! *(throws it into the room)* The devil wrote it—my own heart's mistrust; fear of you, Father; the thought of having murdered my mother. This, and oh, what else more! It drove me to despair. I wanted to be free from the world, and didn't have the determination to lay a hand upon myself. Now let the hangman do it! My child is dead, killed by me!

MASTER: God! Is it possible? *(examines the* child*)* Truly! Most righteous God! How far your creatures can fall after that first misstep.

(Humbrecht *stands with crossed arms, stares at* Evchen, *then at the* child. Evchen *seems neither to see nor hear.* Gröningseck *bursts in, still in his traveling clothes)*

EVCHEN: God! That's the one thing I needed!

VON GRÖNINGSECK: How astounded you all look! How pale! What's going on here? What's the matter?

HUMBRECHT: A bit of work for the lout, nothing more. God! I mean my heart is as heavy as if the whole Muenster Tower were pressing on it. Now I can only take rat poison! Here! *(leads the* Lieutenant *to the baby)* Here! If you have a father's heart! Mine is broken. Adieu! I'll see you again, Eva, in the workhouse. Say your last adieu!

VON GRÖNINGSECK: What! Evchen, gentle Evchen! You couldn't possibly with your own hand . . . your child . . . my child . . .

EVCHEN: Only too possible, sir! But before you reproach me further, read the letter there. Then you may speak.

VON GRÖNINGSECK *(picks up the letter):* Again the hand of Hasenpoth! *(looks at the signature)* In my name! *(glances at it)* The rest I can imagine. Wait! Blackguard! You'll pay for it with your blood, before another hour passes!

(He is about to leave, but bangs into the prosecutor *at the door. The* jailers *stand at the door)*

PROSECUTOR: Not another step, sir! Before the *procès verbal** is set down and signed. *(To the* jailers*)* Has one of you ordered a *porte-chaise†* and guard? *(One* jailer *exits)*

---

*Formal statement.
†Transport.

VON GRÖNINGSECK *(goes over again to* Master Humbrecht*):* The base, cowardly betrayer! Now do you believe, Master, that there are cases where personal vengeance becomes a duty? *(*Master Humbrecht *shrugs his shoulders)* Where is the state in which such monsters, such Hasenpoths, who destroy whole families under the guise of friendship, are punished as they deserve? Ha! How much good it will do me! With what heart's delight I will dance in his blood!

MASTER: It would be more humane, I believe, if you would try to save this poor girl from the gallows, than to heap crime upon crime.

PROSECUTOR: Yes, that would be some saving! The law that condemns the childmurderer to death is clear and has suffered no exceptions for many years. If the facts here are as clear as they seem to be, you can spare yourself the effort.

VON GRÖNINGSECK: And despite you and all your lawman's lack of feeling, I will set off today for Versailles to obtain grace for her at the court itself, or—

EVCHEN: Grace for me! Gröningseck! What are you thinking of? I should die ten thousand deaths! Better today than tomorrow!

PROSECUTOR: Not so fiery, Lieutenant! Of course, much depends on circumstances!

*(*Clerk *and* magistrates *enter)*

EVCHEN: Didn't I tell you, Gröningseck? My fate was to be written in blood.

VON GRÖNINGSECK: It wouldn't be, if you had trusted me. If you had given in less to melancholy and believed somewhat more in honor—or if I had somewhat less.

MASTER *(regards each alternately, sympathetically):* To hide yourselves this way from me!

HUMBRECHT *(tears his vest open, breaking off the buttons):* The whole world is becoming too narrow for me! *(takes a deep breath)* Pooh! *(claps the* Lieutenant *on the shoulder)* If you need money, sir! Traveling expenses! You understand me, right? A thousand, two, three thousand guilders lie ready at my house! And I would give ten thousand if the wretched ball and all its consequences were sent to the devil!

Translated by Betty Senk Waterhouse

STORM AND STRESS
A Play
Friedrich Maximilian Klinger

CHARACTERS

WILD
LA FEU
BLASIUS
LORD BERKLEY
JENNY CAROLINE, *his daughter*
LADY CATHERINE, *her aunt*
LOUISA, *Lady Catherine's niece*
SEA CAPTAIN BOYET
LORD BUSHY
A YOUNG MOOR
INNKEEPER
BETTY

The setting is America.

Act 1

A room in an inn.
Wild, La Feu, *and* Blasius *enter in traveling clothes.*

WILD: Cheers! In tumult and uproar again, so the senses whirl around like weather vanes in a storm. The wild noise has thundered into me such a feeling of well-being that I really begin to feel a little better. To have ridden so many hundreds of miles so as to bring you into the obliterating frenzy! Mad heart! You should thank me for it! Rage and then take it easy! Refresh yourself in confusion!* How are you?

BLASIUS: Go to hell! Is my Donna here?

LA FEU: Keep up your illusions, fool! I will slurp them from my nails like drops of water. Long live illusion! Hey! Hey! In the magic of my fantasy I wander in the rose garden led by the hand of Phyllis.†

WILD: May Apollo embolden you, foolish boy!

LA FEU: I shall not fail to metamorphose the black house over there, gone up in smoke with the old tower, into a fairy palace. Magic, magic fantasy! *(listens)* What lovely, spiritual symphonies strike my ear? By Amor! I want to fall in love with an old crone, live in an old, dilapidated house, bathe my tender carcass in stinking puddles of manure, only to curb my fantasy. Is there no old witch with whom I can flirt madly? Her wrinkles would become for me undulating lines of beauty, her protruding black teeth marble

---

*The word translated here as "confusion" is *Wirrwarr,* Klinger's original title for the play.
†Phyllis: a name (like "Damon," act 3, scene 3) common in eighteenth-century pastoral poetry.

columns of Diana's temple. Her sagging leather breasts would surpass the bosom of Helen. A woman as dried out as I! Hey, my fantastic goddess! I can tell you, Wild, I have conducted myself worthily throughout our travels. I have seen things, felt things, that no mouth tasted, no nose smelled, no eye saw, no mind perceived—

WILD: Especially when I blindfolded you. Ha, ha!

LA FEU: To Hades with you! You raving—! But tell me now once more, where are we right this minute in the real world? In London, right?

WILD: Yeah, sure. Don't you remember that we were on a ship? You were definitely seasick.

LA FEU: I don't know anything about anything. I am not to blame for anything. Is my father still alive? Send news to him then, Wild, and let him say that his son is still alive. I know I came from the Pyrenees Mountains out of Friesland. Beyond that, nothing.

WILD: Out of Friesland?

LA FEU: In what quarter of the city are we now?

WILD: In a fairy palace, La Feu! Don't you see the golden skies? The amors and amoretti? The queens and gnomes?*

LA FEU: Blindfold my eyes! (Wild *does so*) Wild! Jackass! Wild! Blockhead! Not too tight! (Wild *loosens the blindfold*) Ha! Blasius—dear, caustic, sick Blasius—where are we?

BLASIUS: How would I know?

WILD: To help you two out of the dream, I'll tell you that I led you out of Russia to Spain because I believed the king was going to start a war with the Grand Mogul. But the Spanish nation was as lazy as ever, so I packed you up again, and now you're in the middle of the war in America. Ha! Let me feel it to my depths, to stand on American soil, where everything is new, everything is significant. Oh! That I can feel no joy purely!

LA FEU: War and death! Oh, my limbs! Oh, my guardian angel! Give me a fairy tale instead! Woe is me!

BLASIUS: May lightning strike you dead, crazy Wild! What have you done! Is Donna Isabella alive! Hey! Will you speak? My Donna!

WILD: Ha, ha, ha! You've finally shown some anger.

BLASIUS: Anger? Finally? You'll pay for this with your life, Wild! What? I am at least a free man. Does friendship go so far that in

---

*Amors, amoretti, queens, and gnomes are part of the repertory of rococo and pastoral poetry alluded to—and satirized—here and elsewhere in the play.

your madness you can drag people through the world like harnessed dogs? To tie us in the carriage, holding a pistol to our
heads, always further and further, clip, clop! Eating and drinking
in the carriage, so that people would take us for lunatics. Into war
and hurly-burly, away from my passion, the only thing left to
me—

WILD: You love no one, Blasius.

BLASIUS: True, I love no one. I have carried it to the point of loving
no one: loving everyone for a moment, and the next moment
forgetting everyone. I am untrue to all women; therefore, all
women are and have been untrue to me. They have pressed me
and oppressed me something pitiful! I have assumed all possible
poses: I was a dandy, then a madcap, then boorish, then sensitive,
then an Englishman. And my greatest conquest I made by being
nobody at all. That was Donna Isabella. In order to return once
more—your pistols are loaded?

WILD: You're a fool, Blasius, and don't understand a joke.

BLASIUS: Oh, a wonderful joke, this! Take care! As of this moment I
am your enemy.

WILD: To duel with you! See here, Blasius, I'd like nothing better in
the world than to grapple with someone and give my heart its
favorite feast. But with you? Ha, ha! *(holds the pistol before him)*
Look down the barrel and say whether it doesn't look bigger to
you than the Tower of London. Be sensible, friend! I need and love
you, as you do me. The devil could not have brought together
greater fools and prophets of doom than us. Because of that we
must stay together and also share the jokes. Our misfortune
comes from our own temperaments; the world has contributed,
but not as much as we.

BLASIUS: Madman! I am eternally on the spit!

LA FEU: They have skinned me alive and pickled me with pepper.
The dogs!

WILD: Now we are in the middle of the war here. The only ecstasy I
know is to be in the middle of a war. Savor the scenery, do
whatever you want.

LA FEU: I'm not one for war.

BLASIUS: I'm not one for anything.

WILD: May God make you even more useless! Again I'm numbed
out of my mind. Completely hollow. I want to have myself
stretched over a drum so as to take on new dimensions. How my

heart aches again. Oh, if I could but exist in the barrel of this pistol until a hand blasted me into the air. Oh, indecision! How far you lead mankind, and how far astray!

BLASIUS: What's going to become of us in the end?

WILD: That you see nothing! I had to flee to escape the dreadful uneasiness and uncertainty. I thought the earth trembled under me, so uncertain were my steps. My presence tormented all good men who took an interest in me, because they knew they couldn't help me.

BLASIUS: Say instead: didn't want to.

WILD: Yes, they wanted to. But everywhere I had to take flight. I've been everything. I did odd jobs just to do something. I lived in the Alps, tended goats, lay day and night under eternal vaults of heaven, cooled by the wind and burned by an inner fire. Nowhere peace, nowhere repose. The highest noblemen in England wander lost in the world. Ah! And I do not find the magnificent one, the unmatched one who stands there. Look, I am so bursting with power and health, I cannot exhaust myself. I want to join the campaign here as a volunteer. Here my soul can distend itself. If they will do me the service of shooting me down, well and good! You'll take my cash and emigrate.

BLASIUS: The devil take me! No one will shoot you down, noble Wild.

LA FEU: Oh, they could do it.

WILD: Could they do me any greater service? Imagine, when we embarked I saw in the distance the captain on his ship.

BLASIUS: The one who has the mortal antipathy toward you? I thought you shot and killed him in Holland.

WILD: Three times have I faced him in life-and-death situations. Now he will not leave me in peace, though I have never offended the man. I gave him a bullet, and he gave me a stab. It's frightening, how he hates me without cause. And I must confess, I love him. He is a rugged and honorable man. Heaven knows what he has against me. Leave me alone for an hour.

INNKEEPER: The rooms are ready, milords. Is there anything else I can do for you?

WILD: Where are my people?

INNKEEPER: They've eaten and are sleeping.

WILD: Let them be.

INNKEEPER: And you require nothing else?

WILD: Your strongest punch, innkeeper.

LA FEU: Oh yes, that's just what you need, Wild.

WILD: Is the general here?

INNKEEPER: Yes, milord!

WILD: What visitors are in this house? But I don't really want to know. *(exit)*

BLASIUS: I'm sleepy.

LA FEU: I'm hungry.

BLASIUS: Keep your illusion, fool! A damnable world, away from my Donna. *(Exeunt omnes)*

Scene 2

Lord Berkley's *room. Lord Berkley. Miss Caroline. Caroline* sits at a *piano in sweet melancholy, fantasizing.*

BERKLEY *(building a house of cards in a childlike, fanciful manner):* To become so completely a child! Everything golden, everything magnificent and good! To dwell in this castle, rooms, hall, cellar, and stable! All of multicolored, muddled, hazy stuff! I find joy in nothing any more. Happy moments of childhood, to return to them! I find joy in nothing more than this house of cards. Symbol of my confused life! A shove, a heavy step, a light breeze will collapse you, but the solid, unflagging courage of a child will build you up again! Ha! So with my whole soul shall I cut myself off, and think and feel nothing more than how marvelous it is to live and move and have my being in you. Lord Bushy! Yes, my soul! I'll set aside a room for you. So unfriendly to me as you were, you shall dwell in Berkley's best room. Ha! It still wells up in me again and again, obstinate Bushy! Whenever I think back. Driven from hearth and home, merely because Berkley was better off than Bushy. It's scandalous. Nonetheless this room, painted with my story, is at your disposal. Who could comprehend that, my heart is shut up so tight—ha, ha! Lord Berkley! You are fine, now that you have become a child again! Daughter!

CAROLINE: My father!

BERKLEY: Child! You cannot believe how well one can become. Look! I'm building Bushy's room now. How do you like it?

CAROLINE: Very much, milord! Truly I want to be his maid and serve him, for your peace of mind.

BERKLEY: Where might he prowl about, enemy Bushy! From hearth and home! From wife and property! Bushy, it cannot be! To deprive my sweet child of everything! No, milord, we cannot live together. *(strikes down the house of cards)*

CAROLINE: My father!

BERKLEY: What, Miss? You should be ashamed of yourself? Aren't you Berkley's daughter? To serve Bushy? Bushy's maid? Not of any queen. Ha! That could make me fall into a deep sleep and drive me crazy. Bushy's maid, Miss! Wouldn't Miss like to change her mind? Bushy's maid?

CAROLINE: No, milord! Only call me daughter! Oh, that word "miss" is a bitter sound to Berkley's daughter when it comes from Berkley's mouth. *(kisses his hand)*

BERKLEY: Hm! Good Jenny! Long live our dominion as lord and miss. But I cannot live together with him. I would truly be tempted to strangle him in his sleep. Oh, give me childish ideas. I find joy in nothing any more. All my favorite things—my etchings, my paintings, my flowers—it's all the same to me.

CAROLINE: If you would listen to some music . . . perhaps this . . .

BERKLEY: All right! Try it and see.

(Caroline plays for him)

BERKLEY: No! No! Oh, I am still the weak, foolish fellow who can be shaped into anything by a pure tone. It is curious, child—there are notes that through their sound place before my eyes the whole sad picture of my adverse life. And there are others that meet my nerves so happily that when the note strikes my ear, I see again one of the happy scenes of my life. In one, your mother meets me at the park in Yorkshire, skipping so merrily on the wide boulevard, where on one side a brook meanders and babbles, as you may recall. I can hear it all, right down to the flies buzzing about you in summer. I was just about to press her to my heart and tell her something pleasant when you played a different chord.

CAROLINE: Dear father! Oh, my mother! *(rolls her eyes heavenward)*

BERKLEY: Yes, just so, with teary eyes turned heavenward. I know what that is like. She often looked the same way, and her eyes spoke as yours do. Oh, Child! When you just played different notes, it was Bushy and Hubert. You see, then, that won't do. I don't know why it is that there is such strange tautness in me.

CAROLINE: I know what music does, what it gives to the heart. The tones weave a magic spell, and if one looks to see what is there—him, him! The sound and echo of all the notes—him! Heart! My heart! *(frightened, covers her eyes)*

BERKLEY: Hm! Hm! My heart, my heart! Sit down next to me and help me build my castle again. You see, I have gotten on well, thank God, in destroying and rebuilding. Ha, ha! Be merry now! You take the right side and I'll take the left. And when the palace is standing, we'll take the tin soldiers. You command one battalion, and I'll command another. We'll grapple like Bushy and Hubert, then we'll conspire to seize the castle and throw old Berkley out naked, with his little Jenny and his good wife. We'll set it on fire. Fire and flames! Eh, Miss?

CAROLINE *(wiping her eyes, kissing his forehead):* Unhappy thought! May heaven trickle calming oblivion on your gray head, old Berkley! Father, we lack for nothing. We're well. What is Bushy, that noble Berkley in his sixtieth year should think of him?

BERKLEY: I don't *think* of him, foolish child! I can't help that it still swells up so bitterly in me. I only *feel* it.

CAROLINE: Exactly.

BERKLEY: I want to proclaim to you how he treated your father. Take your eyes off me! Now then, I wished I had him—he would lay his head calmly and peacefully on my breast. But you would have to stand by me and not move an inch—otherwise, if he stood before me like that—oh, God! You have constructed us wondrously, wondrously tightened our nerves, wondrously tuned our hearts!

CAROLINE: Didn't Bushy have a son?

BERKLEY: Of course. I would say a brave, robust, wild lad, if it weren't Bushy's son.

CAROLINE: Wasn't he named Carl? Blue eyes, brown hair, taller than any other boy his age. He was a handsome, wild, red-cheeked youth. He was always my cavalier, and fought for me.

BERKLEY: Bushy! Bushy!

CAROLINE: Father! Oh, my father! You're raving again. *(presses against him)*

BERKLEY: Go away! Didn't I have a son, a brave, stormy, headstrong youth, whom I lost that terrible night? A life for a life, if I catch Carl Bushy in the flesh! If my Harry were here now, I would want his fist to be iron, his heart maddened, his teeth eager. I would have him trot throughout the world until he avenged Berkley on Bushy.

CAROLINE: Milord! Spare your daughter!

BERKLEY *(agitated):* Now, then! Let me ponder something for a while . . . yes, ponder something. Do you want to come along, Child? Ha, I want to go to the parade. I think the enemy is going to attack in a few days, and then we will march out. Ha, ha! I am a gray old man. Give me only childhood and foolish things! Ha, ha! It is crazy, Miss, and good that hot remains hot and hate remains hate. As becomes a decent man. Age is not so cold; I'll have you feel that. Pack up my castle then; I don't want this game to lose its charm. Adieu, Miss, the drums sound. *(exit)*

CAROLINE *(calling after him):* Only good times, dear father!

BERKLEY *(comes back hastily):* God knows, Miss, it was around midnight, pitch-dark, when he fell upon us. And when I woke up in the morning after having been rigid and numb, I had no wife, nor any of my children. I screamed, moaned, and groaned in tones . . . in tones . . . hey! And raised my hands to the darkened heavens: give me my children! Make Bushy childless, that he may feel what it is. Childless! Then I found you, wet, cold, and frozen. You hung on my neck and wrapped your tender arms and legs around me. Miss Berkley! I stood there so saddened and dead in endless pain, in endless joy, at having saved one of my children. And with your trembling hand you wiped away the cold sweat from my brow. That was a moment, Miss! *(embraces her, presses her to his heart, remains silent and motionless. Coming to)* Yes, Miss! See! It seizes me like that. And then a messenger: your lady is dead! And then a messenger: your Harry has disappeared! Yes, Miss! And Bushy is to have this house! No, by God, no! Adieu, child! Don't cry.

CAROLINE: Not cry? Your child not cry? Lord Berkley, don't go away just now. It's closing in on me here, Father! *(hand on her heart)*

BERKLEY: No, no! I shall send your aunt and cousin to you. Berkley is a good soldier. When he's had his fun, he's ready and able. Adieu!

CAROLINE *(alone):* What will become of all this? Oh, when he suffers it makes me tremble. War, then! And my tears and pleas are to no avail. Where shall I go? I'm afraid. Ah, so much sorrow, and still afraid. And eternally this longing in my heart? *(at the piano)* Take me under your care! You alone understand me; to me your sound, the echo of my secret feelings, is solace and deliverance. Ah, each note Him! Him! *(plays a few passages, stops suddenly, starts again)* Yes, him! *(sinking into mournful dreaming)*

Scene 3

Caroline. Louisa.

LOUISA *(enters, dancing and skipping):* Good morning, Miss. Yes, just look, dear Cousin. I am in a terrible mood. A day full of vapors. Our aunt and her eternal nagging about the cavaliers! It is not to be endured. "He is courting me, Niece! He said the sweetest things to me!" On and on eternally. If Lady Catherine could only understand that spring is spring and winter is winter, despite all of our efforts! Has Miss had disturbing dreams? Why are you hanging your head so? What's wrong with you, Child?

CAROLINE: Nothing, nothing. My father—

LOUISA: Is he being pigheaded? Is he wild? Yes, what can you say? If only we were out of this hateful country! To London, Cousin! To London! That is the place of glitter and magnificence. *(looks in the mirror)* Why am I here? Why are these playful blue eyes here? All London would be talking about them. What use to me are my talents, my lessons, my French and Italian? To capture hearts is our purpose. Here! Oh, I am lost! Believe me, I'll let myself be carried off by the first Englishman who pleases me.

CAROLINE: You're not serious.

LOUISA: Well, not completely, of course. I am certainly kind to you, and I'm kind in general, provided that I have many suitors on whom to practice my powers. But dearest, you must feel yourself that we are not suited to the place. How many suitors do you think I have now, all at the same time? (Caroline *remains lost in thought)*

LOUISA *(counting them up in her mind, with lively gestures):* I really can't count more than six, because I have to leave out the half-serious ones and the ones I scared away. There's Silly, so long and slender, who always keeps his eyes tightly shut when he speaks to me, as if my look has glued his eyes. Once he was stammering to me so, with eyes still closed, and I kept mimicking him. Aunt almost burst, trying to hold back the laughter. And there's Boyet, who forever says nothing but "Miss, I love you." As if there were no other words in the dictionary of gallantry. Never "Miss, I love you tenderly," or "to death," or anything like that. Oh, his speech is as short as his stature. Ah well, I could always use him as a dwarf, if a real cavalier someday wanders through here. Now, Toby—

CAROLINE: Wasn't Carl Bushy a dear, good youth?

LOUISA: A brave youth of fiery courage and emotion! I banished Captain Dudley, Miss! I don't know what the fool has in mind. Imagine! A few days ago he said so sagely that we women usually have far less love and show far less love than men, and that this was because of our feminine nature. What does the solemn fool mean by that?

CAROLINE: I don't know.

LOUISA: Feminine nature! Think of it! Just because I acted somewhat displeased that he said something to you the other day. I don't know what he said, but the way he said it, and the way he looked when he said it—as if he was feeling something I have not noticed in any of my suitors. I am not jealous, Cousin. You are gentle, sensitive, dear, and good. I am beautiful, wild, and ill-tempered. And then there is Stockley, whom I merely tolerate so that he doesn't visit Miss Tranch. I can't bear *her* at all. In the end I make fools of them all. I spin them around as lads do with a top, but they enjoy it. One should not know love, Auntie says, until one is twenty-five. Then it has its reasons. And I don't even know what it's supposed to mean: to love.

CAROLINE: You are fortunate, Cousin. I don't know either, but—

LOUISA: As long as I amuse myself, dispel my boredom, exercise my moods and caprices, it's good enough. But you know what love is—

CAROLINE *(perplexed)*: What are your suitors' names?

LOUISA: I hear Auntie coughing.

Scene 4

Lady Catherine. Louisa. Caroline.

CATHERINE: Oh, how exasperating! Sniffling and coughing on such a wonderful day! Yes, ladies! Come quickly and prepare yourselves. The air in this country will be the death of me. Louisie, pull yourself together. You don't look as much like yourself as you should.

LOUISA: What's the matter, Auntie?

CATHERINE: I felt a premonition of this. Three strangers have arrived.

CAROLINE: Is that all, Aunt?

LOUISA: Isn't that enough?

CATHERINE: Fine people! Oh, a tall, wild lad among them. I could hardly reach his beard. He cursed and looked to heaven as if he felt something very deeply. I perceived it at once. Oh, ladies, it is a good sign when a young man curses. They are Englishmen. Tell me, Louisie, how do I look? They are Englishmen.

LOUISA: And I, Auntie?

CAROLINE: An Englishman! What did he look like, Aunt?

CATHERINE: They will pay us a visit. Yes! Can I wear green with rose red?

LOUISA: Too young, too old, Auntie. Come, I could never reach a decision on such important matters in less than an hour. We shall seek counsel from Betty. An Englishman! Oh, my Englishman!

CATHERINE: Virtuous and demure, Miss! Don't run so. I'll be out of breath.

LOUISA *(aside):* Because she can't move. Ha, ha! *(takes her by the arm)* Come on, Auntie, we young girls shall skip and hop—

CATHERINE: Nasty thing. *(exeunt)*

Act 2

Scene 1

Betty *leads* Wild, Blasius, *and* La Feu *in.*

BETTY: Here, milords, be so kind as to wait. Miladies will soon have the honor. *(exit).*

LA FEU: Good, my pretty Iris!* *(looking around)* Ah! There's something so endearing, so alluring about first sight. One always feels different in ladies' chambers. My heart flutters so charmingly. Why are you grimacing so, Wild?

WILD: I don't understand myself yet. I feel so good, all things speak to me in this room and attract me. Yet so terrifyingly wretched, so terrifyingly uncertain. I leap from thought to thought; I can't fix myself on anything. Ah, only when it returns in full purity—the eternal high emotion, where my soul loses itself in reverberations, catching sight of her beautiful face in the magnificent distance, in the evening sun, in the moonlight. Ah! Even if I hurry on the rapid wings of love it disappears, is always lost right in front of me. Yes, I am miserable. Living eternally in thought, I am miserable! Ah, me! I thought I would find in this other hemisphere of the world that which was not to be found. But here is like there and there is like here. Thank God that the imagination sees the distant as marvelous. Once he stands on the point so ardently wished for, how the roaming vagabond flees again, in certain faith that *there* the unquiet spirit will find everything. Thus all over the world in magical, urgent fantasy it is always the same here and there. Happy spirit! I shall follow you!

BLASIUS: The centaurs trot along again before your imagination. I

---

*Iris is the goddess of the rainbow and the messenger of the Gods.

am again nothing at all, and want to be nothing at all. Wild, it is shameful how you eternally gad about with ghosts.

WILD: I beg of you—I will find them.

LA FEU: The women are taking so long!

WILD: Listen! You know how I am. If the women make a disagreeable impression on me, be ready with some excuse, for I'll be off.

BLASIUS: And then we'll have to explain your boorishness. Go! Do what you want. I am not at all interested in women. Nevertheless, I must seek out their company, for they amount to so little and I to nothing at all. You nauseate me, Wild! It would be kind of you to leave me alone for a while.

WILD: Was it my idea to seek you out?

BLASIUS: I can't stand you. Your power is repugnant to me. You're crushing me to death, and with your eternal chasing of phantoms—I hate you!

WILD: As you wish. You'll love me again.

BLASIUS *(embracing him):* Who can resist you? Lad! Lad! I am more ill at ease than you. I am torn within and cannot pick up the threads of my life again. Let it be! I want to become melancholy. No, I want to become nothing. You saw my noble steed in Madrid pulling carts; I cried from the depths of my soul, and Isabella wiped away my tears. Splendor of the world! I can no longer pluck your flowers. Yes, whoever has lost this feeling, whoever has lost thee, undying love, thou who sustainest everything in us!

WILD: Blasius, you have more than you believe.

LA FEU: Where are the women keeping themselves? *(rifling through the books)* Miladies' books give me great hope, for they are blessed with sweet fantasy. Ah, novels! Ah, fairy tales! Ah, how marvelous all the lies! How happy are they who can lie to themselves!

Scene 2

Lady Catherine *and* Louisa *enter, paying their respects. Bows and curtsies all around.*

LA FEU *(as he catches sight of them):* Venus Urania!* By the grove of

---

*Venus as goddess of the sky and of higher, purer "heavenly love," as opposed to lust.

Paphos!* *(to* Lady Catherine) Bewitching goddess of this island! Your gaze stirs my heart to tones of love, and my sinews resound with the dearest harmony.

CATHERINE: Milord! *(a curtsy)* Milord! *(coquettishly)* Strangers of your caliber make our sad life light and pleasant. I have the honor to address—

LA FEU: You, Blasius, tell her my name. This is my guardian, milady!

BLASIUS: La Feu, milady! *(to* Louisa) Miss, I wish that I had not seen you, at least not at this moment. I am so little—

LOUISA: Ha, ha! Milord . . . Blasius, right?

BLASIUS: So they call me.

LOUISA: So, Milord Blasius, I am sorry that my countenance pains you so. Indeed, milord *(a mocking bow)* Ha, ha! Auntie's presence makes him a resounding instrument. *La Vache sonnante*† Ha, ha! Oh, that'll kill me! So, milord, so serious?

BLASIUS: I am not merry. Beautiful and stupid! Woe is me!

WILD: Satan couldn't take this hell. *(exit)*

CATHERINE *and* LOUISA: But why is milord leaving?

LA FEU: I must tell you, milady—Blasius, you certainly know why.

BLASIUS: He has attacks of insanity, miladies, and when he's overcome it just carries him away.

LA FEU *(indicating* Catherine): And the sight of this goddess couldn't stop him?

CATHERINE: Oh, milord! How sorry I am for him—such a handsome man, such a robust, wild countenance.

LA FEU: But a madman. Imagine, he wants to go to war.

CATHERINE: And you?

LA FEU *(kneeling):* Here is my battlefield.

LOUISA *(annoyed):* This is insufferable!

CATHERINE *(solemnly pulling* La Feu *to his feet):* Kneeling becomes you, milord. Presumably, therefore—

LA FEU: Ah! You elevate me with such godliness, with such splendor! Surely many a knee has already bent itself sore before milady!

CATHERINE: Oh, milord! Perhaps one doesn't pass through life unnoticed.

*Venus is frequently called the Paphian, an allusion to the legend that after her birth in the sea she landed at Paphos on Cyprus.

†The mooing cow. This is a reference to the *Cow in the Marketplace of Athens* by the ancient Greek sculptor Myron, which was reputed to be so realistic that one imagined it was mooing.

LOUISA *(exasperated and indolent):* Where are you, milord? Still in the other hemisphere?

BLASIUS *(annoyed and bored):* Milady, you command—

LOUISA *(mocking his tone):* Milord!! Nothing—

CATHERINE: And you, milord?

LA FEU: Ah, away, away! Caught in love's spell! Happy, blessed fate, that led me on this path! Finally your wrath has abated, wild unlucky star! I feel the thrill in my veins renewed. Entrancing goddess! I wish I had the tiny, tiny eyes of a gnat, that I might scrutinize every detail of your charm and beauty.

CATHERINE: What a tone! How cheerful and agreeable. Has milord been away from London long? Oh, if milord would only tell us something about London!

LOUISA: Oh, about London! *(aside)* These people are unbearable!

LA FEU: Yes, milady, about London, but I feel only what is before me. London, milady, is supposed to be a great city. I know little of the world. I was born in London. I was just in the Pyrenees. Oh, those are high, high, mountains! Ah, milady, but my love would be even higher, if milady would love me—

CATHERINE *and* LOUISA: Love? Ha, ha!

LA FEU: Does that strike you as amusing, miladies?

LOUISA: Of course, milord! No, we love nothing.

CATHERINE: Be quiet, Niece! The distinction remains, and it all depends on . . .

LA FEU: Yes, charming Lady: on what we have?

LOUISA *(to Blasius):* Milord continues to dream. All my gaiety abandons me around you.

BLASIUS: Forgive me, I am so moved—you are beautiful, Miss!

LOUISA: And you are very entertaining.

BLASIUS *(after a long pause):* You are bored. I am sorry that I cannot entertain you better. My misfortune is that of always being nothing when I should be everything. I love so silently, Miss, as you see, that I am really in decline.

LOUISA: Love, milord! What are you trying to say? To love silently! Oh, the boredom! Does Lord Wild also love so? It's not as though I were curious—I don't have to know! If only you were more lively!

BLASIUS: Yes, lively! *(aside)* I am absolutely bored to death. My heart is so cold and the girl is so beautiful and cheerful.

LOUISA: I'm having an attack of the vapors. Would milords like to take tea in the garden? Perhaps the room does not agree with you.

BLASIUS: Whatever you like.

LOUISA: Oh, heaven! *(smacks him with her fan)* Come to life, already!

BLASIUS: I am still fresh from the sea, and I have . . . I have . . .

CATHERINE *(who throughout this has been quietly talking to La Feu)*: Yes, milord?

LA FEU: Yes, as I was saying, come with me. Oh, my goddess, I have become everything again before your eyes. Who can see so much charm without every fiber of his body being reborn! Yes, my goddess! I want to tell you much, much about the waves of love that chase my fantasy beyond the sun. And milady *(kisses her hand)* I love you.

CATHERINE *(aside):* This is curious! I don't understand him, and yet I like him. *(aloud)* Milord, you are—

LA FEU: Oh, you! It seems to me we are sympathetic.

CATHERINE: What does *sympathetic* mean?

LA FEU: God have mercy! I don't understand myself enough, milady, to know what the word means.

CATHERINE: How spiteful you are, milord!

(Exeunt omnes)

Scene 3

Caroline, *alone.*

CAROLINE: Were those the Englishmen? Far, far eternally far—it's good they're gone. *(lost in silent melancholy)* Yes, just so did he appear as he came from out of my mind and placed himself before me. *(reaches out toward something)* Oh, so dear to my heart! Why does he stay away so long? Ah! I shall never see Carl Bushy again! I may never see Carl Bushy again! Yet do I not see him? *(enraptured)* My eyes look to him, my heart beats for him; my eyes possess him, my heart possesses him.

Scene 4

Wild *enters without knocking, keeping his hat on throughout the scene. Draws back when he becomes aware of* Caroline's *presence.*

CAROLINE *(frightened):* What? Who?

WILD *(regards her fixedly, with his whole soul):* Forgive me, Miss. I have the wrong room.

CAROLINE: Milord. An error that is easy enough in an inn. *(regards him uneasily)*

WILD *(confused, impassioned, inquiring, hanging on her words):* Milady, may I? Milady . . . yes, I'm going . . . going right now . . . *(draws nearer and nearer)* . . . but, milady . . . I'm staying here . . . and if you are an Englishwoman, as I was told . . . if you . . .

CAROLINE *(trying to compose herself):* Milord, may I inquire as to whom I have the pleasure of addressing? My father will be very happy to see a compatriot.

WILD: Your father? Miss! Do you have a father? Ah! Here! Here! That's so good, so brutally good. Yes, milady, I'm an Englishman . . . an unfortunate one. My name is Wild, and I am—yes, milady, at this moment—

CAROLINE *(suffering):* Wild? Aren't you from Yorkshire? Your face . . . your . . . your . . . yes, milord, surely you must be from Yorkshire.

WILD: From Yorkshire? No! My soul is pounding so—ah, here I find what I have been seeking throughout the whole world. *(taking her hand)* You are an angel, milady, a marvelous, sensitive creation. *(looking toward the heavens)* You have saved such a moment for me! Let me speak! I feel it so deeply . . . your eyes . . . yes, your eyes full of soul and suffering . . . and this heart . . . torn in two and deeply, deeply unfortunate. I traveled here to let myself be killed in the next battle . . . and . . . and . . . I want to be killed.

CAROLINE: So confused . . . oh, sir, do you suffer?

WILD: Yes, alas. Oh, suffering is so various in human beings . . . often so wonderful . . . and if I may . . . milady's name?

CAROLINE: My father, milord, is Lord Berkley.

WILD *(starts back):* Lord Berkley! That is . . . the spitting image!

CAROLINE: What's the matter with you? Do you know the unfortunate Lord Berkley?

WILD: Know? No! And you are Jenny Caroline Berkley?

CAROLINE: Yes, sir. *(looks about herself, in extreme consternation):* Oh, sir! Sir! Who are you?

WILD *(kneeling before her, still grasping her hand):* No, Miss, I am . . . my tongue is so weak, so much is in my heart. I am . . . Miss Berkley . . . *(leaps up suddenly)* the happy man who has searched the whole world for you. *(drawing near the door)* The unhappy man—

CAROLINE: Carl Bushy! My Carl!

WILD *(at the door):* Ah, here! Here! *(his arms reach out for her)*

CAROLINE *(hurrying to him):* Carl Bushy, and you would leave me? Is it you? Is it you? Ah, just this word, and then let my soul be free!

WILD *(embracing her):* Yes, I am he! Jenny! I am Carl Bushy! I am the blissful—Jenny! Ah! I've found you!

CAROLINE: Let me gather my thoughts! The joy . . . the anguish . . . you are Carl . . . I believe . . . you are Carl Bushy!

WILD: What are you afraid of? Why do you kill the joy that pulsates through my whole body? I am he who, with your picture in my heart, sought you and your father in every corner of the earth. •

CAROLINE: My father! My father! Save yourself! He hates Bushy and his son. Save yourself! Flee! Ah, forsake me! Flee! I haven't seen you.

WILD: I? Jenny! Flee? I am here in your presence, gaze here into your sweet eyes, and the first joy of my life has returned. Flee? Who will tear me away from here? All the wildness of my mind catches hold of me. Who will tear me away from here? Who will tear Carl Bushy from Miss Berkley? Let your father come! Are you not mine? Were you not mine from the first years of our childhood? I grew up with you; our hearts, souls, and beings were one. You were engaged to me before you knew the meaning of the word. *(coldly)* I'm staying here, Miss! I'm staying here.

CAROLINE: You make me so afraid.

WILD: Should I go? Jenny! Jenny, I have you now.

CAROLINE: Leave me alone for a minute on the balcony.

WILD: Good, Miss! I'll stay here. Nothing will budge me from here. Heaven has formed a bond between us that no human hand can sever. Here I'll wait for the enemy of your new fatherland. I'll await my enemy.

CAROLINE *(gently):* But not with this wild, disturbed look! Promise me not to reveal your name.

WILD: As you wish. Oh, Jenny! If you could feel for a moment the anguish that has driven this heart throughout the world! I have worn myself out; I wanted to destroy myself. Ah, this hour! This hour still remaining to me! And still all of it wretchedness? But I want to feel nothing, to sense nothing any more. I have you now, and defiance, defiance to the stubborn old mule!

CAROLINE: What is this doubt, this frightening disturbance, this fury in your haunted eyes?

WILD: Your father! Yes, your father! My father—both ruined! Miss! I shall not leave you. It seizes me so violently! Yes, Jenny, fly away with me! Fly from this land with me! *(embracing her)*

CAROLINE: Let me be!

WILD: Is your father setting a trap for me? Oh, how good I feel in the midst of tumult! My darling!

CAROLINE: One moment, Carl! What if my father comes?

WILD: And still hates? Still the vindictive Berkley! My dear, sweet, little Miss! Thank God, who has showered so much of His grace on me in these violent emotions. Yes, Miss! Only love has held this machine together, which through its eternal inner war was so close at every moment to its own destruction.

CAROLINE: Good Carl! You are as always a wild, good youth. So have I imagined you. Oh, the years, the years, that have gone by! Can you really believe I was thirteen years old, and you fifteen, when we were torn apart from each other: I to this other half of the world. I came here; you were there. Yes, you were there, and where was there any spot in the world that you did not occupy?

WILD: And you! What now? How all of this tormented me! You are what I sought and required in the whole world to reconcile my heart. I found you, found you in America; where I sought death, I find peace and blessedness in those sweet eyes. *(embraces her)* And so I have you, so I have you, Miss Berkley! And hold you, and what Wild holds—I would strangle your father to possess you. But this is ecstasy, and it is gentle. *(kisses her)*

CAROLINE *(breaking free):* Frightening! Wild! Carl! Where is the gaze to give life to those words?

WILD: Here, Miss! *(kisses her)*

Scene 5

Berkley. Wild, Caroline.

BERKLEY: Hm! Morning—eh! What's this? What's going on here?
WILD *(rigid):* I was kissing milady.
BERKLEY: And you, Miss, you let it happen?
CAROLINE: Milord!
BERKLEY *(bitterly):* Adieu, Miss!
WILD: Milord, do you mean to insult me? I beg you, Miss, remain. It is not possible for Lord Berkley to insult a man he does not know. I am an Englishman, I am called Wild, and I wished to visit you.
BERKLEY: Well done, sir!
WILD: I have suffered in the world, I have suffered and my senses have become somewhat chaotic. They often seize me violently. A miserable man finds so little sympathy in the world: I found it in miss, milord, and when one finds that—I kissed miss and would have done so even if her father had been standing there the whole while.
BERKLEY: So young and yet so miserable? Look at me! At me, milord!
WILD: Yes, milord, so young and yet so miserable, and still more miserable because I am lacking in patience, for my emotions are so strong. I have become bitter; only this moment have I felt that there was still joy in the world.
BERKLEY: I could take an interest in you. Please, sir, seat yourself in another light. I cannot bear certain features on your face.
CAROLINE: Oh, Father, milord suffers so much.
BERKLEY: You may leave us alone. I see that one can be honest with milord. His whole turbulent being speaks so sincerely.
CAROLINE: As you wish. (Wild *holds the doors for her, nodding)*
BERKLEY: As I was saying, milord—you must forgive me. I had an enemy, a horrible enemy, who reduced me to the most frightening condition in which an old man can be, and I saw you, milord. If I catch him, wherever it may be, I shall be compelled to torture him until I see those features, which I criticized in you, disappear from his face. God knows, you seem to be a decent man! It takes all my strength not to fall upon you and press you to my heart as a son. But I also lost a son because of him. And so, milord, you must forgive me.

WILD: As you wish, as you wish.

BERKLEY: Yes, I understand this unease, this doubting tone in which you say that, and looks pass between us that could win one's heart. Have patience! One grows accustomed. If you are miserable and have tasted gall, then we will soon see eye to eye.

WILD: I have, milord—but what does all this mean? Now to my request of you! Could you allow a man like me to join as a volunteer in the campaign against your enemy?

BERKLEY: With all my heart. Welcome! I shall go at once to the general. Come along!

WILD: I came for this very purpose. The sooner the better.

BERKLEY: Oh, milord! I have long hoped for such a day. I'm never better than when I'm in the midst of cannon fire.

WILD: It will be good for me, I hope.

BERKLEY: What part of England are you from?

WILD: London.

BERKLEY: Well then, you must know Lord Berkley's fate.

WILD: I have heard of it.

BERKLEY: But don't just dismiss it indifferently, young man.

WILD: I am not cold, milord, only angry at the people who could have made so many things different.

BERKLEY: Are you in your right mind? Man! Have you a heart? I am Lord Berkley, pursued, displaced, ejected, deprived of wife and son. Have you a heart, young man, or has your own misery made you callous? If so, then hold out your arm and bless the world. Do you know Bushy?

WILD: No, milord!

BERKLEY: Have you heard of him? I ask you, how are things with him? Miserable? Wretched?

WILD: Quite happy, milord.

BERKLEY: Fie on you! Happy! Have you seen my daughter? Do you see my gray hair, my crazed eyes? Happy?

WILD: He had to leave his house and property. He fell out of favor with the king and has become invisible.

BERKLEY: A thousand thanks, milord! A thousand thanks! Hey, Bushy! So I have been in part avenged! Is he really miserable? Well, he can't be wretched enough. Right? He has no home to give him shelter, no one to nurse him in his old age?

WILD: He is happy, milord!

BERKLEY: I must ask you to leave my room. You are a friend of him and thus my enemy. You have his way of speech, his bearing—by

God! I see Bushy in you. Leave now unless you want to drive an old man into a rage.

WILD: Happy, in the sense that he doesn't care. Happy in his own way, I mean.

BERKLEY: Well, he shouldn't be. His hair should become stinging snakes, and the fibers of his heart scorpions. Sir! He should not be able to sleep, nor wake, nor pray, nor swear. That is how I wish to see him. Then I would be magnanimous and put a bullet through his brain. What he's earned is eternal torment, but I would be magnanimous, sir, to please my daughter. If you had known my lady, milord, who died from heartache (*grasps* Wild's *hand;* Wild *pulls it back at the last words*) I know you would raise your hands with me and curse Bushy and his descendants. Tell me, milord, how goes it with Bushy's son?

WILD: He wanders through the world without rest. Miserable in himself, miserable at the fate of his father.

BERKLEY: That is good, milord! That is good! Do you think he's still alive?

WILD: He's in Spain now.

BERKLEY: But I am hoping that his father will never see him again. I am hoping that young Bushy will ruin his body through dissipation and rot away in the prime of his youth. He should never see him again, milord, the joy would be too great. To see his son again! Just think, to see his son again! What that must mean to a man! I could go mad. When I see my Harry, my sweet, stubborn son before me in my thoughts, riding on his nag, calling "Father! Father!" and cracking his whip—he should never see him again! (Wild *is about to leave*) Stay a moment, milord! Tell me, did Bushy come away with his wealth? Milord, if someone wanted to tell me eternally of Bushy's misfortune, I would want to do nothing in the world but listen. Has he come away with his wealth?

WILD: Enough, milord, to live contentedly in his calm fashion.

BERKLEY: I'm sorry to hear it. I wish I could see him begging me for a pound. Do you think I'd give it to him?

WILD: Why not, milord? He would give you what he had.

BERKLEY: Do you think so? If my miss were standing by, perhaps. Perhaps not. Oh, he is a horrible hypocrite, old Bushy. I'm afraid he might even get a pound from me with his hypocritical mien. Isn't he a hypocrite, milord?

WILD: No, definitely not!

BERKLEY: What would you know of it? Of course you take his part; you have his nose.

WILD: Milord, I'm going.

BERKLEY: Forgive me. But just tell me where that jealous Hubert wound up?

WILD: He accompanies old Bushy.

BERKLEY: Thank you, sir. Miserable?

WILD: There is enough occasion for him to exercise his raw envy, so he finds himself well in his humor.

BERKLEY: Take care, sir! I won't stand for this! He must suffer as much as Bushy. I beg you, let him suffer! Lie to me! He suffers!

WILD: Now, milord, I must rejoin my friends. You'll see to it that I am enlisted?

BERKLEY: Yes, milord. Farewell. You have made me very happy. Come back soon. This evening, for dinner. I could almost love you. *(exit* Wild*)* Now I feel well. Ha, ha! Bushy and Hubert, does it weigh heavily on you? Blessed be the king! It gives me a right childish joy. That fellow there is only half to my taste. There is something so fatal and strong in his being, just like Bushy's. The devil knows! I must share this joy with my niece. *(exit)*

Act 3

Twilight
Same room as act 1, scene 1.
Blasius. La Feu.

BLASIUS: Wild is so odd, so extraordinarily joyful. Dashes about, reaches toward heaven as if he wanted to pull it down. I have seen tears shimmering in his eyes. What could be wrong with the man? I can't get him to stay in one place. I'm cold.

LA FEU: Dear, dear Blasius. I'm quite hot.

BLASIUS: You are the eternal fever.

LA FEU: Right, the eternal fever, or else I suffocate. I am in love again. Through my whole body, through veins and limbs, through my whole soul. I am so hot, I'm afraid I may go off like a bomb—if only then it would lift my pure being and lay it down in the bosom of the charming lady!

BLASIUS: The old lady? La Feu!

LA FEU: Old? Old? What is old? Nothing is old, nothing is young. I no longer know any difference. Oh, I am at the point when one begins to be well. Can you believe it, I have forgotten everything, as if I had drunk the waters of Lethe. Nothing bothers me any more. I could take up a crutch and go begging. One must become so at last.

BLASIUS: Oh, if only I were still sitting in the tower!

LA FEU: Nothing bad can happen to one in the tower. Oh, do me the pleasure and fling me inside. I want to dream so happily, so blessedly! Man must dream, dear, dear Blasius, if he wants to be happy and not think, not philosophize. In my youth, Blasius, I was a poet, I had ardent, roving fantasies. But they poured ice water on me until the last spark was extinguished. The dreadful experience, the frightful masks of human faces, when one wants to embrace everyone with love! Derision on one side! Satan on the other! I stood there like an extinct volcano. I traveled through an enchanted kingdom, cold and without a receptive feeling. The most beautiful maidens had as little effect on me as the flies that buzz round the tower. In order to be free from misery my soul was determined to feel differently and discover which of its regions were cold. Now everything is all right, everything is lovely and beautiful!

BLASIUS: If only I were sitting in the tower again, where spiders, mice, and rats were my only society!

LA FEU: Were you sitting in the tower then?

BLASIUS: Of course, of course. In a pretty tower, and looked through a hole that wasn't any larger than an eye. I could see light with only one eye. So I'd peer, first with one eye, and then the other, so as to stay used to the light. There a man can have sensations, La Feu! There the heart swells, and there the heart withers away— and the man dries up too. I could look at one spot for a whole day ... and see ... *(stiff and distracted)* Eh, what? In Madrid, La Feu, and in London. *(bitter)* Praised be the human race! Eh? They meant well with me. I was the most honest fellow in the world.

LA FEU: That was your failing, dear, dear Blasius.

BLASIUS: In Madrid the Inquisition did it because of my carriage. In London because I shot a fellow who robbed me of my money and wanted to rob me of my honor.

LA FEU: Yes, Blasius! Dear Blasius! One need not shoot anyone.

BLASIUS: Oh, if only there were an end to mankind's feelings!

LA FEU: How are you getting on with the lady?

BLASIUS: Leave me alone! I have bored myself. She is merry and beautiful and cold as snow and as chaste as Diana's nightgown. She restrains one; I am dead and drowsy. *(yawning)* Good night, Donna Isabella! Oh, if I were sitting once again at your feet, most charming one! *(falls asleep)*

LA FEU: I must keep watch by the lady's window tonight. She is a quite charming lady, to whom one can say anything, and who understands a person before he or she speaks. I want to write a fairy tale some day.

Scene 2

Wild. Blasius. La Feu.

WILD *(enters in uniform):* How are you?
LA FEU: Good! Good, Wild. Blasius is sleeping and I am dreaming. I must send some verses to the lady.
WILD: Dearest La Feu! *(embraces him)* Dear Blasius! *(embraces him)*
BLASIUS: Hey, what's going on, then? Can't a man have any peace?
WILD: I am well again. Oh, my dear fellows! I have been restored.
BLASIUS: Good for you. I feel awful. *(goes back to sleep).*
WILD: May Heaven protect you. I want to pour out my soul into the air. *(exits)*

Scene 3

Sea Captain Boyet. Innkeeper. La Feu. Blasius. Moor.

INNKEEPER: What do you wish, milord?
CAPTAIN: Nothing, nothing, except for you to leave.
(La Feu sits, writing in ecstasy)
CAPTAIN *(to his people):* You all clear off! Little boy, stay here! So, little fellow!
MOOR: Rough captain, what do you want?
CAPTAIN: Would you still let yourself be shot for me?
MOOR: Here I stand, good lord. You have caused me pain, to be sure. By the gods! You are sometimes as mad as a tiger, you lobster! See, on my back are bruises as large as my fist, harsh lord!
CAPTAIN: Because I like you, little ape!
MOOR *(kissing his forehead):* Flay me! Pull my skin over my head, wild lord! I am your boy, your monkey, your Soley,* your dog. *(twisting around him)* You have given my father life and freedom. *(Captain pinches him)* Oh, ouch, why do you pinch me?
CAPTAIN: I like you. Do you want to be a midshipman, boy?
MOOR: Oh, lord, lord! A sword for me, and put yourself behind me when your enemy comes. Good lord! Tiger! Great lord! The blood in my body loves you and throbs under my skin.

---

*The meaning of *Soley* is unclear.

CAPTAIN: Sugarcane from a Moor boy! Do you want to be beaten?

MOOR: Do you want to be coaxed? Should I stroke your cheeks?

CAPTAIN: Did you see the ship, the one that sailed by?

MOOR: Yes, lord. Why did you attack?

CAPTAIN: So as not to shrink before them. To laugh in their faces, and snatch it from under their noses.

MOOR: But you were hit by a cannonball, and sailors and soldiers are dead.

CAPTAIN: Fill my pipe! Who wants to talk about that? Dead, boy, dead, all that's nothing. Are you afraid of death?

MOOR: While you live, yes. I would want to stay with you.

CAPTAIN: Now let's try it here. Death is afraid of me. Ten years I have faced it, and never a wound, except from that scoundrel of a Scot.

MOOR: If all the mothers and fathers you've made childless came together—

CAPTAIN: Gentle boy! You're not fit for the sea. Hold my pipe! Place a stool under my feet! *(looks about)* Hey, who's there? Boy, go thin out the people a bit. You are so useless. Please, boy, go rap the sleeper there on the nose. I won't have anybody sleep until I'm at rest. And the writer there, so wrapped up in himself—go torment him.

(The Moor *raps* Blasius *on the nose. Goes over to* La Feu *from behind, and snatches his quill as he's writing)*

LA FEU: The shimmer of your eyes! Hey, hey!

BLASIUS: Hmph! Hooligans all!

CAPTAIN: Gentlemen, I would like to make your acquaintance. Are you in the army?

BLASIUS: I'm nothing. *(falls asleep)*

CAPTAIN: That's a lot. And you?

LA FEU: Everything, everything.

CAPTAIN: That's not much. Come here, Mr. Everything! Let's wrestle a little to put my joints in order. *(grabs him)*

LA FEU: Oh me, you centaur! There's nothing there for the imagination! *(sits down)* "The shimmer of your eyes." Stupid rhymes! Eyes, dies, luck, suck—"From whose love I suck!" Terrific!

CAPTAIN: Boy, give no one any peace and don't be afraid. The crazier you act the better. Go wake up the sleeper, boy. *(The* Moor *does so)*

BLASIUS: Lout! Ass! Wild! *(flails about with his fists)* Wild! If you don't leave me alone—

MOOR: A blow! A blow!

CAPTAIN: Wild! Sir! Where is he? Answer me!

BLASIUS: How should I know?

CAPTAIN: I can say this much to you: either you tell me where Wild is, or you'll take a little walk with me.

BLASIUS: Let me alone, and I'll see if it pleases me.

CAPTAIN: If it pleases—Sir!

BLASIUS: Yes, if it pleases me! Then you'll hear.

CAPTAIN: I like that. Well, I'll go look up the general. I brought a pretty ship with me. I rely on your word. It will be good to find you, Sir Wild! Come, boy.

MOOR: I'm right behind you.

BLASIUS: The dog! How in hell did the fellow wind up here? He's the ship's captain or the devil. I must find Wild. Nobody lets me sleep!

LA FEU: Just let me read this to you.

BLASIUS: Leave me alone!

LA FEU: I want to sing it at her window. You promised miladies a walk.

BLASIUS: Perhaps I'll come.

Scene 4

Wild. Preceding.

BLASIUS *(meets* Wild *and the* Captain *at the door):* I almost trudged off to no purpose. *(sits silently)*

(La Feu *reads through his verses. The* Moor *plays with toys)*

CAPTAIN: A stroke of luck that I find you here.

WILD: Good! Very good!

CAPTAIN: You know of course that I cannot stand you?

WILD: I haven't asked you.

CAPTAIN: So, I shall show you. Eh, Scot! May the thunder strike me down, you shall not share God's air with me. Since the first sight of you, I have borne such a hatred for you that my fist grabs for sword and pistol when I see you from afar. Quick, boy, my weapon!

WILD: You know, Captain, that you are crude and offensive, and that I am guilty of no crime against you. You forced me to shoot you in Holland, and by my soul! It pained me to see you fall for no purpose.

CAPTAIN: Your bullet struck deep, but a bullet that stays in the flesh is no bullet and only inflames the human spirit. Believe me, when you fall I'll have my sailors pipe you a funeral song when the wind is at its wildest.

WILD: Thank you, Captain! As you wish.

CAPTAIN: Because I wish and must! Because in my eyes you have such a toadlike, fatal appearance. Because when I see you, my sinews twitch as if one bellowed the most hostile sound into my ears.

WILD: I can tell you that I can put up with you. But nonetheless, even if I don't much care, I'll do it for a joke. I didn't particularly need to throw my life away today, but you're an honest man, and if we can't live in the same place, and I intend to stay here—

CAPTAIN: Charming! Listen, Scot! I must report now to the general, so we shall put our business off until tomorrow.

WILD: That's good too. So I'll see battle.

CAPTAIN: And I with you. But the devil take you if you let yourself be shot. I'm warning you! *(exit)*

Scene 5

The garden. Moonlight.
Lady Catherine *and* Louisa, *walking.*

LOUISA: The evening air, dear aunt! You're coughing so dreadfully.

CATHERINE: Coughing! Stupid thing! Coughing! Ha, ha! Now really, child, oh, child! *(coughing throughout)*

LOUISA: Well, what then?

CATHERINE: It would be a beautiful gift, if you would tell—

LOUISA: Oh, because I'm bored I'll tell you that I have never in my life seen two more tactless boors than the two strangers. I can tell you that again.

CATHERINE: Tactless boors? Ha, ha! La Feu! The sweet English Milord La Feu! A cherub among men! Ha, ha, Niece! A splendid gift it would be if you would help me praise him. Sit down, let's go through all his endearing traits as the night slips away, and when the sun rises let's begin again.

LOUISA: Yes, Wild, Auntie! Wild! Have you seen him? I saw him sneaking through the bushes earlier. Wild, Auntie!

CATHERINE: Not Wild! La Feu! Did you see his eyes?

LOUISA: They are, I believe, somewhat dried up, dull, and weak. At least I didn't see any fire or shine within.

CATHERINE: I beg of you, look at those stars! The shimmering, the glittering—his eyes!

LOUISA: Oh, really!

CATHERINE: Aren't you paying attention to what I say? Oh, he is speaking! Love makes poets, and poets make such comparisons. The splendor of his eyes, the splendor of the stars—and his hair!

LOUISA: We haven't yet agreed on his eyes. Blasius has killed all my cheerfulness with his stupid boredom. Have I stopped having an effect on men, then?

CATHERINE: His hair, Niece! So blond, so sweetly blond!

LOUISA: He was wearing a wig.

CATHERINE: A wig! Ha, ha! Amor in a wig! How can you be so poorly observant, faced with such beauties? No, your taste is not the best.

LOUISA *(annoyed):* His hair is brick red.

CATHERINE: Leave me alone, you willful little thing! And you must not keep calling me Aunt when I'm in the throes of love talk. Say instead: milady.

LOUISA: Where on earth are they? They promised to go walking with us in the moonlight.

CATHERINE: Just wait, La Feu will certainly come.

LOUISA: Auntie! Do you know that I spoke with Wild? He came this way and could not and would not get out of the way. I was quite aloof and asked him his name. Then he stammered very confusedly that his name was Wild, as though it were a lie. I have my own ideas about that. He had been alone so long with Miss Berkley. He's in love with her, by all the stars! In love with her! He turned away from me so coldly and streaked past me like a raw wind.

CATHERINE: Blasius is in love with you.

LOUISA: Oh, him! If we only knew who he was, this Wild.

CATHERINE: La Feu will surely know. We'll ask him.

Scene 6

La Feu. Louisa. Lady Catherine.

LA FEU *(from some distance):* Do I not find you, my love? Where are you, that I might lay this song at your feet? To sing to you the hymn of praise to your charms! To wreathe your fragrant hair!

LOUISA: Your Adonis is calling.

CATHERINE: Quiet! Let him speak! Oh, the words of love are more valuable than frankincense.

LA FEU: I've been wandering the garden back and forth searching for you, my love.

LOUISA: Milord.

CATHERINE: Unfriendly girl! But he didn't hear you. Milord!

LA FEU: Ah, this tone inflames my blood *(rushes to her)* Ah, milady! Hours have I wandered about in love-drunk fantasy. I have braided you a wreath, heavenly Venus! Walk now in the woods wreathed by love. *(crowns her)*

LOUISA: To the madhouse with the fool!

CATHERINE: Oh, milord! How pleasant! How very happy I am!

LA FEU: Happy? Yes, happy! With love, everything is happy; without love, everything is sad. I have established monuments to love that will never decay, even though my heart should decay.

CATHERINE: Oh, milord! Your heart will never decay.

LOUISA: You're coughing more and more, Auntie! Ask him!

CATHERINE: Yes, milord, a question for you. Would you please tell us the real name of your companion Wild?

LA FEU: Wild? Is he still here? Isn't he in the war?

CATHERINE: Not yet, milord. Tomorrow.

LA FEU: Have a good trip!

CATHERINE: But he is in love with my niece.

LA FEU *(pointing to* Louisa): With milady?

LOUISA *(annoyed):* Milord!

CATHERINE: I implore you, by all the gods of love! Tell me his real name.

LA FEU: If I can remember it. Hm! You really want to know this?

CATHERINE: Of course! Quickly!

LA FEU: I have no memory, milady! I mean, he chased off a servant who betrayed it. I think he's forbidden me to tell.

CATHERINE: No, surely not.

LA FEU: You know? I just can't think of it . . . Carl, I think.

LOUISA: Go *on,* milord.

LA FEU: Bu . . . Bu . . . oh, my memory! Carl . . . Bu . . . Bu . . .

LOUISA: Bushy, milord?

LA FEU: Yes, yes, Bushy! I think so.

LOUISA: Now we've got it! Her Carl! Her Bushy!

CATHERINE: My brother must be told.

LA FEU: But take care. No one but you must know. Come now, let's dance the dance of love in the moonlight. *(leaps up with her)*

CATHERINE: Oh, milord!

LOUISA: I shall go along to annoy them. *(they exit down a lane)*

Scene 7

Wild *enters.*

WILD: The night lies so cool, so nicely about me! The clouds drift by so quietly! Ah, otherwise how cheerless and gloomy everything would be! It is good, my heart, that you can again catch this pure feeling of awesomeness; good that the night air sighs around you and you feel love wafted through the vast stillness of nature. Shimmer, stars! Ah, we have become friends again! You are carried with almighty love, as is my heart, and you twinkle in pure love, as does my soul. You were so cold to me in the mountains! And when my love spoke to you, and heavy tears gushed forth, you vanished before my wet eyes and I cried out: "Jenny, my life! Where are you, light of my eyes?" So often have I clung to you, moon, but it went dark around me as I reached for her who was so far away. Ah, that everything is so woven together, so bound together by love. It is good that you again understand the rustling of the trees, the gushing of the stream, the babbling of the brook; that all the tongues of nature are clear to you now. Take me into your lovely coolness, friend of my love! *(lies down under a tree)*

Scene 8

Caroline. Wild.

CAROLINE *(opening the window):* Night! Still night! Let me confide in you. Let me confide in you, meadows! Valleys! Hills and forests! Let me confide in you, moon, and all you stars! No longer to cry over him, no longer to sigh over him. I wander under your light, my friend who was sad! No longer in wailing do you answer me, echo, you that knew no other sound but his name—Carl! Does that not ring sweetly through the night? Carl! Do not my flowers nod to me happily? Do not the winds hurry to carry my voice to his ears? You should rejoice with me, lonely little place. I want to confide in you, gloomy place. *(she becomes aware of Wild's presence)* And you who lie there buried in the shadows, darling eavesdropper!

WILD: Life! My life!

CAROLINE: Friend of my heart!

WILD: On the wings of love I come to you. *(climbs up the tree)*

CAROLINE: Be careful, my dearest, the branches are bending.

WILD: Let them bend, the swayings of love are strong. *(reaching for her hand)* Miss! My Miss!

CAROLINE: Don't be so foolhardy! Don't trust those limbs!

WILD: I hang on your eyes. Let me breathe! Grant me that I may feel, that I may say what it is this moment. Ah, all you sad nights, how quickly you have disappeared! You have wiped them all out, heaven, and have brought me here! Miss! Dear Jenny! How are you? Speak to me, my love. Why are you hiding your sweet eyes from me?

CAROLINE: Speak! Oh, speak!

WILD: Tears, my love?

CAROLINE: The first tears of joy.

WILD: My best, my love!

CAROLINE: And also tears of grief! Wild! What have you done? Retreat, oh, light! Unhappy man, what have you done?

WILD: Jenny, your knees are shaking. What's wrong with you?

CAROLINE: This coat, tomorrow morning—oh, you and my father! Why do you chase death when you needn't?

WILD: To be worthy of you. Forget this coat! I feel so good in it now. Forget it. And this wish is also satisfied!

CAROLINE: Alas! Death!

WILD: Death! And love envelops me. Let me wander in the valley of death; love will lead me back.

CAROLINE: And its message leads me to you.

Scene 9

La Feu, Blasius, Lady Catherine, *and* Louisa *come along the lane.* Caroline. Wild.

LOUISA: What is that on that tree there?

CAROLINE: I hear my cousin, Carl! You must leave!

WILD: Let her come! I'll see you again. *(springs down. Remains at the window in deep inner thought)* Tomorrow! Yes, tomorrow! And what, then, if I lie stretched out! This heart has felt all that creation offers, all that a man can feel. Oh, this night! This night! And the coming day! I shall see you again! And your image stays with me and leads me along—I shall see you again. *(fixedly, to heaven)* I shall see her again! I'll see you again, as now! So sure as the bond that ties you to me! I shall see her again! I lie here, and my breast swells. *(they come nearer)*

LOUISA: Did you see that, aunt? He was there, and so was she! They were together, I say. Did you see him? Did you see her? Do you see him? Oh, I would like to pull away the moonlight, the vile man!

CATHERINE: Does this concern me? Come to my brother, we want to tell him—

LA FEU: What, milady? You want to go? When the night is full of more and more fantasy? The music of the spheres sounds more and more charming. *(Blasius sits down)*

LOUISA: Well, milord?

BLASIUS: I am so tired . . . can't move another step. The walk is so wet and cold, I'm going to be sick—

LOUISA: Shame on you, milord. You could at least keep quiet.

BLASIUS: Yes, quiet, quiet . . . fire is fire and tired is tired. *(rises)*

LOUISA: Let's walk past him. *(they all walk past* Wild. *He takes no notice)* What impertinence!

Act 4

Scene 1

Night. Berkley's room, as before.
Berkley. Servant.

BERKLEY: Battle tomorrow. Ha, ha, ha! That's really something, a
battle. Conduct yourself bravely, old lord! Sleep well tonight! Ha,
ha!
SERVANT: Milord, there is a gentleman outside.
BERKLEY: So late. Let him come in. Sir Wild?
SERVANT: No, he said he was a sea captain.
BERKLEY: Treat him with every consideration, if he is the captain
who brought along the ship. *(Exit* servant*)*

Scene 2

Captain. Moor. Berkley.

CAPTAIN: Milord! The innkeeper told me that an Englishman lived
here. I couldn't go to bed without seeing you.
BERKLEY: Welcome, a thousand times welcome, good, wild seaman!
CAPTAIN: Welcome! I paid you a compliment when I arrived. A rich,
English ship, milord. By the way, I'm tired. *(The* Moor *stands
behind him and plays with his hair)*
BERKLEY: Lie down, sit down. As you wish.
CAPTAIN: Thank you. *(stares at him)* Yes, milord, I'd like to—if I
had arrived at my goal. I am traveling the whole world through—
BERKLEY: It's good, sir, that I see you. You do my soul good. I must
kiss you, sir!

CAPTAIN: Milord! All my obstinate wildness dissolves in your presence.

BERKLEY: Good! Spirit of my Harry! Are you still staying here? Who are you looking for, sir?

CAPTAIN: An old man. Heaven will swear I have traveled ten years on the sea; I'll be lost until I find him.

BERKLEY: Harry? Is it you? You have his soul, you have his—Harry! I suppose I would have to call him forth out of you.

CAPTAIN: Milord, who are you?

BERKLEY: Who am I? God in heaven! In heaven! Harry! Harry! You are—

CAPTAIN: Harry Berkley—

BERKLEY: My son—

CAPTAIN: Father, my father! *(embraces him)*

BERKLEY: My Harry! Eh, my boy! Let me hold you then in my arms! Oh, my Harry! I am so happy, my eyes cloud over.

CAPTAIN: Oh, my father! I have traveled the world searching for you. I have crawled across every island.

BERKLEY: Yes, indeed, you are he. You have the wildness, the tumult of Berkley. The rolling, threatening eyes, the fixedness, the unshakableness, the resolution. Hey, Harry! Harry! Let me now truly rejoice! So gallant a seaman, my Harry! To bring us a ship and my Harry!

CAPTAIN: Oh, my father! That I have, ha, ha.

BERKLEY: I am crazy with joy. I must rest a bit. Joy weakens me so, my limbs cannot support me any longer. *(sits)*

CAPTAIN *(embraces him):* Unhappy father, what you must have suffered!

BERKLEY: If you only . . . if you only . . . you are here now. I have suffered nothing. No, I can't sit. Caroline. Caroline! Caroline! Miss! Miss! For God's sake, Miss!

CAPTAIN: My sister!

BERKLEY: Harry! Caroline! You are here! *(to heaven)* You have given them back to me! Given them back to this heart! I cannot cry now. There he stands—oh, my Harry!

CAPTAIN: My father, the words do not come. But where is my sister? And my mother?

BERKLEY: Mother! Mother! Harry! Oh, Berkley, your wife—Miss! Miss!

Scene 3

Caroline. Preceding.

BERKLEY *(to* Caroline): Will you cry out? Will you shout and leap up?

CAROLINE: Milord!

BERKLEY: He's there! There! There! There he is!

CAPTAIN *(embraces her):* My sister, my dearest!

CAROLINE: Mine! Mine!

BERKLEY: I can say nothing for tears and joy, Harry! Ah, you cannot speak, it makes you so happy. Ha, ha! What are you seeing, old man? Oh, my children! *(embraces them)* Now may heaven give you your son again too, old Bushy!

CAROLINE: Oh, milord! This wish makes your daughter very happy.

MOOR *(kneels before* Berkley *and* Caroline): Old man, I am your slave. Good Miss, I am your slave.

CAPTAIN: So, boy!

BERKLEY: Stand up, black one! Give me your hand!

MOOR: God bless you! I am yours as I stand here. And yours, lady!

CAROLINE: You shall be satisfied with me. Dear brother! Dear Harry! How could you let us cry so long for you?

BERKLEY *(to the* Captain): Speak! Tell us!

CAPTAIN: My mother, milord! I don't see my mother. I have brought so much for her, and for you, Miss. Where is my mother?

BERKLEY: Just enjoy yourself now!

CAROLINE: Dearest! Best! *(cries)*

CAPTAIN: You're crying? Dead! Eh, girl? Out with it! Dead?

BERKLEY: Yes, dead! By heaven! An angel of God! Oh, I could go mad, that my lady doesn't stand here among us, like a shade-giving, refreshing tree, laying her hands on your heads and blessing you. Dear, gentle woman! Did you look down to see your old lord, lying among thorns, walking the raw path of grief? Look down now! That she is not here among us! Damn Bushy! May he never see his son! It is because of him I've lost her!

CAPTAIN: My mother dead? Dead because of him? Cursed thought of mine, to give him to the sea!

BERKLEY: Gave him to the sea? What?

CAROLINE: Brother! My brother! Speak!

CAPTAIN: Revenge, Father! On Bushy and Hubert. Ha! I was only a boy, but I sensed what they did to us and avenged you before I found you.

BERKLEY: You did? Sweet child! Harry! Harry! How? How, sweet youth?

CAROLINE: But they're not dead, Brother?

CAPTAIN: Of course they are. Of course.

CAROLINE: That! That! God in Heaven! *(sinks into a chair)*

CAPTAIN: What's wrong with the child? Eh, Miss?

BERKLEY: I'll wake her up. Hey, Miss! Miss! Bushy, our enemy! He is dead! Are you awake? I would wake from the dead if I heard such news. We are avenged, Miss!

Scene 4

Wild. Preceding.

WILD: Milord! You sent for me—*(catching sight of* Caroline) Miss!

CAPTAIN: Hey, what the hell does the Scot want? Tomorrow we'll be shooting each other.

WILD: Miss . . . Jenny . . . what's going on?

BERKLEY: Eh, milord! So much joy—unfortunate man—so much joy! This is my son, sir!

WILD: The captain? Well, then! That too . . . Miss! Dear Miss!

CAROLINE: Wild! Wild! Please go away!

BERKLEY: Another joy, milord. Another major joy. Be merry, I forgive you for the way you look. My son here has killed old Bushy. He is dead, milord, my friend! What, no joy? Why are your eyes so fixed? Milord!

CAROLINE: Father!

CAPTAIN: I set him adrift—God knows, in one of the most dreadful storms I have ever experienced at sea—with Hubert in a tiny fishing boat. It was night and thundering awfully; the winds blew over the sea with such a melodious roar that my heart pounded in response. What bothered me was that they didn't move a muscle. If they had prayed and beseeched, then by all the elements, I would perhaps have hanged them, or left them on a desert island, for just then the sea surged so high that I wouldn't have trusted my dog to it. They disappeared from my sight almost at the moment they got into the boat. Only when there was lightning could I see them struggling in the distance. It howled so bitterly about me that I could not have the pleasure of seeing them swallowed by the sea, or of hearing their laments. But the storm was no joke.

CAROLINE: It is getting so cold. *(sinks down dully)* So dead—

BERKLEY: Hey, then! What are you doing? Truly there's a pounding deep in my heart.

WILD: In you, milord? And what of me? Ha! Awaken in me—you are so stiff! So wooden. Hey, hey, hey! Miss, hey! Awaken with me! Hey, hey, hey! It's really cold!

CAPTAIN: What chills you then, Scot?

WILD *(draws his sword):* Draw your sword! Hey! Draw your sword! Or I'll strangle you in my fever and tear out your heart with my teeth! And you, old man, eh? Cold! Am I cold? Does my hand tremble? Hey! It reaches for a gun, and will not rest until you lie there and I suck the life from your blood. Am I cold?

CAPTAIN *(draws his sword):* Hey, Scot! If you can't wait any long—

BERKLEY: What? Why are you fighting? What? *(also draws his sword)*

CAROLINE: Father! Brother! Wild! *(sinks into* Wild's *arms)*

CAPTAIN: What has the girl to do with the Scot? Get away! Don't be surprised, Father. We have fought before. I have sworn eternal hate towards him.

BERKLEY: Eternally, eternally. He so resembles Bushy.

CAPTAIN: Will you wait for morning, to shoot face-to-face?

WILD: Yes, yes, of course. See only this heart! Only this brain! *(strikes him on the head)*

CAPTAIN: Are you mad?

CAROLINE: Father! Must I die here then?

BERKLEY: I want—

Scene 5

Lady Catherine. Louisa. Preceding.

CATHERINE: Good evening, Brother! What do all these swords mean? Ay, God! You could frighten a person—and it gives me great pleasure to introduce to you Sir Wild Carl Bushy, your daughter's fiancé.

BERKLEY: Carl Bushy?

LOUISA: Yes, yes, Uncle dear! Quite definitely. His friend La Feu told us everything.

CAPTAIN: Wasn't my feeling justified? Wasn't the impression he made on me right? You have lived too long!

WILD: I am he. Cease to be men! See in me your murderer! And this one is mine, old man! *(takes* Caroline *in his arms)*

BERKLEY: She hates you, now that she knows who you are. Will the miss soon disappear from before my eyes? Harry! I could never stand him. What shall we do to him? *(embraces* Caroline*)* No, I shall do nothing to him, Harry.

CATHERINE: Harry! Harry! What's going on?

BERKLEY: This is my son—enough joy! Now get out of here!

LOUISA: Lovely that he's here.

CATHERINE: Just remember! Mountains and valleys may not come together, but people can. Good evening, Harry.

BERKLEY: Just go!

CAROLINE *(pleading):* Father! Brother!

BERKLEY: Get her out of here!

(Exeunt Catherine, Louisa, *and* Caroline*)*

WILD: Good night, Miss. We'll see one another again.

CAPTAIN: Oh? Certainly not here.

WILD: So you set him adrift at sea, the righteous Bushy?

CAPTAIN: At sea, the righteous Bushy.

WILD: In the middle of a storm?

CAPTAIN: In the middle of a storm, Carl Bushy!

WILD: You didn't do that, Captain!

CAPTAIN: By Satan, I did!

WILD: A weak old man?

CAPTAIN *and* BERKLEY: It was Bushy!

WILD *(jeering):* Oh, let me fall at your feet, Alexander the Great! With only a ship full of men you were able to overpower two feeble old men. Those are trophies! And they didn't raise a hand against you? Didn't open their mouths? From this I recognize Bushy. Should I now begin to sing your victory song? I shall, by Bushy's blood! I shall, gallant hero! A ship filled with men, and two feeble old men! Ha, ha, ha! You knave! You knave! What a great deed!

CAPTAIN: Knave?

WILD: Of course! Worse! Coward! Old Berkley! You should be very proud of having raised such a son! Be proud of your deeds! By God, they are great! And great deeds deserve great rewards. Hee, hee! Just wait, Captain! I'll sing ballads about it in the streets of London, as soon as the tale of murder reaches its end. Hey, hey!

CAPTAIN: Wild! By all the devils, I'll run you through!

WILD: Hee, hee! But wait till I've put my sword away.

MOOR *(to* WILD*)*: Man! If you didn't look so fierce, I'd want to show you something that I stole from one of the old men. A little picture of a white woman. I tore my disheveled hair out over the old man, it hurt me so. The old man was good. Here it is!

CAPTAIN: Boy! *(approaches him)*

MOOR: Oh, woe!

WILD: He *was* good, boy! *(kisses him)* He was good!

MOOR: He was so kind to me! I was ill, and for a whole week he held me against his bosom and stroked my hot head and comforted me until the captain found him.

WILD: All that! Oh, lad! *(looking at the picture)* Mother! My mother! Mother most sweet! If there be nothing more of love in me, ignite the last sparks of passion and let them flare up in wrath and thirst for revenge! Mother! Till another time! I thank you, boy!

MOOR *(secretly)*: I have still more to say to you.

CAPTAIN: Boy! What are you doing?

MOOR *(at his feet)*: Here! *(laying his hands on his breast)* I must!

WILD: In the middle of a storm! Why are you sitting there? Are you brooding about the cowardly killing? Captain! I will be honorable with you. It was good that you told me how vilely you behaved; otherwise I would have knocked you down just now with incredible coldness. I will not attack you unarmed. And so tomorrow. But I cannot sleep until you lie there stretched out! Then shall I fling you into the sea with shouts of joy, by Carl Bushy! I shall!

CAPTAIN: I'll be there tomorrow morning!

BERKLEY: First you should come with me to the battle.

WILD: Yes, old man, yes! The battle. *(to the* Moor*)* Good night, boy. If you think of attacking me tonight with some hundred men, feel free—I'll be on guard.

BERKLEY: Won't you stay for dinner?

WILD: Only a cannibal's dinner, milord! I'm hungry for the captain's flesh. *(exit)*

CAPTAIN: Wait till I've gone rotten.

BERKLEY: Come, my son, let's have dinner.

CAPTAIN: I shall not rest until the man is gone from this world. The sight of him oppresses me. I was his enemy from the outset, even before I knew him.

BERKLEY: He is a Bushy! That is enough. But for now let Bushy be Bushy. Come to my heart, you, my life!

Scene 6

The garden.
Blasius. La Feu. *Both sitting on a grass bank.*

BLASIUS: Are you going to stay here all night, La Feu?

LA FEU: Let me be. Night does me so much good, my heart feels so reborn—

BLASIUS: Oh, under the heavens here, to breathe my last this hour! I feel well now that I have firm hold of that thought again, and it has turned to feeling and deep emotion. Blessed be thou, earth, thou that open'st thyself to us so maternally, taking us into thy arms and protecting us! Ah! If the moon wanes, the stars still shimmer above me. I lie lulled to sleep . . . a deep, sweet sleep. I shall still have this feeling. Thou shalt be with me there, I shall be with thee. So let the storm rage, the winds howl about me. Thou givest peace to thy son. Most gracious mother, my pilgrimage is at an end. I have walked through thorns; I have also known joy. Here I am again!

LA FEU: Oh, Blasius, heavenly Blasius! Here, on your bosom, on your heart, I imbibe with you . . .

BLASIUS: Love! Unfortunate ones, all those I have abandoned, don't cry for me! Forget me! I could give you no peace, no help. I had none. Forgive me! How many thousands of times was my heart torn to pieces, how many thousands of times did my soul tremble when I was so beaten by mankind, so beaten by the wrath of fate? I could not leave here, I could not leave there. I had courage enough to climb mountains, but they soon snapped my power in two. Oh, who here has too much heart, too much feeling! Oh, woe! Lovely air, give me love. La Feu! I feel at this moment no uneasiness. I feel this hour as those who are about to abandon the earth must feel, those whom I always believed to be the most marvelous. My heart trembles so . . . this passing feverish heat . . . ah, the sickness of the soul! Good night, brother! Good night, brother Wild! And all good souls who sigh here and there! Thank you for this moment! Good night!

LA FEU: Blasius! Blasius!

Scene 7

Wild *enters, with drawn sword.*

BLASIUS: Wild! Brother!

LA FEU: What's with you? Oh, dreadful man, don't disturb my soul!

BLASIUS: I beg you, brother! Leave my heart in peace! You're killing me! What's happened to you?

WILD: What's happened to me? Is everything so different with me? Ha! Everything has withered and died! Father! My father!

BLASIUS: Wild, dear Wild!

WILD: Go away! What do you want from me!

LA FEU: What is the matter with you?

WILD: You'll get no answer from me! I am nothing to you or the world until I have revenge! Most terrible revenge! Leave now! And you! Have you power over your tongue? Leave now, if you don't wish to succumb to me!

LA FEU: Brother, I am innocent!

WILD: So go then!

BLASIUS: Now I collapse into myself again, brother!

WILD: Leave me to the barren insensibility in which you see me! (Blasius *and* La Feu *exit.* Wild *remains outside* Caroline's *window*)

Act 5

Berkley's *room.*
Caroline. Betty.

CAROLINE: Betty, dear Betty! Is it not yet over then?

BETTY: No, Miss! All my limbs are trembling. I still hear shooting. But not so much now. They say we've won. Oh, God, so many wounded are coming! So many fine people, Miss! There's one with only half a head. It could break your heart.

CAROLINE: I have courage, Betty! Do you not sense that I have courage?

BETTY: Miss! You tremble as much as I. The dear old lord! And the captain! And the foreign lord!

CAROLINE: Betty!

BETTY: If one of them were killed I'd tear my hair out.

CAROLINE: Betty!

BETTY: Oh, but you're going to faint!

CAROLINE: Just leave me alone! Every shot that I heard struck one of them, struck me. Leave me alone, dear Betty!

BETTY: I'll go see if it's over yet. *(exit)*

CAROLINE *(alone):* Oh, this night, this night! And this morning! How have my delicate nerves survived this? I don't understand it. Where did this strength come from? I was about to flee with him! To let him take revenge, and then flee with him! How did this thought come into my soul? How did it fill me so completely? Ah, how he stood before me in torturous, furious pain. His suffering clouded his senses and made him wild. To let him go from me in this torment! And now perhaps his strength is shattered, his heart turned cold—Carl!

Scene 2

Moor. Caroline.

MOOR *(enters, crying):* I can't find any of them. Ah, my lord, to leave me alone! And I can't find the other good lord, whom I have so much to tell. Wretched boy that I am!

CAROLINE: Good boy! Good morning.

MOOR: Yes, Miss. When I woke up it was truly delightful. I had spent the whole night visiting with my father, Zukai, and my mother. You don't know him. Oh, you should know him, and how the neighbors love him and his enemies fear him. They didn't want me to leave and gave me all sorts of things to eat. Now I am sad.

CAROLINE: Poor boy!

MOOR: Good Miss! Where was I? What is all the banging for? So don't you know where the lord is with whom my lord and his father are so angry? He was as sad as you, and I wanted to make him happy.

CAROLINE: You? Him?

MOOR: Yes, me. What his name is, I don't know. But it's because of his father. I can't tell you, Miss, even though you are good and would not betray me. I've seen them. Hurrah! The old man embraced me! See, Miss, he kissed me and my cheeks were wet, and my chest was so tight I could not get enough air. He is really all right, the old man.

CAROLINE: *Who* is, boy?

MOOR: Be quiet, Miss! Quiet! You could have almost heard it from me; I was prattling it all out. Your father doesn't like him, and there would be no end of the beating and brawling for me. Listen! Someone's coming. That's good. I want to find my lord.

CAROLINE: Come with me!

MOOR: I want to help you cry, Miss. Ah, I often have to cry! You teach us blacks how to cry very early, but then you laugh. *(exit)*

CAROLINE: You shall not cry, boy, with me.

Scene 3

La Feu, Lady Catherine *enter, both bedecked extravagantly with flowers.*

LA FEU: Oh, golden age! Oh, majesty! Ah, the eternal, the eternal spring morning in my sick heart! See now, my love! I should like to metamorphose my entire future life into a poetic, Arcadian dream, far away from everybody. We would sit by a cool fountain, under the shade of the trees, hand in hand, singing the wonders of the heart and of love. That, milady, would be the only way to forget all the tragic situations of my past. We would not complain about men, nor speak of them bitterly, as Blasius does; no, eternal joy should prevail in us, with us, and in everything around us. What men have done to me I forgive as sincerely as I love you. Heaven has given me sensations with which I could never continue to live among human beings. Of course they have ground me down, but, milady, still a corner of this heart remains uncorrupted. It has now come to the fore, and may Heaven forgive him who would disturb me and call me perverse.

CATHERINE: I still don't understand.

LA FEU: Ah, then I shall place my whole feeling in your soul! My Diana! We should dream forever a sweet, gentle dream, ever as sweet as the first kiss of love. But fantastically! A kingdom of flowers!

CATHERINE: You bewitch me!

LA FEU: I am ready to become a shepherd. That has been my idea for a long time. I lacked only a shepherdess, and that I have found in you, lovely soul!

CATHERINE: Oh, milord! And sheep, a shepherd's hut, a shepherd's crook, and shepherd's clothes—white with red trim! I brought just such a costume from London. I could die from joy at your sweet thoughts.

LA FEU: I'll dress as an innocent shepherd. We'll buy a flock. Wild will give us one of his dogs. We shall fantasize our lives away. To live eternally in peace, eternally in love! Oh, the blessedness!

CATHERINE: Milord! Milord! And sheep too?

LA FEU: Yes, milady. And a little hut as well. I am your shepherd!

CATHERINE: And also—ha, milord—to marry?

LA FEU: God forbid! Everything spiritual, everything fantastic. That is the charm of it. Only one thing more. What sort of names shall we take to befit our innocent condition?

CATHERINE: Oh, endearing ones, milord!

LA FEU: Oh, of course, very endearing. I'll be Damon, and you Phyllis.

CATHERINE: Yes, milord! I have always loved those names in poetry. I'll be Phyllis. Let's go make the preparations at once.

Scene 4

Blasius. Louisa. Preceding.

LOUISA: Oh, Aunt! I have a headache. I'm not well. Blasius is as silent as a fish, and when he speaks he tortures his listener. He keeps speaking of marriage.

CATHERINE: Fie!

BLASIUS: I only said that we're ideally suited to it. Because when we're together I am bored and miss is bored. To have this and to endure this is part of marriage. Our virtuosity consists then in that—

LOUISA: Why do you go on? I must tell you that I am thoroughly tired of you. You have driven me to distraction with your annoying behavior so that I have started to become irritable myself. Before, I was a creature of genuine cheer and merriment, one day after another, but now you have spoiled everything, so just go!

BLASIUS: Miss! Truly, your face is often a bright ray of sunshine to me! Let me look at it now and again. Just don't talk!

LOUISA: So! If I tried it you'd take a nap in the sunshine!

BLASIUS: Try to understand.

LOUISA: Shame on you!

BLASIUS: Hm! Hm! I'm getting tense again, may God have mercy on me.

LOUISA: Aunt! We want to play. No, dance! Do you dance, milord?

BLASIUS: Oh, agony!

LOUISA: It's so stupid—those men there.

CATHERINE: I have so much to tell you, dear, so much. Just think, we are going to become shepherds. La Feu a shepherd and I a shepherdess.

LOUISA: Ha, ha, ha!

BLASIUS: Good for you. La Feu! Prosperity and good luck!

LA FEU: Yes, brother! I want to dream until my dying day.

BLASIUS: Be well. And I shall become a hermit. I have tracked down a beautiful overgrown cave. I want to close myself and my remaining feeling off there and begin anew the life we abandoned on the Alps. Heaven and earth have become friends with me this night, as well as all of nature.

LOUISA: Hee, hee! Let us play, and you do what you want.

BLASIUS: What are these alarms, drums, and tumult? My senses have fled me.

CATHERINE: They're returning from the war, milord!

LOUISA: The poor people! How tired they must be of shooting!

Scene 5

Berkley. Captain, *limping*. Preceding.

BERKLEY: Laugh, youth, laugh! Ha, ha, it was hot. It was fierce!

CAPTAIN: The devil take me if I ever fight on land again. The water, Father! By all the elements, he who can swim, let him swim and stay away from land. Somebody get this bullet out of my leg! May thunder strike the land war dead! Somebody get this bullet out of my leg, the damned thing is throbbing. I've nearly bled to death and can hardly stand.

BERKLEY: Is that worth whimpering about? Where is my child? My Jenny?

LA FEU: But how did milord wind up with a bullet in the back of his leg? Were you running away?

CAPTAIN: Go to hell with your questions, Mr. Nosey!

CATHERINE: Not so harsh, Nephew! Come, milord. We want to put our affairs in order.

LA FEU: Yes, dear lady. *(Exeunt LaFeu, Blasius, and Louisa)*

CAPTAIN: I'm glad that they're gone. Oh, Neptune, I'm your sea dog! They shot devilishly at our wings, Father. Wild must have made a pact with Satan. The damned presence, solidity, and strength of the man—this stupid bullet! Father! Join me on my ship! We will be pirates for the colonies. That damned Wild!

BERKLEY: I can tell you, Harry, I have developed a great respect for Wild, and an even greater hate for Bushy.

Scene 6

Caroline. Preceding.

BERKLEY: See, Miss? Here we are.

CAPTAIN: Come here, I need you.

CAROLINE: Father! My father!

BERKLEY: Victory!

CAPTAIN: I'd rather have been killed. Bushy had the most honor in it. He worked wonders with his recruits. He made it thunder with bullets! I couldn't shoot with him today.

CAROLINE: Poor brother, a wound! And Bushy acted heroically?

CAPTAIN: Oh, shut up. My reputation is gone. I'd like to lose myself in madness.

CAROLINE: Has Wild come back, then?

CAPTAIN: What does it matter to you? Of course.

BERKLEY: Don't complain, Harry. You were heroic. Oh, Miss! Take my old head to your bosom. Oh, how marvelous to lie here! It was so foolish of me to go into the fire today. Oh, my children! I cannot bear the joy any longer. I sense that my life has run its course.

Scene 7

Moor. Preceding.

MOOR *(at the captain's feet)*: Oh, lord! Lord! Dear Lord! You're bleeding.

CAPTAIN: Take heart, boy! And get this bullet out of my leg. *(looks at it)* Why, it's not in back! By God, Berkley! An honorable wound! Kiss your son! Eh, Sister!

BERKLEY: God be praised! You've plagued me not a little. *(kisses him)*

MOOR: Oh, agony. What a hole!

CAPTAIN: Fool! Grab it! Hey! I was sure, Father, that I had stood fast.

BERKLEY: But let me get the army surgeon.

CAPTAIN: No! I shall not consider myself wounded!

Scene 8

Wild. Preceding.

WILD: Miss! Dear Miss! Eh, already here, milords! Suppress your emotion, Wild! Good afternoon. So I've come to fetch you, Captain! My wound is deep, and if I'm not to suffocate, I must have revenge.

CAROLINE: Carl! Carl!

WILD: Be still, Miss, and have pity on me. Revenge for Bushy, Captain!

CAPTAIN: I have a bullet here, and can't oblige just now.

WILD: Mount your horse! Hey, coward! If you'd had me on your ship, eh? I'll tear you apart like a wild animal if you don't come right now.

BERKLEY: Hey, Bushy, stop raving. We are here.

WILD: Good, milord.

CAPTAIN: Have a horse saddled for me. Bullet or no bullet, you shall not trumpet like this for long.

WILD: Marvelous! Miss! Farewell, Miss! Oh, Jenny! Farewell!

CAROLINE: You are going . . . going . . . Carl! I shall not leave you!

WILD: Darling! Dearest! Oh, dearest! (*Exeunt* Wild *and* Caroline)

BERKLEY: Hm! I am so confused! So weak! Hey, Harry! You shouldn't duel with him. With the son of an enemy? Ha! For what? Because you avenged your father? I swear by the shadow of my dear lady, you shall not. Though his father has already robbed me of everything, of well-being and good fortune. I would rather tear out my cried-out eyes! You mustn't! Ha! Come!

CAPTAIN: Get this bullet out of me, and I'll get the life out of him! (*exit*)

Scene 9

Garden
Wild. Caroline.

WILD: Oh, Miss! Miss! This was a good day. It did my heart good, but as I come here and as I stand before with these feelings— Jenny! Why did I have to return? Why was I spared? When I saw so many around me fall? I must have revenge, Miss! On your brother! I feel wrath here, I feel love here. Do you feel it, Jenny, do you see? I stand at the abyss of human beginning, at the end of human emotion. For it is torn here, Miss *(points to his chest)* and is born again there! *(points to the stars)* And here your image, which I do not want and want more and more passionately. Jenny, all my torture! All my love!

CAROLINE: Is there nothing, then, to save you? Is there nothing, then, to help? Come here to my arms, dear anguisher! Let me give you peace! Let me give you love! Only not this thirst for blood, this thirst for revenge! Forgive my brother! No, you cannot—Carl! So quiet and dead—and I so wholly wretched without salvation. I would summon up my last bit of strength—but it vanishes. And I! Ah, I had the one for whom I called and sighed! He was given to me! Carl! And so it ends?

WILD: Hide your tears! Hide your sorrow! Hide your love from me! No, give me love, that I may live and feel until the moment of destruction. I have become so deaf, so benumbed. Only the sympathy of your loving eyes dissolves the stiffness and lets me seize something in the frightening inner turmoil, something to hold onto. Oh, Jenny! How can he be your brother? The murderer! Oh, it is sin to bring this to your ears. I sense how it must strike your nerves. It will not come from my tongue, it is so deep in my heart, and swells my bosom—hey! You should have it, yearn, yearn! And so you have taken all my senses prisoner. Miss! Miss! What is the matter?

CAROLINE: Let it now grow darker before my eyes and heavier here. I go to my end, so gladly to my end. You destroy so mightily.

Scene 10

Moor. Preceding.

MOOR: Lord! Lord! Have I found you at last? Ah, I have things to tell you, dear lord. But send the miss away, dear lord!

WILD: Nonsense, boy! Out with it!

MOOR: Oh, lord, lord! I want to tell you about the old man who loves me and whom I love. A gray head, and he is still alive! *(gently)* Believe me! By all the gods! I would rather have been thrown with him into the sea. He is not dead!

WILD: Would you lie to me?

MOOR: They are both alive. Just be kind and I shall tell you. Ah! The ship's lieutenant, a good man, protected them. I begged so long at his feet that he agreed. We lied to the captain that they were in the boat. The boat was set adrift empty. Ha, ha, ha!

WILD: Splendid boy! Miss!

CAROLINE: What, new life! New strength! *(she embraces the* Moor)

MOOR: We hid the old men in a tiny, tiny corner and I stole enough biscuits and water for them. But betray none of this to the captain. You too, Miss! He would kick me out or whip me to death.

WILD: Divine boy! Where are they?

MOOR: Just be quiet and don't betray me.

WILD *(embraces him, raises him, staring at the heavens):* My father lives!

(Caroline *embraces him)*

MOOR: Take care, lord!

Scene 11

Lord Bushy. Preceding.

Lord Bushy *walks with tired, feeble steps. As he becomes aware of his son,* he summons up his strength, meets him, and without a word, sinks into Wild's arms. Wild *is immobile with joy.*

BUSHY *(after a long pause):* Oh, am I here?

WILD: Father! I am again at your heart!

CAROLINE: Milord, as am I!

BUSHY: I am here! Hold me, Carl! So little breath, so little strength to rejoice!

WILD: I have found you again! *(embraces* Caroline *and his* father) My heart! My heart! How well I have become! These silver locks! This look! I have it all again!

BUSHY: All again! All again, your friend and father! Let me just catch my breath a bit.

MOOR *(embraces the old man):* Do you still love me, Father?

BUSHY: Come, dear boy, lie down by me!

MOOR: The captain.

BUSHY: Let him come. I have weapons here. *(points to his heart)*

CAROLINE: Milord! Oh, milord! Don't hate me! If you knew me—

BUSHY: I hate no one, my dear. My eyes have become clouded . . . who are you, Miss?

WILD: You allowed me, Father, to seek out in all corners of the earth the one who had my soul. I have found her. Jenny Caroline! My Jenny! I have found her and only now do I know what I have found.

BUSHY: Berkley's Jenny! Whom I called Daughter before hate divided us, and whom I always loved—come to my arms! Thank you for all the hours that you sweetened with your love, and thank you for this love, Miss! And thank you, good black one, for making sure I lived to see this moment. Do you know, Carl, what you owe to this boy? He described you to me, your suffering, your anguish. Ah, how easily I recognized you! Did he tell you?

WILD: Everything, Father, everything!

BUSHY: Miss, now and forever my daughter! Love has guided my son well. Where is Berkley? Are you reconciled, Carl? Lead me to him!

CAROLINE: Milord! No!

BUSHY: Does he still hate me?

WILD: Oh, Father! I was just on the brink of—let us flee and speak no further. Since you are here, I forgive the captain and the old man. Jenny! Will you leave us alone?

BUSHY: Be calm. I want to show myself to Berkley. Whatever wrath rises in him at the sight of me, he will surely appease it. I have sought him, and since I have found him—I am here. Stay here, Carl!

WILD: I cannot be there and forgive him.

BUSHY: Why not? Peace and calm have returned to my soul; they shall also return to Berkley's. I have found nothing in all my errors but this, and I have found everything.

Scene 12

Captain. Berkley *rushes in*.

BERKLEY: Harry! Harry! Hey, Harry! You mustn't!

CAPTAIN (*to* Wild): Where have you been keeping yourself? What's this, Miss? (*he becomes aware of* Lord Bushy) Is this a dream? Hey, Milord Bushy, are you flesh and blood?

(Berkley *composes himself*)

BUSHY: It's me, Captain.

CAPTAIN: Hellfire and damnation! Is the sea that fond of you? Father, it's Bushy! Old Bushy!

BERKLEY: Yes, I see it. I feel it. Come with me, Harry. My heart is so heavy—

BUSHY: Lord Berkley!

BERKLEY: Not your voice! I fear your voice! What further blows will you deal me?

BUSHY: Blows of peace and love. *(tries to grasp* Berkley's *hand;* Berkley *draws back)* Repenting my past life, forgetting the wild passions! Milord! I have taken all sins upon me and I have ended my pilgrimage here, full of sorrow and suffering. Let me raise here the flag of peace!

BERKLEY: Get out of here! Come, Miss! May I not be led into temptation for this or that.

BUSHY: Berkley! Are you not yet at the point where one is happy to feel at peace?

CAPTAIN: Now, sir! My pistols and horse are ready, my wound forgotten.

WILD: I have forgiven you, Captain, because I found him again.

CAPTAIN: And I have not forgiven you,

BERKLEY: Come with me, Miss. Why do you stand there with the Bushys?

CAROLINE: Oh, Father!

WILD *(embraces her):* She is mine, milord! You gave her to me when I was a boy. She is mine!

BERKLEY: Shall I curse you, Miss? Come, Child!

CAROLINE: Father!

CAPTAIN: Berkley! I am going mad!

WILD *(embraces her):* We shall go far from here, monster! But the miss goes with us. Here are my pistols and here is death! Take them!

CAPTAIN: Let me kill him, milord!

BERKLEY: Dog! You madman! *(*Wild *holds* Caroline *tightly in his arms)* She'd be shot as well, and all the charm of the world would lie in the grave. Look at the girl, so beautiful, so good, and so ugly in Bushy's arms. Dear Miss! He wants to deceive you! Deceive with love! Won't you come, pretty Miss? Won't you? Come then, dear, virtuous child, to your old father! You alone can calm his nerves, that I know. Just come, and I'll let the Bushys go quietly.

WILD: Shall I end my life here, Miss?

CAROLINE: Forgive! Father, forgive and forget! *(reaches toward* Berkley *and held back by* Wild)

BERKLEY: Fie, Miss! Shame on you! I beg of you, girl, don't provoke me! Miss, I beg, I beseech you, by my gray hair, by my old head. Give up my enemies and come this instant to me! Come, Child! You nursed me and took care of me, now I'll nurse you and take care of you. Eh, Miss! Shall I go mad, Miss! Should I loathe and hate my child? Curse you and the world? I shall go mad, Miss!

CAROLINE: I am your child, lord! Your good, true child!

CAPTAIN: They are playing with us, Father!

BERKLEY: Only this grace, dear heaven! That I may forget this child! Get away from this oppressive confusion.

BUSHY: Berkley, we once called ourselves brothers. We lived in friendship and love. An evil spirit divided us. The old feeling has at long last returned to me. Could it not happen to you? Brother!

BERKLEY: Be silent! Bushy, be silent! I hated and hate, loved and love!

BUSHY: Your hate fell hard on me. I deserve it no longer. I stand at the edge of the grave. Thoughts of eternal peace have long filled my soul; they give me strength, even as my weakened body becomes feebler. Berkley, at such a time one does not lie, and I never did. Here, where truth is separated from falsehood, I tell you that I am innocent of the devastation of your house, and of your banishment. He who did it has long lain in the valley of death. Peace to his ashes! His name and his motives will never be revealed by this heart.

BERKLEY: You didn't do it? Old hypocrite!

BUSHY: That's harsh, Berkley. My face speaks for me, and my openness, which has cost me much. Our misfortune was a misunderstanding—we sought a goal, our interests clashed. My passions were too hasty, and yours even more fiery. Oh, milord, what we have done! What have we become? Let us make everything good. Let us live in love!

CAROLINE: Oh, Father! It is all so true, what milord says. *(embraces him)* Your Jenny! You are coming around!

WILD: Noble Berkley!

CAPTAIN: It's disgraceful to get along so well, like womenfolk, at the end.

CAROLINE: Harry! Don't deny your feelings! I see in you that you would gladly—

CAPTAIN: Oh, stop it. I'm going to my ship.

BUSHY: Berkley, I want to vindicate myself before you. Only know that my heart is pure!

BERKLEY: I can't love you . . . stay here.

BUSHY *(embraces him):* I understand you.

BERKLEY: Let me be! I am so confused . . . but stay here.

WILD: Well done, milord! And you, Captain?

CAPTAIN: I don't understand it all yet. Come, boy!

BERKLEY: Stay, Harry!

CAPTAIN: It displeases me. I must first become one with myself before I can be one with another. Moor! Moor!

MOOR: Here, dear lord!

CAPTAIN: Come along and amuse me. *(exit)*

MOOR: Yes, I'll cry for joy, if that amuses you. *(exit)*

BERKLEY: Come, Bushy, down the path. I shall make an attempt to tolerate you. I cannot make any promises about my emotions yet. I still hate you and . . . so much comes to mind . . . just come! *(exeunt)*

(Wild *and* Caroline *embrace in the full passion of their love*)

Translated by Betty Senk Waterhouse

THE ROBBERS
A Play

Friedrich Schiller

What drugs cure not, *iron* will cure;
what iron cures not, *fire* will cure.
                    —Hippocrates

CHARACTERS

COUNT MAXIMILIAN VON MOOR
KARL ⎫
FRANZ ⎭ *his sons*
AMALIA VON EDELREICH, *his niece*
SPIEGELBERG ⎤
SCHWEITZER ⎟
GRIMM ⎟
RATZMANN ⎬ libertines, then bandits
SCHUFTERLE ⎟
ROLLER ⎟
SCHWARZ ⎟
KOSINSKY ⎦
HERMANN, *bastard son of a nobleman*
DANIEL, *Count Moor's servant*
PASTOR MOSER
A PRIEST
ROBBERS, *and others*

The scene of the action is Germany; the duration about two years.

Act 1

Scene 1

A room in Old Moor's *castle in Franconia.*

(Franz von Moor, Old Moor.)

FRANZ: But are you sure you are well, Father? You look so pale.

OLD MOOR: Quite well, my boy; what did you have to tell me?

FRANZ: The post has arrived; a letter from our informant in Leipzig—

OLD MOOR *(eagerly):* News of my son Karl?

FRANZ: Hmm! Hmm! Yes, indeed. But I am afraid—I don't know—whether I should—your health—Father, are you really quite well?

OLD MOOR: As fit as a fiddle! Is it about my son, his letter?—why are you so anxious? That is twice you have asked me.

FRANZ: If you are not well—if you have the slightest suspicion that you are not well, then let me—I will tell you at some more appropriate moment. *(half-aside)* This is no news for a delicate constitution.

OLD MOOR: God in heaven, what can it be?

FRANZ: Let me first turn aside and shed a tear of pity for my lost brother—I ought to hold my peace forever, for he is your son; I ought to conceal his disgrace forever, for he is my brother. But to obey you is my first, sad duty; and so forgive me.

OLD MOOR: Oh, Karl, Karl! If only you knew how your wild ways torture your old father's heart; if only you knew, how a single piece of good news of you would add ten years to my life—would make me young again; while now, ah, every word brings me a step nearer the grave!

FRANZ: If that is so, old man, then good-bye—this very day we should all be tearing out our hair over your coffin.

OLD MOOR: Wait! It is only one single short step more—let him have his own way. *(Sitting down)* The sins of the father are visited upon the third and the fourth generations—let it be accomplished.

FRANZ *(taking the letter from his pocket):* You know our informant. Look! I would give the finger of my right hand to be able to say he was a liar, a black and venomous liar.—Brace yourself! Forgive me if I do not give you the letter to read for yourself—you should not yet hear it in its entirety.

OLD MOOR: Everything, everything—my son, you will spare me the need for crutches.*

FRANZ *(reading):* "Leipzig, May 1st.—If it were not that the most solemn promise binds me not to conceal the slightest piece of information I can come by regarding the fate of your brother, then, my dear friend, never should my innocent pen have exercised such tyranny over you. From a hundred of your letters I can tell how news of this kind must pierce a brother's heart like a dagger; it is as if I could see the worthless wretch—"

(Old Moor *covers his face*)

Father, look! it is only the mildest parts I am reading—"see the wretch already costing you a thousand bitter tears"—ah, they flowed, they poured streaming down my cheeks in pity—"it is as if I could see your good old father, deathly pale already"—Dear God! and so you are, already, before you have heard anything at all?

OLD MOOR: Go on! Go on!

FRANZ:—"deathly pale already, reeling in his chair, and cursing the day those childish lips first framed the name 'Father'." I could not find out everything, and of the little that I know it is only a little that I tell. Your brother, it seems, has run the whole gamut of infamy; I, at any rate, know nothing worse than the things he has done, though his imagination may well surpass the bounds of mine. Last night at midnight he made a grand resolution—since he had run up debts of forty thousand ducats"—a pretty sum, Father—"and as he had robbed a rich banker's daughter here in town of her honor, and fatally wounded her fiancé, a fine young fellow of good birth, in a duel—to flee with seven others whom he had depraved like himself and escape the arm of the law"— Father! In heaven's name, Father! What is the matter?

*That is, Old Moor will not need crutches if bad news causes his premature death.

OLD MOOR: It is enough! Stop, my son!

FRANZ: I will spare you—"he has been declared a wanted man, his victims are crying out for satisfaction, a price has been put on his head—the name of Moor"—no! my miserable lips shall never be my father's murderers! *(tearing up the letter)* Do not believe it, Father! Do not believe one syllable he writes!

OLD MOOR *(weeping bitterly)*: My name! my honorable name!

FRANZ *(throwing his arms round his neck)*: Shameful, thrice shameful Karl! Did I not suspect it, when he was still a boy, and was always following after girls, chasing up hill and down dale with street urchins and ruffians, shunning the sight of the church as a miscreant shuns the jail, and tossing the pennies he had wheedled from you to the first beggar he met, while we sat at home improving our minds with prayer and by reading pious sermons? Did I not suspect it, when he would rather read the adventures of Julius Caesar and Alexander the Great and other such benighted heathens than the story of the penitent Tobias?* A hundred times I prophesied to you—for my love for him always kept the limits set by a son's duty to his father—the boy will yet bring shame and misery upon us all! Oh, that he did not bear the name of Moor! that my heart did not beat so warmly for him! The sinful love for him that I cannot suppress will one day bear witness against me before the judgment seat of God.

OLD MOOR: Ah—my hopes, my golden dreams!

FRANZ: I know; that is what I was saying. The fiery spirit that burns in the lad, so you always said, that makes him yearn so keenly for every kind of beauty and grandeur; the frankness that mirrors his soul in his eyes, the tender feeling that melts him to tears of sympathy at any sight of suffering, the manly courage that sends him climbing hundred-year-old oak trees and leaping ditches and fences and foaming rivers; the youthful ambition, the implacable constancy; all these shining virtues that took root in his father's favorite son, one day will make him a friend's true friend, a model citizen, a hero, a great, great man—and now, Father, look! the fiery spirit has grown, has burgeoned, has brought forth glorious fruit. See how this frankness has so neatly turned to insolence, see how this tenderness coos for any coquette, so readily yields to the

*Tobias, or Tobit, of the Apocrypha, the pious Jew in exile who never loses faith in divine providence and eventually enjoys a happy family reunion and a peaceful death.

seduction of a Phryne!* See how this fiery genius has burnt up the oil of its life in six short years, to the last drop, so that to his very face people can say "Voilà, c'est l'amour qui a fait ça!†" No, just look at this bold imagination, just look at the plans it makes and carries out, so that the heroic deeds of a Cartouche or a Howard‡ pale into insignificance beside them! And only let these magnificent beginnings grow to full maturity—for after all, who can expect perfection at such a tender age? Perhaps, Father, you will live to see the glorious day when he is the commander of an army, ensconced in the stillness of the forests, ready to ease the weary wanderer's journey by taking half his burden from him—perhaps before you are laid to rest you will be able to visit his monument, that he will have erected for him between heaven and earth— perhaps, oh Father, Father, Father—find yourself another name, or shopkeepers and street urchins will point their fingers at you, for they will have seen your fine son's portrait at the market place in Leipzig.

OLD MOOR: And you too, my Franz, you too? Oh, my children! How they pierce my heart!

FRANZ: You see, I have my wits about me too; but my wit is the bite of a scorpion.—And then that everyday dullard, that cold, wooden Franz, and all the other names that the contrast between the two of us so often prompted when he sat on your lap or pinched your cheek—one day he will die within the walls of his own estate and rot and be forgotten, while the fame of this virtuoso flies from pole to pole. Ah! gracious Heaven, see him join his hands in thanks, this dry, cold, wooden Franz—that he is not like him!

OLD MOOR: Forgive me, my son; do not be angry with a father whose expectations have been dashed. The God who sends me tears through Karl will wipe them away, my Franz, by your hand.

FRANZ: Yes, Father, my hand shall wipe them away. Your Franz will make it his life's work to lengthen your days. Your life shall be the oracle that I will consult above all else in all my doings; the glass in which I shall see all things. No duty shall be too sacred for me to break it in the service of your precious life. Do you believe me?

*Phryne is a famous fourth-century B.C. Greek courtesan.
†There, love did that!
‡L. D. Cartouche (d. 1721) and the fictitious Captain Zachary Howard were notorious highwaymen.

OLD MOOR: You bear a heavy burden of duty, my son—God bless you for what you have been and for what you shall be to me!

FRANZ: But tell me, now—if you did not have to call this son your own, would you be a happy man?

OLD MOOR: Stop!—When the midwife brought him to me, I lifted him up to heaven and cried: am I not a happy man?

FRANZ: So you said. And now do you find it so? You envy the wretchedest of your peasants that he is not this son's father.— Sorrow will be yours as long as you have this son. That grief will grow with Karl. That sorrow will undermine your days.

OLD MOOR: Oh! it has made me like a man of fourscore years.

FRANZ: Why, then—if you were to disown this son of yours?

OLD MOOR *(starting up):* Franz! Franz! What are you saying?

FRANZ: Is it not your love for him that brings you all this grief? Without that love, he exists for you no longer. Without this criminal love, this sinful love, he is dead for you—he was never born to you. Not flesh and blood, the heart makes fathers and sons. Love him no more, and this degenerate is no longer your son, even if he was cut from the flesh of your own body. he was the apple of your eye, but it is written, if thine eye offend thee, pluck it out; it is better for thee to enter into the kingdom of God with one eye, than having two eyes to be cast into hellfire. Better to enter childless into the kingdom of God, than that Father and Son should be cast into hellfire. It is the word of God!

OLD MOOR: You would have me curse my son?

FRANZ: Not so, not so! It is not your son that I would have you curse. What is he that you call your son? he whom you gave his life, while he spares no effort to shorten yours?

OLD MOOR: Oh, it is true, it is all too true! it is a judgment upon me! The Lord wills it so!

FRANZ: See how the child of your bosom treats its father. Through your father's sympathy he strangles you, murders you through your love, has even stabbed your father's heart to strike the final blow. When once you are no more, he is master of your estates and king of his passions. The dam is broken, and the torrent of his desires can rage freely on. Imagine yourself in his place! How often he must wish them under the earth—his father, his brother, who stand pitiless in the way of his excesses? But is that love for love? Is that filial gratitude for a father's tenderness? When he sacrifices ten years of your life to a moment's lust? when he gambles the good name of his fathers, unspotted for seven centuries, on the pleasure of a fleeting minute? Is that he whom you call your son? Answer! Do you call that a son?

OLD MOOR: An unloving child! Oh! but still my child! still my child!

FRANZ: A precious, darling child, whose sole pursuit it is not to know it has a father. Oh, if only you would learn to see it as it is! If only the scales would fall from your eyes! But your indulgence can only confirm him in his depravity, your support give it legitimacy. Yes, indeed, you will turn aside the curse from his head; upon you, Father, upon you will the curse of damnation fall.

OLD MOOR: It is just! it is only just! Mine, mine is all the fault!

FRANZ: How many thousands who have drained the cup of pleasure to the dregs have been brought by suffering to see the error of their ways! And does not the bodily pain which accompanies every excess bear the fingerprint of the divine will? Should man by cruel mercifulness turn it aside? Shall a father let go to eternal damnation what is entrusted to him?—Think, Father, if you deliver him up to his misery for a little while, will he not have to mend his ways and learn to be a better man? or else he will remain a scoundrel, even in that great school of misery, and then—woe to the father who flouted the decrees of a higher wisdom by his tenderness!—What then, Father?

OLD MOOR: I will write and say that he no longer has my support.

FRANZ: What you do is just and wise.

OLD MOOR: That he shall not show his face before me.

FRANZ: It will work to his salvation.

OLD MOOR *(tenderly):* Until he mend his ways!

FRANZ: Very well, very well! But if then he should come with the mask of the hypocrite, should gain your pity by his tears and your forgiveness by his flattery, and then the next day should mock your weakness in the arms of his whores? No, Father! He will come of his own accord when his conscience is clear.

OLD MOOR: Then I will write this moment and tell him so.

FRANZ: Stop! just one more word, Father! Your indignation, I fear, might dictate too harsh words for your pen, words that would rend his heart—and then—do you not think he might even take it as a token of forgiveness, that you deign to write to him with your own hand? It will be better to let me write for you.

OLD MOOR: Do so, my son.—Ah! it would have broken my heart! Tell him—

FRANZ *(quickly):* Shall I, then?

OLD MOOR: Tell him that a thousand tears of blood—tell him that a thousand sleepless nights—but do not drive my son to despair.

FRANZ: Should you not go to bed, Father? It was hard for you to bear.

OLD MOOR: Tell him that his father's bosom—I tell you, do not drive my son to despair. *(exit, sadly)*

FRANZ *(watching him go, and laughing):* Console yourself, old man, you will never clasp him to that bosom; the path to your bosom is as firmly barricaded to him, as heaven is to hell.—He was torn from your arms before you knew that you could want so—I should be a poor hand at it if I could not manage to pry a son from his father's heart, even if he were bound to it with fetters of brass—I have drawn a magic circle of curses about you that he will not be able to cross.—Good luck, Franz! The favorite is gone; things are looking brighter. I must pick up all these pieces of paper—someone might easily recognize my hand—*(collecting the torn pieces of the letter)* And the old man's grief will soon put an end to him; and *she*—I must drive her precious Karl from her thoughts too, even if half her life should depend on him. I have every right to be resentful of nature; and by my honor, I will make my rights known! Why was I not the first to creep out of our mother's womb? Why not the only one? Why did nature burden me with this ugliness? why me? Just as if she had been bankrupt when I was born. Why should I have this Laplander's nose? Why should I have these blackamoor's lips, these Hottentot's eyes? I truly think she made a heap of the most hideous parts of every human kind as the ingredients for me. Death and damnation! Who gave her the power to make him like that, and to keep it from me? Could anyone pay court to her before he came along? Or offend her, before he existed? Why was she so partial about her own creation? No, no! I do her an injustice. After all, she gave us the gift of ingenuity too when she set us naked and miserable upon the shores of this great ocean of the world: swim whoever can, and let sink whoever is too clumsy! She gave me nothing; what I can make of myself is up to me. Each man has the same right to the greatest and the least; claim destroys claim, impulse destroys impulse, force destroys force. Might is right, and the limits of our strength our only law. It is true, there are certain conventions men have made to rule the pulses that turn the world. Honorable reputation! A valuable coin indeed, one to drive a fine bargain with for the man who knows how to use it. Conscience—yes, indeed! an excellent scarecrow to keep the sparrows from the cherry trees! and a well-written check to help the bankrupt, too, at the last moment. Yes indeed, most admirable devices to keep fools respectful and to hold down the mob, so that clever people can live in better comfort. It must be admitted, most ingenious devices! They remind me of the hedges my peasants plant so cunningly around their fields so that the rabbits cannot jump over—no, not on your life, not one single rabbit!—but their lord and master sets spur to his horse and gallops freely over the crops. Poor little rabbit! It's a sad part to play, to be a rabbit in this world! But your lord and master needs his rabbits! So, away we go! Fear nothing, and you are as powerful as if all fear you. It is the fashion nowadays to lace one's breeches so that one can wear them tight or loose as one pleases. We will have ourselves a conscience made in the latest style, so that we can let it out nicely as we grow. How can we help it? Go to the tailor! I have heard a great deal of idle talk about something called love of one's kin, enough to turn a sound man's head.—He is your brother! which, being interpreted, is: he was baked in the same oven that you were; so let him be sacred to you!—Just consider this extraordinary conclusion, this ridiculous argument from the proximity of bodies to the harmony of minds; from the identity of domicile to the identity of feeling; from the uniformity of diet to the uniformity of inclination. But there is more to it—he is your father! He gave you life, you are his flesh and blood; so let him be sacred to you! Another cunning conclusion! I should like to know *why* he made me? Not out of love for me, surely, since there was no *me* to love. Did he know me before he made me? Or did he think of me while he was making me? Or did he wish for me as he was making me? Did he know what I should be like? I hope not, or I should want to punish him for making me regardless! Can I feel any gratitude to him for my being a man? No more than I could grudge it him if he had made me a woman. Can I acknowledge any love that does not rest on respect for my person? Could respect for my person exist, when my person could only come into being through that for which it must be the condition? And what is so sacred about it all? The act itself through which I was created? As if that were anything but the animal gratification of animal desires? Or the result of that act, when that is nothing but brute necessity that one would gladly be rid of if one could, if it were not at the cost of flesh and blood. Am I to speak well of him for loving me? That is vanity, the professional sin of all artists, who fancy their own work, however ugly it may be.—There it is then, the witchcraft that they veil in clouds of holy incense to abuse our fearful nature. Am I, too, to let myself be led along by it, like a little boy? Very well, then! courage, and to work! I will crush everything that stands in the way of my becoming master. And master I must be, to force my way to goals that I shall never gain by kindness. *(exit)*

Scene 2

A tavern on the borders of Saxony.

(Karl von Moor *deep in a book,* Spiegelberg *drinking at the table*)

MOOR *(laying the book aside):* I hate this age of scribblers, when I can pick up my Plutarch and read of great men.

SPIEGELBERG *(puts a glass before him. Drinking):* Josephus* is the man you should read.

MOOR: The bright spark of Promethean fire is burnt out. All we have now is a flash of witch meal†—stage lightning, not flame enough to light a pipe of tobacco. Here we scratch about like rats at Hercules' club, and addle our miserable brains with speculation over what he had between his legs. A French cleric proclaims that Alexander was a coward, a consumptive professor with a bottle of smelling-salts under his nose gives lectures on energy. Fellows who faint when they have had a girl write commentaries on the tactics of Hannibal—boys still wet behind the ears crib their proses from Livy on the battle of Cannae, and snivel over Scipio's victories because they have to describe them.

SPIEGELBERG: Said in true Alexandrine style.

MOOR: A fine reward for your valor on the battlefield, to live on in the grammar school and be dragged around immortal in a schoolboy's satchel. A worthy repayment for the blood you shed, to be wrapped round buns by a Nuremberg confectioner, or if

---

*Flavius Josephus, Jewish historian and general of the first century A.D.
†Witch meal is lycopodium powder, made from the spores of club mosses and used on the stage to produce flashes of fire.

you're lucky to be hoisted onto stilts by a French tragedian and pulled about like puppets on a string! Haha!

SPIEGELBERG *(drinking):* I tell you, you should read Josephus.

MOOR: Pah! An age of eunuchs, fit for nothing but chewing over the deeds of bygone days, mutilating the heroes of old with their learned interpretations and mocking them with their tragedies. The strength of their loins is dried up, and the dregs of a beer barrel must help to propagate mankind.

SPIEGELBERG: Tea, brother, tea!

MOOR: There they go, smothering healthy nature with their ridiculous conventions. Haven't the courage to drain a glass, because they would have to wish "Good health!" Fawn on the man who polishes His Highness's boots, and make life a misery for the wretch they have no need to fear. Praise each other to the skies for the sake of a dinner, and would gladly poison each other when they lose a bedstead at an auction. Damn the Sadducee who doesn't show himself enough in church, and reckon up their filthy lucre at the altar; fall on their knees so that they can show off their coattails the better; don't take their eye off the preacher, so as not to miss the cut of his wig.—Fall in a faint if they see a goose bleeding and clap their hands when their rival goes bankrupt— No, however much I pleaded—"Just one more day!"—no! to jail with him, the dog!—Pleas! Oaths! Tears! *(Stamping his foot)* Hell and damnation!

SPIEGELBERG: And all for a few thousand miserable ducats—

MOOR: No, I'll not think of it. I am supposed to lace my body in a corset and straitjacket my will with laws. The law has cramped the flight of eagles to a snail's pace. The law never yet made a great man, but freedom will breed a giant, a colossus. They ensconce themselves in a tyrant's belly, humor every whim of his digestion, and draw in their breath when his guts rumble.—Oh, if only Arminius's* spirit still glowed in the ashes!—Give me an army of fellows like me to command, and I'll turn Germany into a republic that will make Rome and Sparta look like nunneries. *(tosses his sword onto the table and stands up)*

SPIEGELBERG *(jumping up):* Bravo! bravissimo! just what I wanted to talk to you about! Look, Moor, I'll tell you something I've been

*Arminius, or Hermann, chief of the Cheruscans, is credited with deterring the Roman legions under Varus and thereby preventing the Roman Empire from expanding east of the Rhine.

thinking about for a long time, you're just the man for it—drink up, have another—suppose we all turned Jews, and started talking about the Kingdom again?

MOOR *(laughing out loud):* Ha! I see, I see! You want to put foreskins out of fashion, because the barber has had yours already?

SPIEGELBERG: You clown! It is true, I do happen, strangely enough, to be circumcised in advance. But look, isn't it a brave and cunning plan? We'll send out a manifesto to all the corners of the world and summon everyone who won't eat pork to Palestine. I shall have authentic documents to prove that Herod the Tetrarch was my great-great-grandfather, and so on. Man, what a jubilation, when they find their feet again, and can build Jerusalem anew. Then clear the Turks out of Asia while the iron is still hot, cut down the cedars of Lebanon, build ships, and flog ribbons and old tat to all the nations. And then—

MOOR *(smiling, and taking him by the hand):* Now, friend! No more pranks of that kind.

SPIEGELBERG *(taken aback):* Bah, you're not going to play the prodigal son now, are you? A fellow like you, who has written enough on faces with his sword to fill three attorneys' books in a leap year? Do you want me to tell the tale of the dog's funeral? What? I shall have to remind you of your own doings; that will put a spark into you again, if nothing else can stir you up. Do you remember? Those fellows on the council had had your mastiff's leg shot off, and to pay them back, you proclaimed a fast in the whole town. People grumbled about it. But you lost no time, bought up all the meat in Leipzig, so that in eight hours there wasn't a bone left to gnaw in the whole place, and the price of fish began to rise. The town council and the worthies were plotting revenge. Seventeen hundred of us lads out on the streets, and you leading us, and butchers and tailors and grocers following, and publicans and barbers and all the tradesmen, and swore they would wreck the town if anyone touched a hair on our heads. So it went like the shooting at Hornberg* and they went off with their tails between their legs. You sent for a whole panel of doctors, and offered three ducats to the one who would write a prescription for the dog. We thought the gentlemen would think

---

*At the proverbial "shooting at Hornberg" there was in fact no shooting at all, because the opponents lacked the courage to fight.

it beneath their dignity and say no, and had already agreed we were going to force them to do it. But that wasn't necessary; they fought for the three ducats, even when it was knocked down to threepence, they wrote a dozen prescriptions in the hour, and that soon finished the brute off.

MOOR: Miserable creatures!

SPIEGELBERG: The funeral was arranged with all pomp and ceremony, there were odes in honor of the departed dog, and we went out at night, nearly a thousand of us, a lantern in one hand and sword in the other, and so on through the town with bells and music till we had buried the dog. Then we stuffed ourselves with food till it was broad daylight, and you thanked the gentlemen for their heartfelt sympathy and sold all the meat at half price. *Mort de ma vie!** They respected us then, like a garrison in a conquered fortress—

MOOR: And you are not ashamed to boast of such a thing? Haven't even shame enough to be ashamed of playing such tricks?

SPIEGELBERG: Go, go! I don't recognize Moor any longer. Don't you remember how you have railed a thousand times against the old skinflint, and said: let him pinch and scrape, so that you could swill to your heart's content! Don't you remember? eh? don't you remember? Oh, you Godforsaken coxcomb, that was spoken like a man, like a man of breeding, but now—

MOOR: Curse you for reminding me of it! Curse myself for saying it! But it was only in the heat of the wine, and my heart knew not the vain things my tongue spoke.

SPIEGELBERG *(shaking his head):* No, no, no! it cannot be! No, Brother, you can never be in earnest. My dear fellow, is it hardship that makes you so downcast? Come, let me tell you one of my exploits when I was a lad. There beside my house was a ditch, eight feet wide at least, and we lads used to have contests, trying to jump across it. But it was no good. Flop! there you lay, and they hissed and laughed at you, and threw snowballs at you, one after the other. Next door to our house a ranger kept his dog on a chain, a bad-tempered brute that used to bite, it would catch the girls by the skirt in no time if they didn't look out and went a shade too close. It was the best thing I knew to tease that dog whenever I could, and I would laugh till I was half-dead to see the

*Literally, "death of my life!"

creature glowering so and longing to take a jump at me, if it could only get free. What happened? Another time I was giving it my usual treatment, and threw a stone and hit it so hard in the ribs that it broke the chain, it was so furious, and was at me, and I was off and away like greased lightning. But hell's bells! there was the damned ditch in my way. What then? The dog at my heels, mad with rage, so never say die, a quick run up and—over I go. That jump saved my skin; the brute would have torn me to pieces.

MOOR: But why are you telling me this?

SPIEGELBERG: Why, to make you see—that necessity brings out the best in us! That's why I shan't be afraid if it comes to the worst. Danger fortifies our courage; our strength grows in adversity. Fate must intend to make a great man of me, since it crosses me so often.

MOOR *(irritated):* What should we need courage for, that we have not dared already?

SPIEGELBERG: What? So you will let your talents molder? Hide your light under a bushel? Do you really think your tomfooleries in Leipzig exhaust the range of human wit? Just wait till we have seen the wide world! Paris and London!—where you earn a box on the ears for calling anyone an honest man. It's a sight for sore eyes to see business done on the grand scale!—You'll stare! Your eyes will pop out! How to forge a signature—how to load dice—how to pick a lock—how to pour out the insides of a safe—just wait, and Spiegelberg will show you! The first gallows we come to, for the milksop who will rather go hungry than get his fingers dirty.

MOOR *(absently):* What? You have done all that, and more, I suppose?

SPIEGELBERG: I do believe you don't trust me. Just wait, let me really get warmed up; you shall have the surprise of your life, your brain will turn somersaults in your head, when my wits are delivered of their progeny. *(standing up, heatedly)* Why, I see it all now! Great thoughts are taking shape in my soul! Mighty plans are fermenting in my ingenious mind! Curse me for sleeping! *(striking his forehead)* for letting my energies lie fettered, my prospects barred and thwarted; I am awake, I feel what I am—what I must and shall be!

MOOR: You are a fool. The wine has gone to your head.

SPIEGELBERG *(in greater excitement):* Spiegelberg, they will say, are you a magician, Spiegelberg? What a pity you did not become a general, Spiegelberg, the king will say, you would have beaten the Austrians into a cocked hat. Yes, I can hear the doctors complaining, it is wicked that he didn't take up medicine, he would have discovered a new powder for the goiter. Ah! and that he didn't study economics, the Sullys* will sigh in their treasuries, he would have conjured louis d'or from stones. And Spiegelberg will be the name, in east and west, and into the mud with you, cowards and toads, as Spiegelberg spreads his wings and flies high into the temple of fame.

MOOR: Good fortune to you! Climb up on pillars of shame to the summits of glory. In the shady groves of my father's home, in my Amalia's arms, a nobler pleasure waits for me. A week ago and more I wrote to my father begging his forgiveness. I did not conceal the slightest detail from him, and where there is honesty, there too is compassion and a helping hand. Let us say good-bye, Moritz. We shall see no more of each other after today. The post has arrived. My father's forgiveness is already within the walls of this town.

(Enter Schweitzer, Grimm, Roller, Schufterle, Ratzmann.)

ROLLER: Do you know they are looking for us already?

GRIMM: That we are not safe from arrest at any moment?

MOOR: I am not surprised. Let it be as it will! Didn't you see Schwarz? Didn't he say anything about a letter he had for me?

ROLLER: He has been looking for you for a long time; I think it's something of the kind.

MOOR: Where is he, where, where? *(making as if to hurry away)*

ROLLER: Don't go! We told him to come here. You are shaking?

MOOR: I am not shaking. Why should I be shaking? Comrades! that letter—rejoice with me! I am the happiest man on earth, why should I tremble?

(Enter SCHWARZ)

MOOR *(rushing to meet him)*: Brother! Brother! the letter, the letter!

SCHWARZ *(giving him the letter, which he hurriedly opens)*: What is it? You are as white as a sheet!

MOOR: My brother's hand!

SCHWARZ: What is the matter with Spiegelberg?

---

*Maximilien de Béthune, duc de Sully (1560–1641), the advisor to Henry IV who restored French prosperity and left a surplus in the treasury.

GRIMM: The fellow is crazy. He looks as though he has caught Saint Vitus's dance.

SCHUFTERLE: He must be out of his mind. I think he is composing verses.

RATZMANN: Spiegelberg! Hey, Spiegelberg!—The brute won't listen.

GRIMM (*shaking him*): Man, are you dreaming, or—?

SPIEGELBERG (*who has all the while been miming a mountebank's act in the corner of the room, jumping up wildly*): *La bourse ou la vie!**

(*He seizes* Schweitzer *by the throat;* Schweitzer *calmly pushes him back against the wall.* Moor *drops the letter on the ground and runs out. All start back*)

ROLLER (*after him*): Moor! Where are you going, Moor? What are you doing?

GRIMM: What's the matter, what's the matter? He's as pale as a corpse!

SCHWEITZER: Fine news that must be! Let's see!

ROLLER (*picks up the letter, and reads*): "Unfortunate brother!" That's a jolly way to begin. "I am obliged to tell you in brief that your hopes are in vain; Father asks me to tell you that you are to go wherever your disgraceful deeds may take you. He also says that you are to entertain no hope of ever weeping your way to forgiveness at his feet, unless you are prepared to live on bread and water in the deepest of his dungeons, till your hairs are grown like eagles' feathers, and your nails like birds' claws. These are his very words. He commands me to write no more. Farewell forever! I pity you—Franz von Moor."

SCHWEITZER: A sweet, charming brother! Indeed, Franz is the creature's name?

SPIEGELBERG (*creeping up quietly*): Bread and water, do I hear? That's a fine life! But I have made other plans for you! Didn't I say I should have to think for you all one day?

SCHWEITZER: What's the sheep's head saying? That jackass wants to think for us all?

SPIEGELBERG: Cowards, cripples, lame dogs is what you are, all of you, if you have not the courage for a great venture!

ROLLER: Well, that's true, so we should be; but is it going to get us out of this damned fix, your great venture? Is it?

*Your money or your life!

SPIEGELBERG *(laughing contemptuously):* You poor fool! Get you out of this fix? Ha, ha! Out of this fix? Is that all your thimbleful of brain can think of? Is that enough to see your horses home? Spiegelberg would be a rogue if that was all he had in mind. Heroes, I tell you, lords, princes, gods it will make of you!

RATZMANN: That's enough at one blow, to be sure! But it will be a breakneck job, it will cost us our heads at least.

SPIEGELBERG: It will cost nothing but courage, for I will supply what wits are needed. Courage, I say, Schweitzer! Courage, Roller, Grimm, Ratzmann, Schufterle! Courage!

SCHWEITZER: Courage? Is that all? I've enough courage to go barefoot through hell.

SCHUFTERLE: Courage enough to scrap with the devil at the gallows' foot for a poor sinner's soul.

SPIEGELBERG: That's what I like to hear! If you have courage, let one amongst you say he still has anything to lose, and not everything to gain!

SCHWARZ: Indeed, there would be plenty to lose, if I were to lose what I still have to gain!

RATZMANN: Yes, in hell's name! and plenty to gain, if I were to gain what I can't lose!

SCHUFTERLE: If I were to lose everything I have on me that's borrowed, then by tomorrow I should have nothing left to lose.

SPIEGELBERG: Very well, then! *(he takes his place in the midst of them, and adopts an imperious tone)* If there is still one drop of heroic German blood running in your veins—then come! We will hide in the forest of Bohemia, raise a robber band, and—why are you staring at me? Has your little bit of courage melted away already?

ROLLER: I don't suppose you are the first rogue to overlook the gallows—and yet—what else is there we can do?

SPIEGELBERG: What else? Nothing else! There is no choice in the matter! Do you want to sit starving in the debtors' prison till the last trumpet blows? Do you want to scratch with spade and hope for a scrap of stale bread? Do you want to beg for alms, singing ballads at people's windows? Do you want to take the king's shilling—if they would trust the looks of you, that's the first question—and do your stint in Purgatory while you are still on earth, at the mercy of some splenetic tyrant of a corporal? Or be drummed out to run the gauntlet, or tramp the galleys and drag the whole arsenal of Vulcan's smithy behind you? That is what else there is, that is all the choice you have!

ROLLER: It's not such a bad idea of Spiegelberg's. I have been making plans too, but it is the same kind of thing. How would it be, I thought, if you all sat down and cooked up an anthology or an almanac or something like that, or wrote reviews for a shilling or two? It's all the rage nowadays.

SCHUFTERLE: I'll be hanged if your plans aren't very much like mine. I was thinking to myself, what if you were to turn evangelical, and hold weekly classes in spiritual improvement?

GRIMM: That's it! and if that was no good, turn atheist, blaspheme against the four Gospels, have our book burnt by the hangman, and we should do a roaring trade.

RATZMANN: Or we could set up to cure the pox—I know a doctor who built himself a house on a foundation of mercury, so the motto over the door says.

SCHWEITZER *(stands up and gives* Spiegelberg *his hand):* Moritz, you are a great man—or a blind pig has found an acorn.

SCHWARZ: Excellent plans! most reputable professions! How great minds think alike! All that's left now is to turn into women and become bawds, or even sell our own virginity on the streets.

SPIEGELBERG: Nonsense, nonsense! And what is to stop you being most of these things in one person? My plan will still do the best for you, and make you famous and immortal too! Look, you poor things! As far ahead as that you must think! Think of the fame that will live after you, the sweet feeling that you will never be forgotten—

ROLLER: And at the top of the list of honest people! You are a master orator, Spiegelberg, when it comes to turning an honest man into a villain.—But doesn't anyone know where Moor is?

SPIEGELBERG: Honest, do you say? What, do you think it will make you any less of an honest man than you are today? What do you call being honest? Relieving rich skinflints of a third of their worries, which only disturb their golden slumbers, anyway; bringing idle money into circulation, restoring the fair distribution of wealth, in a word bringing back the golden age; taking away some of the good Lord's burdens, so that he can be rid of them without war, pestilence, famine, and doctors—that's what I call being an honest man, that's what I call being a worthy instrument in the hand of Providence; and with every joint you roast to be able to flatter yourself with the thought that it's your own cunning, your own lion's courage, your own long vigils that have earned it; to be respected by great and small—

ROLLER: And in the end to be hoisted up to heaven in the flesh, and come wind come weather, in spite of old Father Time and his greedy appetite, to swing there with sun and moon and all the stars in the firmament, while the birds sing a heavenly concert at the feast and the long-tailed angels sit in sacred council? What? And while monarchs and potentates make a feast for moths and worms, to have the honor of being visited by Jove's royal bird? Moritz, Moritz, Moritz! Beware, beware the three-legged beast!*

SPIEGELBERG: And that frightens you, coward? Why, there's many a virtuoso rotting on the gibbet who might have reformed the world, and won't such a one be spoken of for hundreds and thousands of years, while many a king and many an elector might be left out of history altogether, if it weren't that the historians were afraid to leave a gap in the line of succession, and if it weren't that it made their books a few pages thicker and brought in more cash from the publisher. And if the passerby does see you floating back and forth in the wind, why, he'll think to himself, that must have been no ordinary fellow, and he'll sigh that the world has gone to the dogs.

SCHWEITZER *(slapping him on the back):* Superb, Spiegelberg! Superb! Why the devil do you stand there hesitating?

SCHWARZ: And even if it meant degradation—what more can there be? One can always have a pinch of powder with one, to speed one across the Acheron† if it should come to that, so that one will never hear the cock crow again. No, friend Moritz! it's a good proposal. That's my catechism too.

SCHUFTERLE: Hell! And mine as well. Spiegelberg, I'm your man!

RATZMANN: Like another Orpheus, you have sung my howling brute of a conscience to sleep. Take me as I am!

GRIMM: *Si omnes consentiunt ego non dissentio.* With no comma, mind.‡ They are holding an auction in my head: evangelist, quack doctor, reviewer, and rogue. I'm to be had for the best offer. Here, Moritz, my hand!

*A reference to the three posts of the eighteenth-century gallows.
†Along with the Styx, one of the rivers separating the living from the dead in Greek mythology.
‡ "If all give their assent, I do not withhold mine." A comma after *non* gives the sense "I do not, I withhold mine."

ROLLER: And you too, Schweitzer? *(offering* Spiegelberg *his right hand)* Then the devil can take my soul.

SPIEGELBERG: But your name shall be written in the stars! What does it matter where your soul goes? When troops of couriers gallop ahead to announce our descent, so that the devils put on their Sunday best, rub the soot of millennia out of their eyes, and horned heads in their thousands poke from the smoky chimneys of their sulphur ovens to see our arrival? Comrades! *(Jumping up)* Away! Comrades! Is there anything in the world so glorious, so thrilling? Come, comrades, and away!

ROLLER: Gently now, gently! where are you going? the beast must have its head, children!

SPIEGELBERG *(venomously):* What words of hesitation are there? Wasn't the head there before a single limb stirred? follow me, comrades!

ROLLER: Steady on, I say. Even liberty must have its master. Without a head, Rome and Sparta were destroyed.

SPIEGELBERG *(ingratiatingly):* Yes—wait, Roller is right. And the head must be a brilliant one. Do you understand? A shrewd political head it must be. Yes, if I think of what you were an hour ago, and what you are now—are by virtue of a single lucky idea— yes, of course, of course you must have a chief—and the man who thought up that idea, tell me, mustn't he have a brilliant, political head?

ROLLER: If we could only hope—if we could only dream—but I am afraid he will not do it.

SPIEGELBERG: Why not? Speak your mind, friend! Heavy though the task may be of steering the struggling ship against the gale, heavy though the weight of a crown may weigh—speak without fear, Roller! Perhaps he will do it after all.

ROLLER: And the whole thing falls to pieces if he will not. Without Moor we're a body without a soul.

SPIEGELBERG *(turning away from him in disgust):* Blockhead!

(Enter Moor in wild agitation. He paces violently up and down the room, talking to himself)

MOOR: Men, men! False breed of hypocrites and crocodiles! Their eyes water, but their hearts are of iron! Kisses on their lips, but swords in their bosom! Lions and leopards feed their young, ravens take their chicks to feast on corpses, and *he, he.*—Wickedness I have learned to endure. I can smile when my archenemy is drinking my heart's blood; but when blood kinship turns traitor, when a father's love becomes a raging fury; oh, then catch fire, manly resignation, be as a ravening tiger, gentle lamb, and let every fiber stiffen to hatred and destruction!

ROLLER: Listen, Moor! What do you think? A robber's life is better than bread and water in the deepest dungeon after all, isn't it?

MOOR: Why was this spirit not formed into a tiger, that fastens its savage jaws in human flesh? Is this a father's devotion? Is this love for love? Would that I were a bear, and could raise the bears of the north against this race of murderers—repentance, and no forgiveness! Oh, would that I might poison the ocean, that they might drink death from every spring! Trust, submission that none could turn away, and no pity!

ROLLER: Moor, listen to what I am saying!

MOOR: It is unbelievable, it is a dream, a delusion—such moving pleas, such keen representation of my misery and my melting repentance—a brute beast would have wept in compassion! Stones would have shed tears, and yet—it would be thought a wicked slur on all mankind, if I were to say so—and yet, and yet—oh, would that I could blow the trumpet of rebellion throughout the realm of nature, to stir up earth, sky, and sea to battle against this brood of hyenas!

GRIMM: Listen, will you! You are so mad you do not hear.

MOOR: Get away from me! Are you not a man? Are you not born of woman? Out of my sight, you creature with man's face!—I loved him so unspeakably! no son loved so, my life I would a thousand times—*(foaming, stamping on the ground)* ha! he who should put a sword into my hand, to deal a deadly blow to this generation of vipers! he who should say to me: if I can pierce the heart of its life, crush it, strangle it—that man shall be my friend, my angel, my god—I will worship him!

ROLLER: We want to be those friends of yours, let us tell you!

SCHWARZ: Come with us into the forests of Bohemia! We are going to raise a band of robbers, and you—

(Moor *stares at him*)

SCHWEITZER: You are to be our captain! you must be our captain!

SPIEGELBERG *(hurling himself into a chair in fury)*: Slaves and cowards!

MOOR: Who gave you that idea? Listen, fellow! *(seizing* Schwarz *fiercely)* It did not come from your man's soul! Who prompted you? Yes, by the thousand arms of death! we shall, we must! a thought fit for gods! Robbers and murderers! As sure as my soul breathes, I am your captain!

ALL *(shouting aloud):* Long live our captain!

SPIEGELBERG *(jumping up, aside):* Until I see him off!

MOOR: See, the scales have fallen from my eyes! What a fool I was, to seek to return to the cage! My spirit thirsts for deeds, my lungs for freedom—murderers, robbers! at that word I trampled the law beneath my feet—men showed me no humanity, when to humanity I appealed; so let me forget sympathy and human feeling! I have no father now, I have no love now, and blood and death shall teach me to forget that ever I held anything dear! Oh, my amusement shall be the terror of the earth—it is agreed, I shall be your captain! and good fortune to the champion among you who lights the fiercest fires, who does the foulest murders, for I say to you, he shall have a kingly reward! Gather round me every one, and swear loyalty and obedience till death! Swear by this man's right hand of mine!

ALL *(reaching him their hands):* We swear loyalty and obedience to you till death!

MOOR: Now, and by this man's right hand of mine! I swear to you to remain your captain in loyalty and constancy till death! If any show cowardice or hesitation or retreat, this arm shall strike him down on the spot; the same fate meet me from any and every one of you, if I offend against my oath! Are you agreed?

(Spiegelberg paces furiously up and down)

ALL *(throwing their hats in the air):* We are agreed!

MOOR: Very well then, let us go! Fear not death or danger, for an inflexible fate rules over us all. We must endure our going hence, be it on soft pillows of down, be it in the hurly-burly of battle, or be it on the gallows and the wheel! One or the other must be our lot! *(exeunt)*

SPIEGELBERG *(watching them go, after a pause):* There is one missing in your list. Poison you have forgotten. *(exit)*

Scene 3

Old Moor's *castle*. Amalia's *rooms*.

(Franz, Amalia)

FRANZ: You look away, Amalia? Am I less worthy than he whom my father has cursed?

AMALIA: Away!—Oh, merciful, loving father, who will cast his son to the wolves and the wild beasts! while he at home is refreshed with sweet, precious wine, and cossets his feeble limbs in pillows of eiderdown, while his great and glorious son may perish! Shame on you, inhuman creatures! shame on you, you monsters, you abomination of mankind! His only son!

FRANZ: I thought that he had two.

AMALIA: Yes, it is sons like you that he deserves. On his deathbed he will stretch out his withered hands in vain to seek his Karl, and start back in horror when he catches the icy hand of his Franz— oh, it is sweet, it is a sweet and noble thing, to earn your father's curse! Speak, Franz, good soul, good brother, what must one do if one would earn his curse?

FRANZ: My poor love, your fantasy is leading you astray.

AMALIA: Oh, I beg you—do you pity your brother? No, inhuman creature, you hate him! and you hate me too?

FRANZ: I love you as I love myself, Amalia.

AMALIA: If you love me, can you refuse me one request?

FRANZ: Not one, not one! if it is not more than my life.

AMALIA: Oh, if that is true! One request, that you will fulfill so easily, so gladly—*(proudly)* Hate me! I cannot but blush crimson with shame, if I think of Karl and realize that you do not hate me. You promise me? Now go, and leave me—let me be alone!

FRANZ: My sweet dreamer! how I adore your gentle loving heart. *(touching her breast)* Here, here Karl reigned like a god in his temple, Karl stood before you while you were awake, Karl ruled your dreams, all creation seemed to you to be dissolved in him, to reflect him, to echo him and him alone.

AMALIA *(moved):* Yes, it is true, I admit it. In spite of you, barbarians, I confess it to all the world—I love him!

FRANZ: Inhuman, cruel! To reward such love like this! To forget the one—

AMALIA *(starting up):* What, to forget me?

FRANZ: Did you not put a ring upon his finger? a diamond ring, as a pledge of your constancy? But after all, how can a young man withstand a courtesan's charms? Who can blame him when he had nothing left to give away? And did she not pay him with interest for it, with her embraces, with her caresses?

AMALIA *(indignantly):* A courtesan, my ring?

FRANZ: Pah! it is shameful. But if that was all! A ring, however precious, any Jew can replace, if it comes to that—perhaps he did not like the setting, perhaps he changed it for a better one.

AMALIA *(angrily):* But *my* ring, *my* ring, I say?

FRANZ: The very same, Amalia—ah, such a jewel, on my finger—and from Amalia!—death itself could not have torn it from me—is it not so, Amalia? it is not the size of the diamond, it is not the skill of the cutting—it is love that makes it precious—dearest child, you are weeping? Cursed be he who makes these heavenly eyes shed their precious drops—oh, and if only you knew everything, if only you could see him, as he is now!—

AMALIA: Monster! What do you mean, as he is now?

FRANZ: Be still, sweet creature, do not ask me! *(as if to himself, but aloud)* If only there were some veil that could hide it, that filthy vice, so that it could creep out of sight of the world! But no! it shows in all its vileness, in the yellow leaden ring round the eye; the deathly pallor of the sunken cheeks betrays it, and the hideous protruding bones—the stifled, strangled voice mutters of it—the tottering, decrepit frame proclaims it aloud in all its horror—it gnaws the very marrow of the bones, and saps the bold youth's strength—there, there! the suppurating juices start forth from forehead and cheeks and lips and cover the whole body with their loathsome sores, and fester in the dark hollows of bestial disgrace—pah! it revolts me. Nose, ears, eyes shudder at it—you saw him, Amalia, that wretch who coughed out his soul in our infirmary, the modest eye of shame seemed to turn aside from the sight of him—alas for him, you cried! Think of it, summon up that vision once more before your mind's eye, and it is Karl that you see!—His kisses are a pestilence, his lips would poison yours!

AMALIA *(striking him):* Shameless slanderer!

FRANZ: Does it fill you with horror, the thought of such a Karl? Does even my pale sketch disgust you? Go, gape at him himself, your handsome, angelic, divine Karl! Go, breathe in the perfume of his breath, let the sweet vapors that his throat streams forth envelop you; one breath from his lips, and you would feel the same black swoon of death upon you as if you smelled a rotting corpse or saw the carrion of a battlefield.

(Amalia *turns her face away*)

FRANZ: What surging tide of love! What bliss in his embrace!—But is it not unjust to damn a man for the sickness of his body? Even the most miserable cripple of an Aesop may hide a great and noble soul, as the mud hides the ruby. *(smiling maliciously)* Even scabbed lips may breathe of love—but yet, if vice has sapped the strength of his character as well, if virtue has fled with chastity, as the perfume fades from the withered rose—if with the body the spirit too is crippled—

AMALIA *(starting up, joyfully):* Ah, Karl! Now I see you truly again! you are still your own true self! It was all a lie! Do you not know, wicked creature, that these things can never touch my Karl?

(Franz *stands for a while deep in thought, then turns suddenly as if to go*)

Where are you hurrying to, would you fly from your own shame?

FRANZ *(hiding his face):* Let me go, let me go! let my tears flow—tyrant of a father! to cast the best of your sons into such misery—to expose him to shame on every side—let me go, Amalia! I will fall on my knees at his feet, I will implore him to let me, me bear the curse that he spoke—to disinherit me—me—to—my life, my blood—everything—

AMALIA *(throwing her arms round his neck):* Oh, my Karl's brother, dearest, most precious Franz!

FRANZ: Oh, Amalia! how I love you for your unshakable constancy to my brother—forgive me, for presuming to put your love to so harsh a test! How perfectly you vindicate my hopes! With these your tears, these your sighs, this your heavenly displeasure—for me, me too—our souls were always as one.

AMALIA: No, that they never were!

FRANZ: Oh, they were as one, in such sweet harmony, I always thought that we should have been twins! and if it were not for the unhappy difference in outward looks between us, which I admit is not to his advantage, then ten times the one might have been taken for the other. Yes, you are, I said to myself so often, you are Karl himself, his echo, his living image!

AMALIA *(shaking her head):* No, no! by the chaste light of heaven! not one drop of his blood, not one spark of his spirit!

FRANZ: So alike in all our tastes: the rose was his favorite flower—what flower did I ever rate above the rose? He loved music more than words can tell, and I! you stars are my witnesses, how often you have heard me at the keyboard in the silence of the night, when all around me lay buried in shadows and sleep—how can you doubt it still, Amalia, when our love coincided in the same point of perfection, and if love is one, how can its children deny their ancestry?

(Amalia *stares at him in amazement*)

FRANZ: It was a clear, still evening, the last night before he set off for Leipzig, when he took me with him to the arbor where you so often sat together, dreaming of love—we sat there long in silence—at last he took my hand and spoke softly and with tears in his eyes: I am leaving Amalia, I do not know—I feel that it may be forever—do not leave her, brother! be her friend—her Karl—if Karl should—not—return.—! *(He falls on his knees before her and kisses her hand passionately)* No, he will not return, never, never, and I have promised him with a sacred oath!

AMALIA *(drawing back sharply):* Traitor, I have found you out! In this same arbor he made me swear never to love another—if he should not—see, how blasphemously, how vilely you—out of my sight!

FRANZ: You mistake me, Amalia, you are quite mistaken in me!

AMALIA: Oh, I am not mistaken in you, I know you from this moment—and you would be his equal? And you say it was to you he wept for my sake? To you? He would sooner have written my name upon the pillory! Go, this instant!

FRANZ: You do me an injustice!

AMALIA: Go, I say! You have robbed me of a precious hour, let your life be so much the shorter.

FRANZ: You hate me.

AMALIA: I despise you, go!

FRANZ *(stamping his foot):* Wait! I will make you tremble before me! To sacrifice me to a beggar? *(exit, angrily)*

AMALIA: Go, base creature!—now I am with Karl again—a beggar did he say? Why then, the world is turned upside-down, beggars are kings and kings are beggars! I would not change the rags he wears for the purple of the anointed—the look with which he begs for alms must be a noble and a kingly look—a look to wither the pomp and splendor, the triumph of the great and rich! Into the dust with you, idle jewels! *(tearing the pearls from her throat)* Be condemned, you great and rich, to wear your gold and silver and your precious stones, to glut yourselves at feasts and banquets, to stretch your limbs on the soft couch of ease! Karl! Karl! You see that I am worthy of you. *(exit)*

Act 2

Scene 1

(Franz von Moor, *brooding in his room.*)

FRANZ: It takes too long for my liking—the doctor says he is on the mend—an old man's life is an eternity! And now my path would be clear and smooth before me, but for this miserable lump of tough flesh that bars the way to my treasures like the magic subterranean dog in the fairy tale.* But must my plans submit to the iron yoke of mechanical laws? Is my high-flying spirit to be bound to the snail's pace of material necessity?—Blow out a light that in any case is only stretching the last drop of oil—that is all there is to it; and yet I would rather not have done it myself, on account of what people will say. I would not have him killed, but put down. I should like to do it like a skilled doctor—only the other way around: not to put a spoke in nature's wheel, but to help her in her own design. And if we can prolong the conditions of life as we can, why should we not be able to abbreviate them? Doctors and philosophers have taught me how finely the motions of the mind are attuned to those of the machine that houses it. Convulsive attacks are accompanied by dissonant vibrations in the machine; passions disturb the vital force; the overburdened spirit weighs down its vehicle. What then? If one could discover how to smooth death this untrodden path into the citadel of life? to destroy the body through the soul?—ha! a masterpiece! The man who could do that—? A work of genius! Think, Moor! An art that deserved you for its discoverer! After all, poisoning has

---

*The dog that guards an underground treasure is a motif in numerous sagas, e.g., "Die Entstehung der Bergwerke auf dem Rammelsberg." Franz makes a similar allusion again in act 3, scene 1.

now been raised almost to the rank of a full-blown science, and experiments have forced nature to make known her limitations, so that the beats of the heart can now be reckoned out years in advance and one can say to the pulse: thus far, and no further!* Is not this a field where one might try one's wings? And how must I set about it, now, to disturb the sweet peace and harmony of body and soul? What species of sensation shall I have to choose? Which will be the deadliest enemies of the flower of life? Anger?—a ravening wolf that devours its prey too quickly. Care?—a worm that gnaws too slowly. Sorrow?—a snake that creeps too sluggishly. Fear?—when hope will always check its growth? What? Has man no other executioners? Is the arsenal of death so soon exhausted? *(brooding)* What? Well? No!—Ah! *(starting up)* Terror! What can terror not accomplish? What can reason or religion do to stay the monster's icy embrace?—And yet?—If he could withstand that assault? If he could?—Oh, then come to my aid, grief, and you, repentance, fury of hell, burrowing serpent that chew again what you have once devoured, and feed again upon your own filth; eternal destroyers and eternal breeders of your poison; and you, howling self-reproach, who make desolate your own house, and wound your own mother's heart—and come you too to my aid, you beneficent graces yourselves, soft smiling past, and future with your cornucopia overflowing with blossoms, show him in your glass the joys of heaven, and then let your fleeting foot escape his greedy arm.—Blow upon blow, storm upon storm I will bring down upon this fragile life, till at last there comes, to crown the troop of furies—despair! Triumph! triumph! the plan is made—tight and cunning as could be— safe—foolproof; for *(mockingly)* there will be no trace of a wound nor corrosive poison for the anatomist's knife to reveal. *(resolutely)* Very well, then!

(Enter Hermann*)*

Ha! *Deus ex machina!* Hermann!

HERMANN: At your service, young Master!

FRANZ *(giving him his hand):* I am not ungrateful for it.

HERMANN: I have proof of that.

---

*Schiller's note: "A woman in Paris is said to have achieved such success in systematic experiments with doses of poison that she could give the date of death in advance with some measure of reliability. Shame on our doctors, that this woman excels them in prognosis!"

FRANZ: You shall have more very soon—very soon, Hermann!—I have something to tell you, Hermann.

HERMANN: I am all ears.

FRANZ: I know you, you are a resolute fellow—a soldier's heart—a man of courage.—My father did you a great injustice, Hermann!

HERMANN: The devil take me if ever I forget it!

FRANZ: Spoken like a man! Revenge is sweet, and a man deserves it. I like you, Hermann. Take this purse, Hermann. It would be heavier, if only I were lord here.

HERMANN: That is my only wish, young Master. I thank you.

FRANZ: Truly, Hermann? do you truly wish that I was lord?—But my father is as strong as a lion, and I am the younger son.

HERMANN: I wish you were the elder son, and I wish your father were as strong as a consumptive girl.

FRANZ: Oh, how the elder son would reward you then! how he would raise you from this ignoble dust, that suits so ill your spirit and nobility, raise you up into the light!—Then you should be covered with gold, just as you are, and rattle through the streets with four horses, indeed you should!—But I am forgetting what I wanted to say to you. Have you forgotten the Lady Amalia, Hermann?

HERMANN: Damnation! why do you remind me of that?

FRANZ: My brother whisked her away from you.

HERMANN: He'll pay for it!

FRANZ: She turned you down. I believe he even threw you down the stairs.

HERMANN: I'll hurl him into hell for it.

FRANZ: He said people were whispering that you were caught between the roast beef and the horseradish, and your father could never look at you without beating his breast and sighing: God have mercy on me, miserable sinner!

HERMANN *(furiously)*: By the burning fiery furnace! be silent!

FRANZ: He told you to auction your patent of nobility, and have your breeches patched with it.

HERMANN: By all the devils! I'll tear out his eyes with my nails!

FRANZ: What? you are angry? what can make you angry with him? What can you do to him? How can a rat hurt a lion? Your anger will only make his triumph sweeter. You can do nothing but grit your teeth and vent your rage on a piece of stale bread.

HERMANN *(stamping on the floor)*: I'll grind him to dust.

FRANZ *(clapping him on the shoulder):* Pah, Hermann! You are a gentleman. You must not be content to bear these insults. You must not let the lady go, no, you must not do that for all the world, Hermann! Hell and damnation! I would stop at nothing if I were in your shoes.

HERMANN: I will not rest till I have him, and have him under the ground.

FRANZ: Not so wild, Hermann! Come closer—you shall have Amalia!

HERMANN: I must, come Satan himself! I must!

FRANZ: You shall have her, I tell you, and I shall help you to her. Come closer, I say!—perhaps you did not know that Karl is as good as disinherited?

HERMANN *(coming closer):* Incredible! It is the first I have heard of it.

FRANZ: Keep calm, and listen! I will tell you more about it another time—yes, I say, as good as banished, eleven months ago. But the old man is already regretting his hasty step—and after all *(laughing)*, I believe it was not his own doing. And my Lady Amalia besieges him every day with her reproaches and her lamentations. Sooner or later he will send to the four corners of the earth to look for him and then good night, Hermann! if he finds him. You can swallow your pride and hold the carriage door for him when he drives to the church with her for their wedding.

HERMANN: I'll throttle him before the altar!

FRANZ: Father will soon hand affairs over to him and retire to live in peace on his estates. Then the proud hothead will have the reins in his hands, then he will laugh at those who hated him and envied him—and I, Hermann, I who would have made you a great man, a man to be looked up to, will be bowing my knee at his door—

HERMANN *(heatedly):* No! as true as my name is Hermann you shall not! not if a spark of wit still glimmers in my brain! you shall not!

FRANZ: Will you be able to stop it? you too, my dear Hermann, will be feeling his whip, he will spit in your face if you meet him in the street, and woe betide you then if you shrug your shoulder or curl your lip—there, that is what will come of your suit to the lady, of your prospects, of your designs.

HERMANN: Tell me, what am I to do?

FRANZ: Listen, then, Hermann! so that you may see what a good friend I am to you, how nearly your fate touches my heart—go, put on different clothes, disguise yourself so that no one will know you, and have yourself announced to the old man—say that you have come straight from Bohemia, that you were with my brother at the battle of Prague, that you saw him breathe his last on the battlefield—

HERMANN: Will they believe me?

FRANZ: Aha, let me take care of that! Take this packet. Here you will find everything set out for you to do. And documents that would convince doubt itself—look to it now, be on your way, and don't be seen! through the back door into the courtyard, jump over the garden wall—leave the climax of this tragicomedy to me!

HERMANN: And that will be: long live our new lord and master, Franciscus von Moor!

FRANZ (*stroking his cheek*): Clever, are you not?—for do you see, in this way we shall achieve all our goals at once, and quickly. Amalia will give up all hope of him. The old man will blame himself for his son's death, and—he is sickly—a rickety building does not need an earthquake to bring it crashing down—he will not survive the news. Then I shall be his only son—Amalia will have lost all support, and will be the plaything of my will, you can imagine—in short, everything will be as we would have it—but you must not take back your word!

HERMANN: What are you saying? [*jubilant*] Sooner may the bullet turn in its flight and tear the marksman's own bowels—count on me! Leave everything to me.—Adieu!

FRANZ (*calling after him*): The harvest is yours, my dear Hermann!—When the ox has carted the corn to the barn, he has to make do with hay. A stablemaid for you, and no Amalia! (*exit*)

Scene 2

Old Moor's *bedroom.*

(*Old Moor, asleep in an armchair.* Amalia)

AMALIA (*creeping softly in*): Softly, softly, he is asleep! (*standing before him as he sleeps*) How handsome, how venerable!—venerable like the portrait of a saint—no, I cannot be angry with you! Dear white head, with you I cannot be angry! Rest asleep, wake joyfully—I alone will go my way in suffering.

OLD MOOR *(dreaming):* My son! my son! my son!

AMALIA *(taking his hand):* Hark, hark! his son is in his dreams.

OLD MOOR: Is it you? is it really you? ah, how wretchedly you look! Do not turn that sorrowful gaze upon me! I am wretched enough!

AMALIA *(waking him quicklv):* Look about you, sweet old man! You only dreamed. Have courage!

OLD MOOR *(half awake):* He was not there? Did I not hold his hands in mine? Cruel Franz! will you tear him even from my dreams?

AMALIA: Do you hear, Ámalia?

OLD MOOR *(more cheerfully):* Where is he? where? Where am I? You here, Amalia?

AMALIA: How is it with you? You were asleep, your rest has refreshed you.

OLD MOOR: I was dreaming of my son. Why could I not dream on? I might have heard his lips speak forgiveness.

AMALIA: Angels bear no grudge—he has forgiven you. *(taking his hand sorrowfully)* Father of my Karl! I forgive you.

OLD MOOR: No, my daughter! His father stands condemned by the deathly pallor of your face. Unhappy girl! I robbed you of the joys of your youth—oh, do not curse me!

AMALIA *(kissing his hand tenderly):* You?

OLD MOOR: Do you know this portrait, my daughter?

AMALIA: Karl's!

OLD MOOR: So he looked, when he was in his sixteenth year. Now he is different—oh, my breast is aflame,—this gentleness is wrath, this smile despair—is it not so, Amalia? It was his birthday when you painted him, in the jasmine arbor?—Oh, my daughter! Your love brought me such joy.

AMALIA *(not taking her eyes off the portrait):* No, no! it is not he. In heaven's name, that is not Karl. Here, here—*(pointing to her heart and her forehead)* The whole, so different. These dull colors cannot reflect the divine spirit that shone in his fiery eye. Away with it! this is a mere man. I was but a bungler.

OLD MOOR: This warm look of devotion—if he had stood before my bed, in the midst of death I had lived! Never, never should I have died!

AMALIA: Never, never should you have died! A leap it would have been, as one springs from one thought to another and a finer— this look would have lighted your path beyond the grave. This look would have borne you on beyond the stars!

OLD MOOR: It is sad, it is hard to endure! I am dying, and my son Karl is not here—I shall be carried to my grave, and he will not be at my grave to weep—how sweet it is to be lulled into the sleep of death by a son's prayer—it is like a lullaby.

AMALIA *(rapturously):* Yes, sweet, sweet as heaven it is, to be lulled into the sleep of death by a lover's song—perhaps we may dream on still in the grave—one long eternal never-ending dream of Karl until the bell tolls for the day of resurrection *(leaping to her feet in ecstasy)*—and from that moment on, in his arms forever. *(pause. She goes to the keyboard, and plays)*

> Hector, wilt thou bid farewell forever,
> Now Achilles with his murd'rous quiver
> Fearful vengeance for Patroclus swears?
> Who will teach thy tender son to fight,
> To cast his spear, and fear the Gods of right,
> When my corpse grim Xanthus downward bears?

OLD MOOR: A beautiful song, my daughter. You must play it for me before I die.

AMALIA: It is the farewell of Andromache and Hector—Karl and I have often sung it to the lute together. *(continuing)*

> Dearest wife, go, fetch the fateful lance,
> Let me go to tread war's horrid dance,
> On my back the weight of Ilium;
> The Gods shield Astyanax with their hand!
> Hector falls, to save his fatherland,
> We shall greet each other in Elysium.

(Enter Daniel)

DANIEL: There is a man waiting for you outside. He asks to be allowed to see you, he says he has an important piece of news for you.

OLD MOOR: Only one thing in the world is important to me, you know what that is, Amalia—is it a man fallen on ill luck, who has need of help from me? He shall not go sighing on his way.

AMALIA: If it is a beggar, make haste and send him up.

(Exit Daniel)

OLD MOOR: Amalia, Amalia! have pity on me!

AMALIA *(continuing to play):*
>   Never shall I hear thy weapons sing,
>   In thy hall thy arms lie moldering;
>   Priam's race of heroes is passed by!
>   Thou art gone where never daylight gleams,
>   Where Cocytus through the desert streams,
>   In dread Lethe's flood thy love will die.
>
>   All my thoughts, ambition's crown
>   Shall dread Lethe's flood in blackness drown,
>   But never yet my love!
>   Hark now! at the walls, the wild one raving—
>   Gird my sword about me, cease thy grieving!
>   Lethe shall not drown thy Hector's love!

(Enter Franz, Hermann *in disguise,* Daniel*)*

FRANZ: Here is the man. Terrible news, he says, awaits you. Can you bear to hear it?

OLD MOOR: It can be only one thing. Come here, friend, and do not spare me! Give him a cup of wine.

HERMANN *(disguising his voice):* My lord! do not punish a poor man, if against his own will he should pierce your heart. I am a stranger in this land, but you I know well, you are Karl von Moor's father.

OLD MOOR: How do you know?

HERMANN: I knew your son—

AMALIA *(starting up):* He is alive? alive? You know him? where is he, where, where? *(making as if to run out)*

OLD MOOR: You can tell me what has happened to my son?

HERMANN: He was a student in Leipzig. From there he went on his wanderings, I do not know how far. He wandered all over Germany, bareheaded, as he told me, and without shoes, and begged his bread at men's doors. Five months later, the hateful war broke out between Prussia and Austria, and as he had nothing left to hope for in this world, King Frederick's victorious drum summoned him to Bohemia. Let me die, he said, to the great Schwerin,* let me die the death of a hero, as I have no father more!

OLD MOOR *(burying his face in the pillow):* Oh, peace, oh peace!

*Kurt Christoph, Count von Schwerin (1684–1757), Prussian general and close advisor of Frederick the Great.

HERMANN: A week later came the great fight at Prague—I can tell you, your son stood his ground like a true warrior. He did miracles before the army's eyes. Five times they had to relieve the regiment beside him; he stood firm. Grenades fell to left and to right of him; your son stood firm. A bullet shattered his right hand; your son took the standard in his left, and stood firm—

AMALIA *(ecstatically)*: Hector, Hector! Stood firm, you hear it, stood firm—

HERMANN: I found him on the evening of the battle, lying there with the bullets whistling round, with his left hand trying to stem the flow of blood, his right he had buried in the ground. Brother! he cried out when he saw me. There was a rumor in the ranks that the general was killed an hour ago—killed! I cried, and you?— Why then, he cried, and took his left hand away, let every true soldier follow his general with me! Soon after he breathed out his mighty soul, to follow where the hero led.

FRANZ *(attacking Hermann savagely)*: May death seal your accursed lips! Have you come here to deal our father his deathblow?— Father! Amalia! Father!

HERMANN: It was my dying comrade's last wish. Take my sword, he groaned, take it, give it to my old father; it is stained with his son's blood. He is avenged; let him rejoice. Tell him it was his curse that drove me to battle, war, and death. Tell him I am fallen in despair! His last gasp was—Amalia!

AMALIA *(as if roused from a sleep of death)*: His last gasp, Amalia!

OLD MOOR *(crying out horribly, tearing his hair)*: My curse that drove him to death! fallen in despair!

FRANZ *(pacing about the room)*: Oh, Father, what have you done? My Karl, my brother!

HERMANN: Here is the sword, and here too is a portrait that he took from his bosom! It is this lady, to the life! Give this to my brother Franz, he said—I do not know what he meant by it.

FRANZ *(as if amazed)*: To me! Amalia's portrait? To me, Karl, Amalia? Me?

AMALIA *(attacking Hermann furiously)*: Vile deceiver, who has paid you, who has bribed you? *(seizing him)*

HERMANN: No one, my lady. See for yourself if it is not your portrait—you must have given it to him yourself.

FRANZ: Dear God, Amalia, it is yours! It is truly yours!

AMALIA *(returning the portrait):* Mine, mine! Oh, heaven and earth!

OLD MOOR *(crying out, clawing at his face):* Woe, woe! my curse that drove him to death! fallen in despair!

FRANZ: And he could think of me in the last terrible hour of his departing, of me! Soul of an angel—as death's black banner already swept over him—of me!

OLD MOOR *(babbling):* My curse that drove him, to death, fallen, my son, in despair!

HERMANN: This grief is more than I can bear. Farewell, old Lord! *(softly to Franz)* Why did you have to go so far, young Master? *(exit, quickly)*

AMALIA *(jumping up, running after him):* Stay, stay! What were his last words?

HERMANN *(calling over his shoulder):* His last gasp was Amalia. *(exit)*

AMALIA: His last gasp was Amalia!—No, you are not deceiving us! So it is true—true—he is dead—dead! *(swaying to and fro, and finally falling to the ground)* Dead—Karl is dead—

FRANZ: What do I see? What is this on the sword? words written in the blood—Amalia!

AMALIA: His words?

FRANZ: Do I see aright, or am I dreaming? Look there, letters of blood: Franz, do not desert my Amalia! Look, look! and on the other side: Amalia, all-powerful death releases you from your oath—Do you see, do you see? He wrote it as his fingers stiffened, wrote it in his heart's warm blood, wrote it upon the solemn brink of eternity! his fleeting spirit stayed a moment, that Franz and Amalia might be joined.

AMALIA: God in Heaven! it is his hand.—He never loved me! *(hurrying off)*

FRANZ *(stamping on the floor):* Desperation! all my art is foiled by such obstinacy!

OLD MOOR: Woe, woe! Do you leave me, my daughter!—Franz, Franz! give me back my son!

FRANZ: Who was it that cursed him? Who was it that drove his son to battle and death and despair?—Oh! he was an angel! a jewel in heaven's crown! Curses upon them that slew him! Curses, curses upon you yourself!—

OLD MOOR *(striking breast and forehead with his clenched fist):* He was an angel, a jewel in heaven's crown! Curses, curses, destruction and curses upon myself! I am the father that slew his mighty son! Me, me he loved unto death! To avenge me he hurled himself into battle and death! Monster, monster! *(venting his rage upon himself)*

FRANZ: He is gone, it is too late for remorse! *(laughing scornfully)* It is easier to murder than to bring to life. You will never raise him from his grave again.

OLD MOOR: Never, never, never raise him from his grave again! Gone, gone, lost forever!—And it was you who talked me into cursing him, you—you—Give me back my son!

FRANZ: Do not tempt my wrath! I will leave you to die!

OLD MOOR: Vampire! vampire! give me my son again! *(Springing up from his chair and attempting to seize* Franz *by the throat;* Franz *hurls him back)*

FRANZ: Feeble old bag of bones! You dare—die! despair!

OLD MOOR: A thousand curses ring about your ears! You stole my son from my very arms. *(twisting and turning in his chair in despair)* Woe, woe! To despair, but not to die! They flee, they leave me to die—my good angels flee from me, all that is holy flees the cold gray murderer—Woe! woe! is there no one to hold my head, is there no one to free my struggling soul from its prison? No sons! no daughters! no friends!—only men—is there none, alone—abandoned—woe! woe!—To despair, but not to die!

(Enter Amalia, *her eyes red with weeping)*

OLD MOOR: Amalia! Messenger of heaven! Have you come to free my soul?

AMALIA *(in a gentler tone):* You have lost a glorious son.

OLD MOOR: Murdered him, you mean to say. Laden with this accusation shall I step before God's judgment seat!

AMALIA: Not so, old man who grieve so greatly! Our Heavenly Father summoned him. We should have been too happy in this world.—There, there beyond the stars—we shall see him again.

OLD MOOR: See him again, see him again! Oh, it shall be as a sword to smite my soul—if I a saint find him among the ranks of the saints—in the midst of heaven I shall be encompassed with the terrors of hell! In the sight of the Eternal, bowed down as I recall: it was I that slew my son!

AMALIA: Oh, he will smile the recollection and the pain from your soul, be of good cheer, dear Father, even as I am! Has he not already sung the name Amalia to the angel's harp, for the heavenly hosts to hear, and the hosts of heaven whispered it after him? His last gasp was—Amalia; will he not cry out in his jubilation: Amalia! before all?

OLD MOOR: Heavenly comfort drops from your lips! He will smile, you say? forgive me? You must stay at my side, my Karl's true love, when I am dying.

AMALIA: To die is to fly to his arms! Oh, happy! I envy you. Why are these bones not brittle? Why are the hairs on this head not gray? Alas, for the strength of youth! Welcome, feeble old age! to bring me nearer to heaven and my Karl.

(Enter Franz*)*

OLD MOOR: Come to me! my son! Forgive me if I was too harsh with you before! I forgive you everything. I would so gladly breathe my last in peace.

FRANZ: Have you done with weeping for your son?—as far as I can see, you have only the one.

OLD MOOR: Jacob's sons were twelve, but for the one he wept tears of blood.

FRANZ: Humph!

OLD MOOR: Go and fetch the Bible, my daughter, and read me the story of Jacob and Joseph! It moved me always so to hear it, and then I was not yet a Jacob.

AMALIA: What part shall I read you? *(she takes the Bible and turns the pages)*

OLD MOOR: Read me the grief of him in his bereavement, when he could not find him among his children—and waited in vain for him, in the circle of the eleven—and his lamentation as he heard his Joseph was taken from him forever.

AMALIA *(reads):* "And they took Joseph's coat, and killed a kid of the goats, and dipped the coat in the blood; and they rent the coat of many colors, and they brought it to their father; and said, This have we found: know now whether it be thy son's coat or no?"

(Franz hurries suddenly away)

"And he knew it, and said, It is my son's coat; an evil beast hath devoured him; Joseph is without doubt rent in pieces."

OLD MOOR *(falls back upon the pillow):* Rent in pieces! An evil beast hath devoured him!

AMALIA *(reading on):* "And Jacob rent his clothes, and put sackcloth upon his loins, and mourned for his son many days. And all his sons and all his daughters rose up to comfort him; but he refused to be comforted; and he said, For I will go down into the grave unto my son mourning.—"

OLD MOOR: Stop, stop! I am not well!

AMALIA *(rushing to his side, dropping the book):* Heaven protect us! What is this?

OLD MOOR: It is death! Black—swimming—before—my eyes—I beg you—call the pastor—that I may—take the sacrament.—Where is—my son Franz?

AMALIA: He is fled! God have mercy upon us!

OLD MOOR: Fled—fled from the bedside of the dying?—And this all—all—two sons, full of hope—the Lord gave—the Lord hath—taken away—blessed be the name of—

AMALIA *(crying out suddenly):* Dead! All dead! *(exit, in despair)*

(Enter Franz, *skipping for joy)*

FRANZ: Dead! they cry, dead! Now I am your lord and master. A hue and cry in all the castle: dead!—But what, perhaps he is only asleep? to be sure! a sleep that surely is that will never hear a good morning again—sleep and death are but twins. Let us just confuse the names! Welcome, brave sleep! We will call you death. *(closing his father's eyes)* Who will come now, and dare to summon me before the courts? or say to my face: you are a villain! Away then with this burdensome mask of gentleness and virtue! Now you shall see Franz naked as he is, and cringe in terror! My father sugared his commands, made his territories one happy family, sat smiling at the gate, and called everyone brother and sister.—My brows shall beetle over you like stormclouds, my imperious name hover like a threatening comet over those mountaintops, my forehead shall be your barometer! He stroked and fondled the necks that would not bow, but rose in spite against him. I am not one for stroking and fondling. I will set my pointed spurs into your flesh, and see what a keen whip will do.—In my lands the day will come when potatoes and beer make a holiday feast, and woe betide any I meet with full and rosy cheeks! Ashenwhite of poverty and slavish fear is my favorite color: that is the livery I will have you wear! *(exit)*

Scene 3

The forest of Bohemia.

(Spiegelberg, Ratzmann, Robbers)

RATZMANN: Are you there? Is it really you? Ah, Moritz, Moritz, brother of my heart, I could hug you to pulp! Welcome to the forest of Bohemia! Why, you've grown big and strong. Hell's bells, buckets of blood! New men too, a whole gang you've brought! That's what I call recruiting!

SPIEGELBERG: Isn't it, brother, isn't it? And fine fellows too! —Do you not think the hand of God is upon me, poor hungry wretch that I was, with my staff I passed over this Jordan, and now there are seventy-eight of us; mostly bankrupt shopkeepers, bachelors who've failed their disputations, clerks from the Swabian provinces, what a body of men! charming fellows, who would steal each other's flybuttons, and won't sleep beside each other without their guns loaded—who keep their pistols primed, and have a reputation for a hundred miles around, you'd never believe it. You'll not find a newspaper without a little item about Spiegelberg the mastermind—it's the only reason I take them—descriptions of me from head to toe, you'd think you could see me with your own eyes—they've not left out the buttons on my jacket. But we have been leading them around by the nose. One day I went to a printer's, told him I had seen the notorious Spiegelberg, and dictated to a scribbler that was sitting there the spitting likeness of some miserable quack doctor in town; the thing gets around, the fellow is arrested, interrogated *par force,* and the fool is so frightened that damn me if he doesn't confess that he is your notorious Spiegelberg! Hell's teeth! I was near jumping up to go and complain to the magistrates about the scurvy creature abusing my name—anyhow, three months later there he swings. I had to take a strong pinch of snuff, I can tell you, when I strolled by the gibbet and saw pseudo-Spiegelberg up there in all his glory—and while Spiegelberg dangles, Spiegelberg slips quietly out of the noose, and cocks a snook at wise-owl Justice behind her back—it's enough to make you weep!

RATZMANN (*laughing*): You're still the same as ever.

SPIEGELBERG: I am indeed, as you see, body and soul. Fool!—I must tell you the trick I played at St. Cecilia's Convent. I reached the convent on my wanderings one evening as it was getting dark, and as I hadn't fired a single shot that day—you know I hate the thought of *diem perdidi** like poison, so it was high time to brighten up the night with some escapade, even if it meant singeing the devil's ears! We wait quietly until late at night. Everything is as quiet as a mouse. The lights go out. We reckon the nuns will be between the sheets. Now I take my comrade Grimm with me, tell the others to wait outside the gate until they hear my whistle—take care of the convent porter, get his keys off him, creep in where the girls are sleeping, whisk their clothes away, and pile them all up outside the gate. On we go, one cell after the other, take all the sisters' clothes in turn, last of all the abbess's—then I whistle, and my fellows outside kick up a commotion as if it was the Day of Judgment, and into the sisters' cells, roaring like wild beasts!—Ha, ha, ha! you should have seen the sport we had, the poor creatures fumbling around in the dark for their petticoats, and weeping and wailing, when they found the devil had taken them! and us upon them like a whirlwind, and them rolling themselves up in their blankets, so surprised and scared they were, or creeping under the stove like cats, and some of them wetting themselves with fright, poor things, you could have learned to swim in there, and the hue and cry and lamentation, and last of all the old hag of an abbess, dressed like Eve before the Fall—brother, you know there is no creature in all this world I hate more than a spider and an old woman, and just imagine now that wizened, hairy old dragon dancing about in front of me, conjuring me by her maiden's honor—the devil! I was already putting my fists up to knock her last few teeth all the way through her guts—make up your mind! either out with the silver, the treasure chest and all those dear little shiny sovereigns, or—my fellows knew what I meant—I tell you, I cleaned out that convent of more than a thousand's worth, and had the fun too, and my fellows left them a memento to carry around for the next nine months.

RATZMANN: Damnation, why wasn't I there?
SPIEGELBERG: You see? Go on, tell me, isn't that a life of luxury? and it keeps you fit and strong, and the corpus is all in one piece, and growing every hour like a bishop's belly—I don't know, there

*I have lost a day.

must be something magnetic about me that attracts all the rogues and vagabonds on God's earth like iron and steel.

RATZMANN: A fine magnet you are! But hang me, I should like to know what witchcraft you use!

SPIEGELBERG: Witchcraft? No need of witchcraft—you must just have your wits about you! A certain practical expertise, that doesn't grow on trees, I admit—what I always say is, you see: you can make an honest man out of any old stick, but for a villain, you need gray matter—and you want a certain national talent too, a kind of, so to speak, villain's climate, and I'll tell you what: go to Graubünden—That's the Mecca of rogues today.*

RATZMANN: Ah, Brother! Italy, they tell me, is a good place altogether.

SPIEGELBERG: Oh yes, yes! everyone must have his due, Italy has had its share of good men, and if Germany goes on as it is going today, and they abolish the Bible completely, as there is every appearance, then Germany may produce something worthwhile too, in time—but altogether, let me tell you, climate makes very little difference. Genius will thrive in any soil, and the rest, Brother—well, you know, a crab won't turn into a pineapple even in the Garden of Eden—but, as I was explaining to you—where was I?

RATZMANN: You were coming to the tricks of the trade.

SPIEGELBERG: Yes, the tricks of the trade! Well then, the first thing you must do when you come to any town is to find out from the police, the jailer and the poorhouse keeper who it is they see most of, who comes to present his compliments most often, and these are the customers you must look for—then, you establish yourself in the coffeehouses, the brothels, and the inns, keep your eyes open, sound people out, see who complains the loudest about their miserable five percent these days, or about the pestilential increase in law and order, who curses the government most, or holds forth about the fashion for physiognomy and that kind of thing! Then you know where you are, brother! Honesty wobbles like a hollow tooth; just get out your pincers—or, better and quicker: you go and drop a purse full of money in the street where everyone can see it, hide yourself somewhere by, and see who

*The Swiss canton of Graubünden officially protested this line, resulting in a severe reprimand of Schiller by the duke of Württemberg.

picks it up; then after a bit you come chasing after, looking around, and crying out, and ask him, just as it might be in passing, did the gentleman not fund a purse of money? If he says yes, well, then the devil was watching; but if he denies it? You will excuse me, sir—I really cannot remember—I am sorry, *(jumping up)* victory, brother, victory! Put out your light, cunning Diogenes!*—you have found the man you wanted.

RATZMANN: You are an expert practitioner.

SPIEGELBERG: God! as if I had ever doubted it.—Now that you have got your man on the hook, you must be careful how you go about landing him! Look, my lad, this is how I have always done it. As soon as I was on the trail, I stuck to my candidate like a burr, drank and swore friendship with him, and nota bene! you must pay for every round! It will cost you a tidy penny, but you must not mind that—on you go, introduce him to gaming and doubtful company, get him involved in a fight, and mischief of one kind and another, till he is bankrupt of strength and resistance and money and conscience and good name; and by the by, I must tell you, you will get nowhere unless you destroy both body and soul—believe me, brother! I must have drawn the conclusion fifty times in my extensive operations, that once the honest man is chased from his nest, the devil is master—it's as easy a step—oh, as easy a step as from a whore to a pious old maid.—But hark! was that a shot?

RATZMANN: It was the thunder, go on!

SPIEGELBERG: A still quicker, better way is this: you rob your man of house and home, till he hasn't the shirt left on his back, then he'll come to you of his own accord—don't ask me the tricks, brother, just ask that red-faced fellow over there—the pox! I outfitted him nicely—I showed him forty ducats, said they were his if he would take a pressing of his master's keys in wax for me—imagine! the stupid brute does it, devil take me if he doesn't bring me the keys and ask for his money.—My good fellow, says I, let me tell you that I shall take these keys straight to the superintendent of police and book you a place on the gibbet!—Strike me dead! you should have seen the fellow: his eyes popped and he shivered like a wet poodle—"In heaven's name! will the gentleman not be reasonable? I will—I will—" "What then, man? Will you tuck up your

*Diogenes, of the fourth century B.C., is the main representative of the Cynic school of philosophy. He is said to have searched, lamp in hand, for an honest man.

pigtail and go to the devil with me?"—"Oh yes, with pleasure, anything you say"—Ha, ha, ha! poor simpleton, mice like cheese, don't they?—Have a good laugh at him, Ratzmann! ha, ha!

RATZMANN: Yes, yes, I must admit. I will inscribe your lesson in golden characters on the tablets of my memory. Satan must know his man, choosing you for his scout.

SPIEGELBERG: Don't you think so, brother? And I reckon if I catch ten more for him he will let me go free—a publisher gives his agent one free copy in ten, why should the devil be such a Jew?—Ratzmann! I can smell powder.

RATZMANN: Confound it! I have smelled it for a long time. Mark my words, something will be up not far from here!—Yes, yes, I tell you, Moritz—the captain will be glad to see you and your recruits—he has enlisted some fine fellows, too.

SPIEGELBERG: But mine! mine! Pah—

RATZMANN: Yes, they look light-fingered enough—but I tell you, our captain's reputation has led honest men into temptation too.

SPIEGELBERG: I hope not!

RATZMANN: Sans jest! and they're not ashamed to serve under him. He doesn't murder for plunder as we do—he didn't seem to care about the money, as long as he could keep his pistols primed, and even the third of the booty that is his by right he would give away to orphans, or to promising lads from poor homes so that they could study. But if there is a squire to be fleeced, one that drives his peasants like cattle, or if we get hold of some gold-braided scoundrel that twists the laws to his own advantage, and makes justice wink with silver, or any fine fellow of that kind—man! then he's in his element, and the devil's in him, as if every nerve of his body was a fury.

SPIEGELBERG: Hmm, hmm!

RATZMANN: Not so long ago we were in an inn, and got wind that a rich count was on his way from Regensburg, who had just won a case worth a million, thanks to a crafty lawyer—he was sitting at the table playing backgammon—how many of us are there? he asked me, and jumped to his feet. I saw him biting his lip, as he only does when he is in a real rage—five at the most! I said—it's enough! he said, threw the money for the landlady on the table, left the wine untouched that he had ordered—we set off on our way. The whole time he didn't speak a word, went aside by himself, only asked us from time to time whether we could not hear anything yet, and told us to put our ears to the ground. At last, there comes the count riding along, his carriage weighed down with baggage, the lawyer sitting inside with him, one man riding ahead, two servants alongside—then you should have seen the man, bounding up to the carriage ahead of us, with two pistols in his hand! and his voice, as he shouted, "Stop!" The coachman didn't want to stop, but he had to take a dive from the box, the count shot out of the carriage door, but it was useless, the riders fled—"Your money, scum!" he cried, in a voice like thunder—he lay like a bullock under the ax—"And are you the villain who makes a whore of justice?" The lawyer shook so that you could hear his teeth chattering—then there was a dagger in his belly, sticking up like a stake in a vineyard—"I have done my part!" he cried, and turned away from us in his proud fashion—"plundering is your business." And with that he disappeared into the woods—

SPIEGELBERG: Hmm, hmm!—brother, what I told you just now was between ourselves, he needn't know about it. Do you understand?

RATZMANN: Yes, yes, I understand!

SPIEGELBERG: You know what he is like? He has his whims. You understand me.

RATZMANN: Very well, I understand.

(Enter Schwarz, *at full speed)*

SCHWARZ: Quick, quick! where are the others? By all the sacraments! you standing there, and talking? Don't you know—don't you know, then?—and Roller—

RATZMANN: What then, what then?

SCHWARZ: Roller has been hanged, and four others too.

RATZMANN: Roller? The plague! but when—how do you know?

SCHWARZ: Three weeks and more he was inside, and we heard nothing, three times they have had him up, and we heard nothing, they tortured him to find out where the captain was—he gave nothing away, stout lad, yesterday they tried him and this morning he was sent by express to the devil.

RATZMANN: Damnation! Does the captain know?

SCHWARZ: He only heard about it yesterday. He was foaming like a wild boar. You know Roller was always his favorite, and now torture—he had ropes and ladders brought to the prison, but it was no use—he dressed up as a friar himself and got in there, and wanted to take Roller's place, but Roller turned it down flat, now he has sworn an oath that made our blood freeze that he will light him a funeral pyre such as no king ever had, one that will burn them black-and-blue. I wouldn't like to be in that town. He has had it in for them for a long time because they are such miserable bigots, and you know, when he says: I will do it! it's as much as if you or I had already done it.

RATZMANN: That's true! I know the captain. If he had given the devil his word that he would go to hell, he would never say a prayer, even though he could save himself with half an Our Father! But oh! poor Roller! poor Roller!

SPIEGELBERG: *Memento mori!* But it makes no difference to me. *(singing)*
> As I go past the gallows tree,
> I turn my head and blink my eye,
> And think, as you swing there so free,
> Who's the fool now, you or I?

RATZMANN *(jumping up):* Hark! a shot.
(Shooting and noises)

SPIEGELBERG: Another!

RATZMANN: And another! the captain!

VOICES *(singing offstage):*
> In Nuremberg you'll never hang,
> Unless they catch you first. *(da capo.)*

SCHWEITZER, ROLLER *(offstage):* Hey, hallo! halloo, ho!

RATZMANN: Roller, Roller! Ten devils take me!

SCHWEITZER, ROLLER *(offstage):* Ratzmann! Schwarz! Spiegelberg! Ratzmann!

RATZMANN: Roller! Schweitzer! Death, devils, hell, and damnation! *(running to meet them)*

(Enter Robber Moor *on horseback;* Schweitzer, Roller, Grimm, Schufterle, *and a troop of* Robbers, *covered with dust and dirt)*

MOOR *(jumping down from his horse):* Freedom, freedom!—you are home and dry, Roller! Schweitzer, take my horse and wash him down with wine. *(throwing himself on the ground)* That was warm work!

RATZMANN *(to Roller):* By Pluto's fiery furnace! are you resurrected from the wheel?

SCHWARZ: Are you his ghost? or am I a fool? or is it really you?

ROLLER *(recovering his breath):* It is. Flesh and blood, entire. Where do you think I've come from?

SCHWARZ: Ask the Sibyl! the judge had put on his black cap for you.
ROLLER: That he had, and that's not all. I've come express from the
gallows. Just let me get my breath back. Schweitzer here will tell
you. Get me a glass of brandy!—You here again too, Moritz? I
thought I should be seeing you in another place—get me a glass of
brandy, will you? my bones are falling apart—oh, Captain!
Where's the captain?
SCHWARZ: Straightaway, straightaway!—but tell us, say! how did you
get away? how have we got you again? My head is spinning. From
the gallows, you say?
ROLLER *(drinking a bottle of brandy):* Ah, that's good, that warms
your heart! Straight from the gallows, I tell you! There you stand
gasping, and can't imagine it—I was only three steps from the
blessed ladder that was going to take me up to Abraham's
bosom—so near, so near! sold to the dissecting theater already,
head to foot, inside and out! you could have had my life for a
pinch of snuff, but I owe the captain breath, life, and liberty.
SCHWEITZER: It's a tale worth telling. The day before, we had heard
from our spies that Roller was in a pretty pickle, and if the skies
didn't fall in time, then the next morning at break of day—that
would be today—he would have to go the way of all flesh.—"Up!"
says the captain, "what won't we do for a friend. We'll save him,
or if we can't save him, then at least we'll light him a funeral pyre
such as no king ever had, one that will burn them black-and-
blue." The whole band turned out. We sent a fast messenger to
him with a note of what we were going to do, to drop in his soup.
ROLLER: I never believed they would succeed.
SCHWEITZER: We bided our time till all the alleys were empty. All the
town had gone out to see the show, on horseback and on foot and
in carriages all jostling together. You could hear the din and the
penitential psalm a long way off. Now, says the captain, set alight,
set alight! Our fellows flew like arrows, set fire to the town in
thirty-three places at once, threw down burning firebrands near
the powder magazine, in the churches and the barns—by God,
before a quarter of an hour was up, the northeast wind came and
served us a treat—he must have had his grudge against the town
too!—and helped the fire on its way to the topmost gables. And
us meanwhile up and down the streets like furies—fire, fire! all
through the town—shrieks and howls and rampage—the firebells
start to ring, then up goes the powder magazine in the air, as if the

earth were split in two, and heaven burst, and hell sunk ten thousand fathoms deeper.

ROLLER: And now my escorts looked over their shoulders—there lay the town like Sodom and Gomorrah, the whole horizon was fire and smoke and brimstone, forty hills echoing the hellish blast all around, everyone falls to the ground in panic—I seize the opportunity, and whish! like the wind—they had untied me, we were as close to it as that—with my company staring back petrified like Lot's wife, away! through the crowds, and off! Sixty yards on and I throw off my clothes, jump into the river, swim under the water till I thought I was out of their sight. The captain ready and waiting with clothes and horses—and so I escaped. Moor, Moor! I only hope you land in such a stew, so that I can repay you in the same coin!

RATZMANN: A brute of a wish, that you deserve to be hanged for—but what a trick to pull off!

ROLLER: It was rescue in my darkest hour, you'll never know what it was like. You should have been there, with the rope round your neck, marching wide awake to the grave like me, and all their accursed rituals and hangman's ceremonies, and every tottering, frightened step nearer and nearer to the loathsome contrivance where I was going to be installed, rising in the hideous glow of the morning sun, and the hangman's assistants lurking, and the horrible music—I can still hear it ringing in my ears—and the hungry ravens croaking, thirty of them perched there on my half-rotten predecessor, and all that, all that—and the foretaste of the eternal bliss that was waiting for me too! Brother, brother! and all of a sudden, the password to freedom—a bang as if heaven had burst its hoops—listen, you vermin! I tell you, if you were to jump from the glowing furnace into icy water, you would not feel such a difference as I did when I reached the opposite bank.

SPIEGELBERG *(laughing):* Poor bastard! Now it's out of your system. *(drinks to him)* Here's to your happy resurrection!

ROLLER *(throwing his glass away):* No, by all the treasures of Mammon! I shouldn't care to live through that again. Dying is more than a harlequinade, and the fear of death is worse than dying itself.

SPIEGELBERG: And the powder magazine blown up—you see now, Ratzmann? That was why the air smelled of sulphur for miles around, as if Moloch's privy had been aired beneath the firmament—it was a masterstroke, Captain! I envy you for it.

SCHWEITZER: If the town makes a holiday out of seeing my comrade done away with like a baited pig, why the devil should we have any qualms at setting off the town for the sake of our comrade? And on top of that, our fellows had the chance of plundering scot-free. Tell us, what did you get?

ONE OF THE BAND: I crept into St. Stephen's in the confusion and cut the gold trimmings off the altar cloth—the good Lord is a rich man, I said, and can spin gold out of old rope.

SCHWEITZER: Well done!—What is the use of that stuff in a church? They dedicate it to the Creator, who laughs at their trumpery—and his creatures go hungry—And you, Spangeler—where did you cast your net?

ANOTHER: Bügel and I raided a store and have brought enough gear for fifty of us.

A THIRD: Two golden fob watches I've spirited away, and a dozen silver spoons too.

SCHWEITZER: Good, good! And we have given them enough to keep them busy for a fortnight. If they want to put the fire out they will have to ruin the town with water.—Schufterle, didn't you hear how many dead there were?

SCHUFTERLE: Eighty-three, they say. The magazine alone blew sixty to smithereens.

MOOR (*very gravely*): Roller, your life is dearly bought.

SCHUFTERLE: Pah! what do you mean? Now if it had been men; but it was only babes in arms still dirtying their linen, wrinkled grandmothers chasing the flies from them, shriveled old stay-at-homes who couldn't find their way to the door, hypochondriacs whining for the doctor while he had gone out to follow the mob at his own solemn pace.—Everyone with a sound pair of legs had run to see the spectacle, and only the dregs of the town was left behind to mind the houses.

MOOR: Oh, the poor, miserable creatures! Children, you say, the old and the sick?—

SCHUFTERLE: Yes, the devil take them! and women in childbed, and pregnant ones afraid of aborting under the gallows, and young wives who thought the hangman's tricks might give them a shock and brand the child in their womb with a gallows mark, the poor poets who had no shoes to put on because their only pair was at the menders', and riffraff of that kind, not worth the trouble of talking about. I happened to be going past a row of cottages there and heard a howling and peeped in, and when I took a good look, what was it? A baby, lying there as right as rain under the table, and the table just about to catch fire—Poor little brute! I said, you're freezing! and threw it into the flames—

MOOR: Did you, Schufterle? And may those flames burn in your breast till the day eternity grows gray!—Away, monster! Never let me see you in my band again! What, are you murmuring? Are you hesitating? Who can hesitate when I command? Away with him, I say—there are others among you who are ripe for my wrath. I know you, Spiegelberg. But I shall come amongst you, and terrible shall be my judgment upon you.

(Exeunt Robbers, *trembling, leaving* Moor *alone, pacing violently up and down)*

MOOR: Hear them not, avenger in heaven! How can I prevent it? How can you prevent it, when your pestilence, your famine, your floods devour the just man with the wicked? Who can command the flame, and bid it spare the hallowed crops when it shall destroy the hornets' nest? Oh shame upon the murder of children! of women! of the sick! How this deed bows my head! It has poisoned my finest works—see the boy standing there, flushed with disgrace and mocked before the eyes of heaven, he who ventured to play with Jove's thunderbolt, and hurled down pygmies when his task was to shatter titans—go, go! you are not the man to wield the highest tribunal's avenging sword, the first stroke was too much for your strength—here I renounce the impertinent plan, go to hide myself in some crevice of the earth, where the daylight shrinks before my shame. *(as if to flee)*

(Enter Robbers, *in haste)*

A ROBBER: Look out, Captain! The forest is alive! Whole troops of Bohemian cavalry are on the rampage.—Hell's constable must have put them up to it.

MORE ROBBERS: Captain, Captain! They have trailed us here—thousands of them are cordoning off the woods around us!

MORE ROBBERS: Help, help! They have caught us, we shall be hanged and quartered! Thousands and thousands of hussars and dragoons and scouts are riding up the hillside and have cut off our escape routes.

(Exit Moor. *Enter* Schweitzer, Grimm, Roller, Schwarz, Schufterle, Spiegelberg, Ratzmann, *and the* Robber Band*)*

SCHWEITZER: Have we shaken them out of their beds? Cheer up, Roller! That's what I have been waiting for for a long time, to cross swords with some of these cook-house champions—where is the captain? Is the whole band together? We have powder enough, haven't we?

RATZMANN: Powder and plenty to spare. But there are no more than eighty of us—we're scarcely one to twenty.

SCHWEITZER: All the better! and if it was fifty of them to my fingernail! Didn't they sit tight till we set fire to the straw under their arses? Brothers! brothers! there's nothing to worry about! They gamble their lives for ten kreutzers, aren't we fighting for our necks and our freedom? We shall be upon them like the flood and rain down on their heads like thunderbolts.—Where in the devil's name is the captain?

SPIEGELBERG: He has left us in our hour of need. Can't we get away?

SCHWEITZER: Get away?

SPIEGELBERG: Oh, why didn't I stay in Jerusalem!

SCHWEITZER: Why, then I hope you drown in a sewer, you miserable rat! When it's naked nuns you've enough to say for yourself, but when you see a pair of fists—coward, let us see now what you are made of, or we'll sew you into a sow's skin and set the dogs on you!

RATZMANN: The captain, the captain!

(Enter MOOR*)*

MOOR *(slowly, aside):* I have let them encircle us completely, now these fellows will have to fight in desperation. *(aloud)* Now, lads! Now is the time! We are lost, or we must fight like wild boars at bay.

SCHWEITZER: Ha! I'll rip their bellies with my tusks till their tripe comes bursting out by the yard! Lead on, Captain! We will follow you into the jaws of death!

MOOR: Load all weapons. There is no shortage of powder?

SCHWEITZER *(bounding up):* No, powder enough to blow the earth sky-high!

RATZMANN: Every man has five pairs of pistols loaded, every man three rifles as well.

MOOR: Good, good! And now some of you must climb the trees, or hide among the thickets, and fire at them from the rear—

SCHWEITZER: That is your place, Spiegelberg!

MOOR: The rest of us, like furies, will fall upon their flank.

SCHWEITZER: That's the place for me!

MOOR: At the same time everyone must let them hear him whistle, and move around in the woods, so that our numbers will seem more formidable; and we must let all the dogs loose, and set them amongst their ranks, to separate and spread them out and drive them into your fire. We three, Roller, Schweitzer, and I, will fight in the thick of it.

SCHWEITZER: Masterly, superb! We will beat them so that they do not know where the blows are coming from. I can shoot a cherry out of a man's mouth—just let them come!

(Schufterle tugs at Schweitzer's sleeve; Schweitzer goes on one side with the captain and speaks quietly with him)

MOOR: Silence!

SCHWEITZER: I beg you—

MOOR: Away! Let him thank his disgrace, it has saved his life. He shall not die when I and my Schweitzer die, and my Roller. Take his clothes from him, I will say he was a passerby and I robbed him.—Calm yourself, Schweitzer! I swear he will yet be hanged one day.

(Enter a Priest.)

PRIEST *(aside, taken aback):* Is this the dragon's lair?—By your leave, gentlemen! I am a servant of the church, and out there are seventeen hundred men, set to guard every hair of my head.

SCHWEITZER: Bravo, bravo! a fine speech to keep one's belly warm.

MOOR: Silence, comrade!—Speak, Father, and be brief! What business have you with us?

PRIEST: I am sent by the authorities, whose word is life and death—you thieves—you murderous incendiaries—you scoundrels—poisonous brood of vipers, that creep in darkness, and sting where no man sees—plague upon the face of mankind—generation of hell—feast for ravens and vermin—colony for the gallows and the wheel—

SCHWEITZER: Dog! enough of your abuse, or—*(thrusting a rifle butt into his face)*

MOOR: Shame on you, Schweitzer! You have spoilt his peroration—he has learned his sermon so perfectly by heart—go on, sir!—"for the gallows and the wheel. . ."?

PRIEST: And you, glorious Captain! Duke of cutpurses! King of villains! Great mogul of all the scoundrels under the sun! Image of that first loathsome rabble-rouser who stirred up a thousand legions of innocent angels to fiery rebellion and dragged them down with him to the pit of damnation—the accusing cries of abandoned mothers howl at your heels, blood is the water you drink, men weigh on your murderous dagger no more than a bubble of air.—

MOOR: Very true, very true! Go on!

PRIEST: What? Very true, very true? Is that your answer?

MOOR: What, sir? That was not quite what you expected? Go on, go on! What more did you have to say?

PRIEST *(heatedly):* Terrible man! get thee behind me! Does not the murdered count's blood stick to your accursed fingers? Have not you with thieving hands violated the Lord's sanctuary, and villainously seized the consecrated vessels of the sacrament? What? Did not you hurl brands of fire into our God-fearing city, and blow up its magazine over the heads of pious Christians? *(clasping his hands together)* Hideous, hideous sins that stink to high heaven and call the Last Judgment to arms, that it may break upon you! Ripe for retribution, ready for the last trumpet!

MOOR: Masterly, so far! but to the matter! What is it that the right worshipful gentlemen would have you tell me?

PRIEST: That which you are not worthy to hear!—Look about you, incendiary and murderer! As far as your eye can see, you are pinned in by our cavalry—there is no room for you to escape now—as sure as cherries will grow upon these oaks, and these pinetrees bear peaches, so surely will you turn your back upon these oaks and pines unharmed.

MOOR: Do you hear, Schweitzer?—But go on!

PRIEST: Hear then, how graciously, how patiently justice has born with your iniquities. If you will crawl upon your knees to the cross, and beg for grace and mercy, then see, severity itself will yield to pity, justice will be as a loving mother—she will turn a blind eye to the half of your crimes, and—consider!—you will only be broken on the wheel.

SCHWEITZER: Do you hear, Captain! Shall I go and squeeze this worn-out sheepdog by the throat till he sweats blood from every pore?—

ROLLER: Captain! Death, devils, and hell! Captain!—see how he chews his lip between his teeth! shall I turn the fellow upside down beneath the firmament like a ninepin?

SCHWEITZER: Me, me! Let me kneel, let me beg at your feet! Let me have the pleasure of grinding him to powder!

(Priest *cries out*)

MOOR: Leave him alone! Let no one dare to touch him! *(to the* priest, *drawing his sword)* Look, Father! here stand seventy-nine men, whose captain I am, and none of them will fly at a command, or dance to the music of your cannons; and out there stand seventeen hundred who have grown gray beneath their muskets—but hear me! thus says Moor, captain of murderers and incendiaries. It is true, I killed the count, I plundered the Dominican Church and set it alight, I cast firebrands into your city of bigots, I blew up the powder magazine over the heads of pious Christians—but that is not all. *(stretching out his right hand)* Look at these four precious rings that I wear, one on each finger—go and tell the worshipful gentlemen with their powers of life and death, tell them point by point, what you are about to see and hear.—This ruby I took from the finger of a minister whom I laid low at his prince's feet when he was hunting. He was a man of the common people, who had made his way by flattery to his master's highest favor—his neighbor's fall was the footstool of his exaltation—orphan's tears bore him aloft. This diamond I took from a minister of finance, who sold offices and honors to the highest bidder, and turned the sorrowing patriot away from his door. This agate I wear in honor of one of your cloth, whom I strangled with my own hands after he had lamented in the pulpit, before his congregation, that the Inquisition had declined so.—I could tell you many more stories of my rings, if it were not that I already regretted the few words I have wasted upon you—

PRIEST: O Pharaoh, Pharaoh!

MOOR: Do you hear? Did you mark him groan? Does he not stand there as if he would call down fire from heaven upon the Company of Korah* with prayer? Judging with a shrug of his shoulders, damning with a Christian sigh! Can a man be so blind? He who has Argus's hundred eyes to spy out his brother's spots, can

---

*"The Company of Korah" refers to the 250 men of the tribes of Levi and Reuben who were swallowed by the earth and burned to death after defying Moses and Aaron when they strayed from a prescribed form of worship (Numbers 16:1–40).

he be so blind to his own?—Gentleness and tolerance they thunder from their clouds, and offer the God of love human sacrifices like a fiery-armed Moloch—they preach the love of their neighbor, and they curse the blind octogenarian at their door—they fulminate against covetousness, and they have slaughtered Peru for the sake of golden brooches and harnessed the pagans like beasts of burden to drag their wagons—they rack their brains in wonder that nature could have brought forth a Judas Iscariot, and he is not the meanest of them who would betray God's Holy Trinity for ten pieces of silver! Oh, you Pharisees, you forgers of the truth, you apes and mockers of God! You are not ashamed to kneel before cross and altar, to flay your backs with scourges and to mortify your flesh with fasting, and you think these miserable mountebank's tricks will deceive him whom you fools yet call all-knowing—just as one mocks the great most bitterly by flattering them that they hate flatterers; you boast of your honesty and upright life, and the God who looks into your hearts would be seized with rage against the creator, if it were not He himself who created the monster of the Nile.—Take him out of my sight.

PRIEST: That the wicked can be so proud!

MOOR: Not enough!—now I will speak with pride. Go and tell the right worshipful gentleman who settle matters of life and death on the throwing of a die—I am no thief that conspires with midnight and with sleep, and plays the great man when he scales the wall—what I have done, doubtless I shall read one day in the ledgers of heaven, but with their miserable hirelings I will waste my words no more. Tell them my trade is retribution—vengeance is my calling. *(turning his back on him)*

PRIEST: So you do not seek grace and mercy? Very well, I have nothing more to say to you. *(turning to the band)* You then, listen to what I have to tell you in the name of justice!—If you will now lay hands on this condemned criminal, bind him and deliver him up, then see! you shall be spared punishment for the horrors you have committed—the memory of them shall be wiped out—Holy Mother Church will receive you once again into her loving bosom like sheep that have strayed, and to each one of you the way to rank and honor shall be open. *(smiling triumphantly)* What then! What do you say to that, Your Majesty?—Hurry then! Bind him and you are free!

MOOR: Do you hear? Do you hear him? Why do you hesitate? Do

you not know what to do? Justice offers you freedom, and you are in truth her prisoners.—She grants you your lives, and those are no empty words, for you are in truth condemned men.—She promises you rank and honor, and what can be your lot, even if you were to be victorious, other than shame and curses and persecution?—She speaks to you with heaven's voice of reconciliation, and you are in truth damned. There is not a hair upon your heads, not upon one of you, that is not destined for hell. Will you still consider? Are you still in doubt? Is it so hard to choose between heaven and hell? Will you not help them, Father!

PRIEST *(aside):* Is the fellow mad?—What, do you think perhaps it is a trap to catch you all alive? Read for yourselves, here is the general pardon, signed and sealed. *(handing* Schweitzer *a paper)* Can you still be in doubt?

MOOR: Look, look! What more can you ask? Signed with his own hand—mercy beyond bounds—or are you afraid they will break their word, have you heard that no faith is kept with traitors?—Oh, have no fear! Politics could make them keep their word, even if they had given it to Satan himself. Who would ever believe them again? Would they ever be able to play the trick again?—I would swear that they mean it! They know it is I who have stirred you up and embittered you, you they think are innocent. Your crimes they interpret as the errors of hasty youth. It is I alone whom they seek, I alone who must pay the penalty. Is it not so, Father?

PRIEST: What is the devil called that speaks out of him?—Yes, yes, it is so—the fellow has me spinning.

MOOR: What, still no reply? Surely you do not think you can break out by force of arms? Look about you, look about you! surely you cannot think that! such confidence would be but childish folly.—Or do you flatter ourselves, thinking to die the death of heroes, because you saw how I rejoiced at the thought of battle?—Oh, do not believe it! You are not Moor.—You are nothing but a gang of thieves! Miserable instruments of my greater designs, like the rope contemptible in the hangman's hand! Thieves cannot die the death of heroes. Life is the thief's profit, after it come terrors.—Thieves have the right to be afraid of death.—Hear how their trumpets sound! See how their threatening sabers flash! What? Still undecided? are you mad? are you out of your minds?—It is unforgivable! I will not owe my life to you, I despise your sacrifice!

PRIEST *(in astonishment):* He will drive me mad, I must fly from this place! Whoever heard such things as this?

MOOR: Or are you afraid that I will kill myself, and by my suicide invalidate the treaty that counted only while I was alive? No, children! that is an idle fear. Here I throw away my dagger, here my pistols and my phial of poison that I had in readiness—so wretched I am, I have even lost power over my own life.—What, still undecided? Or do you think I will resist if you attempt to bind me? Look! see me lash my right hand to this oak tree's branch, I am defenseless, a child can conquer me.—Who will be the first to abandon his captain in his hour of need?

ROLLER *(in furious excitement):* And if nine circles of hell surrounded us! *(brandishing his sword)* Every man who is not a dog, save your captain!

SCHWEITZER *(tearing up the pardon, and throwing the pieces in the Priest's face):* Pardon, in our bullets! Away, vermin! tell the magistrates who sent you that in Moor's band you could not find a single traitor.—Save, save the captain!

ALL *(shouting):* Save, save, save the captain!

MOOR *(tearing himself free, joyfully):* Now we are free.—Comrades! I feel an army in my fist—death or liberty!—at least they shall take none of us alive!

(The trumpets sound the attack. Noise and tumult. Exeunt, with drawn swords)

Act 3

(Amalia *in her garden, playing upon the lute.*)

AMALIA:
> Fair as angels, full of heaven's delight,
> Fairer far than other youths was he,
> His gaze as Maytime sunbeams tender-bright,
> Mirrored in the heavenly azure sea.
>
> His embrace—O raging ecstasies!
> Fiery hearts around each other furled,
> Our lips and ears entranced—before our eyes
> The night—and our two spirits heavenward whirled.
>
> And his kiss—O taste of paradise!
> As two burning flames will grasp and cling,
> As two harps will join their melodies
> And their heavenly harmonies will sing,
>
> Plunging, racing, soaring, spirits bound,
> Lip and cheek a-tremble and ablaze,
> Soul joined with soul and heaven and earth around
> The lovers lost and melted in the haze.
>
> He is gone! alas, it is in vain
> The timid sigh recalls him to our grasp!
> He is gone—and life is now but pain,
> All joy expiring in a dying gasp.

(*Enter* Franz)

FRANZ: Here again, willful dreamer? You crept away from our merry feast and spoiled our guests' pleasure.

AMALIA: I am sorry for these innocent delights! When the dirge must still be ringing in your ears that sang your father to his grave—

FRANZ: Would you mourn forever? Let the dead sleep, and make the living happy! I have come—

AMALIA: And when will you be gone again?

FRANZ: Oh, Amalia! Let me not see these black, proud looks! You grieve me. I have come to tell you—

AMALIA: I suppose I must hear that Franz von Moor has succeeded to the title.

FRANZ: Yes, I came to hear what you would say—Maximilian has been laid to rest with his forefathers. I am your lord and master. But Amalia, I would be so in every respect.—You remember what you have been to our family, Moor treated you as his daughter, his love for you lives on even after his death—can you ever forget that?

AMALIA: Never, never. Who could be so thoughtless as to drown those memories in feasting!

FRANZ: My father's love for you must be repaid to his sons, and Karl is dead—you wonder? you are giddy? Yes, truly, the thought of it is so grand, so flattering, that it must even numb a woman's pride. Franz tramples upon the hopes of the noblest young ladies in the land, Franz comes and offers his heart and his hand to a poor orphan who would be helpless without him, and with it all his gold and all his castles and forests. Franz, whom men envy and fear, comes of his own free will to declare himself Amalia's slave—

AMALIA: Why does not the lightning split the blaspheming tongue that speaks such shameful words? You, you murdered my love, and Amalia should call you husband! you—

FRANZ: Not so hasty, Your Most Gracious Highness!—It is true, Franz cannot mop and mow like a cooing Celadon before you— true, he has not learned to moan his lover's plaint to the echo of the rocks and caves like a languishing Arcadian swain—Franz speaks, and if he hears no answer, he will—command.

AMALIA: Command! You, reptile, command? command me?—and if I throw your command back in your face with scorn?

FRANZ: You will not do that. I know a way that will nicely tame your blind obstinate pride—a convent cell!

AMALIA: Bravo! excellent! in a convent cell, spared your basilisk's look forever, and with time enough to think of Karl, to cling to his memory. Welcome with your convent! Let your cell enfold me!

FRANZ: Ha! is it so!—beware! Now you have taught me the art of tormenting you—the sight of me shall scourge this everlasting fancy of Karl from your head like a fury with locks of fire, the terrifying specter of Franz shall lurk behind your lover's image like the dog in the fairy tale that lay on the underground treasure—by your hair I will drag you into the chapel with my sword in my hand, force the oath of matrimony out of your soul, take your virgin bed by storm, and conquer your proud innocence with my greater pride.

AMALIA *(striking him across the face)*: Take this for your dowry!

FRANZ *(provoked)*: Ha! ten times and ten times more you shall be paid back for that! Not my wife—you shall not have the honor—no, I will have you for my mistress, and honest peasant women will point their fingers at you if you dare to cross the street. Yes, gnash your teeth—spit fire and venom from your eyes—I like a woman to be angry, it makes you more beautiful, more desirable. Come—your struggling will be sauce to my triumph and spice to my pleasure when I force my embraces on you.—Come with me to my room—I am burning with desire—now, this minute you shall go with me! *(attempting to drag her off)*

AMALIA *(falling upon him)*: Forgive me, Franz! *(as he is about to embrace her, she snatches his sword from his side and steps quickly back)* Look, villain, what I can do to you now! I am a woman, but a woman in desperation—once dare to lay your lustful hands upon my body—this steel shall pierce your loathsome breast, and my uncle's spirit will guide my hand! Away, this minute *(drives him away)* Ah! how good, how good—now I can breathe—I felt I was strong as a fiery steed, fierce as the tigress pursuing the triumphant robber of her cubs.—A convent, he said! Thanks, for this happy discovery! Now love betrayed has found its resting place—a convent—the Redeemer's cross is the resting place for love betrayed. *(about to go)*

(Enter Hermann, *timidly)*

HERMANN: Lady Amalia! Lady Amalia!

AMALIA: Wretch, why do you disturb me?

HERMANN: I must shed this weight from my soul before it drags me down to hell—*(falling at her feet)* Forgive me! forgive me! I have wronged you grievously, Lady Amalia!

AMALIA: Stand up! Leave me! I do not want to hear!

HERMANN *(detaining her):* No! Stay! In God's name! In God's eternal name, you shall hear it all!

AMALIA: Not another sound—I forgive you—go home in peace! *(hurrying away)*

HERMANN: Then hear me this one word—it will give you peace again!

AMALIA *(comes back and looks at him in amazement):* What, friend!—who, what on earth or in heaven can give me peace again?

HERMANN: One single word from my lips—listen to me!

AMALIA *(seizing his hand with pity):* Good fellow—can a statement from your lips draw back the bolts of eternity?

HERMANN *(standing up):* Karl is alive!

AMALIA *(crying out):* Miserable wretch!

HERMANN: It is so—And one more thing—your uncle—

AMALIA *(rushing at him):* You are lying—

HERMANN: Your uncle—

AMALIA: Karl is alive!

HERMANN: And your uncle—

AMALIA: Karl is alive?

HERMANN: Your uncle too.—Do not betray me. *(Rushes off)*

AMALIA *(standing as if petrified, then starting up wildly and rushing after him):* Karl is alive!

Scene 2

A country scene, near the Danube.

(The Robbers, *camped on rising ground beneath trees. The horses are grazing downhill.)*

MOOR: Here I must lie and rest *(throwing himself on the ground)*. My limbs are shattered and my tongue is as dry as a potsherd. *(Schweitzer creeps off unnoticed)*

I would bid you fetch me a handful of water from the river, but you are all weary unto death.

SCHWARZ: And the wine in our wineskins is no more.

MOOR: See how fair the corn stands! The trees almost breaking beneath their fruits. The vine full of promise.

GRIMM: It will be a fine harvest.

MOOR: You think so? Then one man is repaid for the sweat of his brow. One?—And yet the night may bring hail, and all may be beaten to the ground.

SCHWARZ: It may well be. All can be beaten to the ground a few hours before the reapers come.

MOOR: It is as I say. All will be beaten to nothingness. Why should a human being succeed where he imitates the ant and be thwarted where he is like the gods? Or is this the limit destined for his endeavor?

SCHWARZ: I do not know.

MOOR: Well said, and, it were better still that you should never seek to know!—Brother—I have seen men, their insect worries, and their giant designs; their godlike schemes and their mouse's scurryings, their wondrous chasing after happiness; this one trusting the leap of his horse—another, his donkey's nose—another, his own legs; this many-colored lottery of life, where so many stake their innocence, their hopes of heaven, to draw the winning number, and—blanks, blanks every one—there was no lucky number there. Brothers, a spectacle to draw tears from your eyes, just as it stirs your belly to laughter!

SCHWARZ: What a glorious sunset!

MOOR *(lost in the sight):* That is how a hero dies—Worthy of adoration!

GRIMM: You seem deeply moved.

MOOR: When I was a boy, my dearest wish was—to live like that, to die like that—*(biting back his anguish)* A foolish boy's wish!

GRIMM: I should think so!

MOOR *(pulling his hat down over his eyes):* There was a time— Leave me alone, comrades!

SCHWARZ: Moor, Moor! What, in the devil's name—? See how pale he has turned!

GRIMM: Why, confound it! what's the matter? is he sick?

MOOR: There was a time when I could not sleep at night if I had not said my prayers—

GRIMM: Have you lost your wits? Would you take lessons from when you were a boy?

MOOR *(laying his head on* Grimm's *breast):* Brother! brother!

GRIMM: What? look! are you a child?

MOOR: Oh, if I were—if only I were again!

GRIMM: Fie, shame!

SCHWARZ: Take courage! Look at the beauty of the landscape, see how fine the evening is!

MOOR: Yes, friends, this world is so fair.

SCHWARZ: Now, that was well-spoken!

MOOR: This earth is so glorious.

GRIMM: Yes, yes—that is what I like to hear.

MOOR *(sinking back):* And I so hideous in this fair world—and I, a monster on this glorious earth.

GRIMM: Oh, in God's name!

MOOR: My innocence! my innocence!—Look! Everyone has gone out to bask in the peaceful sunbeams of spring.—Why must I, I alone draw hell from the joys of heaven? All so happy, all kin through the spirit of peace! the whole world one family, a father there above—a father, but not mine—I alone cast out, I alone set apart from the ranks of the blessed—not for me the sweet name of child—not for me the lover's melting glance—never, never more the bosom friend's embrace. *(starting back wildly)* Set about with murderers, in the midst of hissing vipers—fettered to vice with bands of iron—rocked giddily over the abyss of destruction on the frail reed of vice—I, I alone cast out, a howling Abaddon* amidst the fair world's happy blossoms!

SCHWARZ *(to the others):* Incredible! I have never seen him like this.

MOOR *(sorrowfully):* Oh, that I might enter again into my mother's womb! Oh, that I might be born a beggar! No! I would ask for no more, oh ye heavens—than that I might be as one of those who earn their daily bread! Oh, I would labor till the blood sprang from my brow—to buy the sweet joy of a single afternoon's rest— the bliss of a single tear.

GRIMM *(to the others):* Patience! the fit will soon have left him.

MOOR: There was a time when they would flow so freely—oh, you days when I was at peace! You, my father's castle—you green

*Friedrich Gottlieb Klopstock (1724–1803) uses the name Abaddon (German *Abbadona*) for the contrite and melancholy devil in his epic poem *Der Messias* (The Messiah) (1748–73).

dreaming valleys! Oh, Elysium of my childhood!—Will you never return! never cool my burning breast with your sweet murmurings? Mourn with me, nature.—Never, never will they return, never cool my burning breast with their sweet murmurings.— Gone! gone! gone beyond recall!—

(Enter Schweizer, with water in his hat)

SCHWEITZER: Drink your belly full, Captain—here's water in plenty, and cold as ice.

SCHWARZ: You're bleeding—what have you been doing?

SCHWEITZER: Fool, it might have cost me two broken legs—and a broken neck. There I was going along one of those sandbanks by the river, whoosh! the stuff slips away from under my feet and down I go, a good ten-foot drop—and when I'd picked myself up and got my wits back, there was the clearest water you could ask for, running between the stones. Enough of a caper for this time, I thought, this is what the captain wants.

MOOR *(giving him back his hat, and wiping his face for him)*: Let me—we do not often see the scars the cavalrymen left on your forehead, back there in Bohemia—your water was good, Schweitzer—these scars suit you well.

SCHWEITZER: Pah! there's room for thirty more!

MOOR: Yes, children—it was a warm afternoon's work—and only one man lost—my Roller died a fine death. There would be a monument on his grave if he had not died for my sake. This will have to serve *(wiping his eyes)*. How many was it of our enemies that we killed?

SCHWEITZER: A hundred and sixty hussars—ninety-three dragoons, forty or so riflemen—three hundred in all.

MOOR: Three hundred against one!—Each one of you has a claim on this head. *(baring his head)* Here I raise my dagger—as truly as my soul draws breath I swear—swear I will never forsake you.

SCHWEITZER: Do not swear! One day, you do not know! your good luck may return, and you will regret it.

MOOR: By my Roller's bones! I swear I will never forsake you!

(Enter Kosinsky)

KOSINSKY *(aside)*: Hereabouts they told me I should find him— hallo! what faces are these? Is it—might they—they are, they are! I will speak to them.

SCHWARZ: Look out! Who goes there?

KOSINSKY: Gentlemen, forgive me! I do not know, is this the right way?

MOOR: And who might we be, if it is?

KOSINSKY: Men!

SCHWEITZER: Haven't we proved it, Captain?

KOSINSKY: Men, I am seeking, who can look death in the face and let danger play about them like a charmed snake, who value freedom more than life and honor, whose very name, sweet sound to the poor and the oppressed, strikes terror in the valiant and turns the tyrant pale.

SCHWEITZER *(to the* captain*):* I like this lad. Listen, friend! We are the ones you are looking for.

KOSINSKY: I think you are, and I hope we shall soon be brothers.— Then you can show me the way to the man I want, your captain I mean, the great Count Moor.

SCHWEITZER *(giving him his hand, warmly):* You're a lad after my own heart!

MOOR *(coming closer):* And do you know their captain?

KOSINSKY: You are he—these features—who could look upon them and seek another? *(gazing at him for a long time)* I have always wished that I could see the man with destruction in his eye, there as he sat upon the ruins of Carthage*—now I need wish it no longer.

SCHWEITZER: This is a fine fellow!

MOOR: And what brings you to me?

KOSINSKY: Oh, Captain! my more than cruel destiny—I have been shipwrecked in the rough seas of this world, have seen my life's hopes sink beneath the ocean, and nothing left to me but the memory of what I had lost, a torment that would drive me insane if I had not sought to stifle it in distractions.

MOOR: Another with a grievance against God!—Go on.

KOSINSKY: I joined the army. Still my ill luck pursued me—I went on a journey to the East Indies, my ship ran aground on the rocks—nothing but frustrated plans! At last, I heard tell everywhere of your deeds—of your murder and arson, as they called them—and I have traveled thirty leagues firmly resolved to serve with you, if you will accept my services—I beg you, noble Captain, do not turn me away!

SCHWEITZER *(with a bound):* Hurrah, hurrah! Roller again, a thousand times over! A real assassin for our band!

---

*Gaius Marius (157–86 B.C.), when he was ordered to leave Africa, is said to have replied: "Tell the praetor that you have seen Gaius Marius sitting, a fugitive, amid the ruins of Carthage."

MOOR: What is your name?

KOSINSKY: Kosinsky.

MOOR: What, Kosinsky? And do you realize that you are a rash and foolish boy, taking the great step of your life as thoughtlessly as a careless girl?—This is not like throwing a ball, or bowling, as you may think.

KOSINSKY: I know what you mean—I am twenty-four years old, but I have seen swords flash, and heard bullets whistle by me.

MOOR: Indeed, young sir?—and have you only learned to fence so that you can strike down poor travelers for a few shillings, or run women through from behind? Go, go! you have run away from your governess because she threatened to whip you.

SCHWEITZER: What the devil, Captain! what are you thinking of? you'll not send this Hercules away? Doesn't he look the man to chase the Marshal of Saxony over the Ganges with a kitchen ladle?

MOOR: Because your rags and tatters of schemes have come to nothing, you come here to be a villain, a cutthroat?—Murder, boy, do you know what the word means? You could chop down poppies and go to sleep with a clear conscience, but to bear murder on your soul—

KOSINSKY: I will answer for every murder you bid me commit.

MOOR: What? are you so clever? Do you think to catch a man with your flatteries? How do you know that I never have bad dreams, or that I will not turn pale on my deathbed? What have you done already to make you think of answering for it?

KOSINSKY: Little indeed—but I have come to you, Count Moor!

MOOR: Has your tutor been telling you tales of Robin Hood?—They should clap such careless creatures in irons, and send them to the galleys—exciting your childish imagination, and infecting you with delusions of greatness? Do you itch for fame and honor? would you buy immortality with murder and arson? Be warned, ambitious youth! Murderers earn no laurels! Bandits win no triumphs with their victories—only curses, danger, death, and shame—do you not see the gallows on the hilltop there?

SPIEGELBERG (*pacing up and down in irritation*): Senseless! hideously, unforgivably stupid! that's not the way! that's not how I used to do it!

KOSINSKY: What should I fear, if I do not fear death?

MOOR: Splendid! incomparable! You learned your lessons like a good boy, I see you know your Seneca by heart.—But my friend, fine phrases like that will not talk away the sufferings of your flesh, will never blunt the darts of your pain. Consider well, my son! *(taking him by the hand)* Let me advise you as a father—see how deep is the abyss, before you jump into it! If there is still one single joy known to you in this world—there could be moments, when you—wake up—and then—find it was too late. Here you step beyond the bounds of humanity—you must either be more than a man, or you are a devil.—Once more, my son! if one single spark of hope gleams anywhere within your life, then leave this terrible alliance which only despair can make—unless a higher wisdom founded it—we can easily be mistaken.—Believe me, a man can think it strength of mind, and yet at the last it is despair.—Believe me! Believe me! and go back, as quickly as you can.

KOSINSKY: No, there is no turning back for me. If my pleas cannot move you, then hear the story of my misfortune. After that you will thrust the dagger into my hand yourself; you will—sit round me here on the ground, and listen carefully!

MOOR: I will listen.

KOSINSKY: Let me tell you, then, that I come of a noble family in Bohemia, and through my father's early death inherited a sizable estate. My lands were like a paradise—for they contained an angel—a girl with all the charms that the bloom of youth can endow, and chaste as the light of heaven.—But why do I tell you this? it can only fall on deaf ears—you have never loved, have never been loved—

SCHWEITZER: Be still! our captain is as red as fire.

MOOR: Stop! I will hear it another time—tomorrow, soon, or—when I have seen blood.

KOSINSKY: Blood, blood—let me go on! My tale will fill your soul with blood. She was from Germany, a commoner's daughter—but the sight of her would melt any nobleman's prejudice. As shy and modest as could be, she accepted the ring from my hand, and within a few days I was to lead my Amalia to the altar.

(Moor leaps to his feet)

Amidst the dizziness of the joys that awaited me, in the middle of my wedding preparations, I was summoned to court by an express messenger. I presented myself. I was shown letters that I was supposed to have written, full of treasonable utterances.

I was inflamed at this wickedness—my sword was taken from me, I was thrown senseless into prison—

SCHWEITZER: And meanwhile—go on! I think I can tell what was brewing.

KOSINSKY: I lay there for a month, and did not know what was happening to me. I was afraid for my Amalia, who would be suffering the pains of death every minute on my account. At last the chief minister of the court appeared, congratulated me with honeyed words on the establishment of my innocence, read me the proclamation of my release, gave me back my sword. Now in triumph to my castle, to fly to my Amalia's arms—she was gone. At midnight they said she had been taken away, no one knew where, and had not been seen since. It flashed across my mind like lightning—away! to the city, I sound them out at court—all eyes were on me, no one would tell me anything—at last I catch sight of her through a secret grating in the palace—she threw me a note.

SCHWEITZER: Didn't I say so?

KOSINSKY: Death, hell, and devils! there it was! they had offered her the choice of seeing me die or of becoming the prince's mistress. Forced to decide between her honor and her love—she chose the second, and *(laughing)* I was saved!

SCHWEITZER: What did you do?

KOSINSKY: I stood there, thunderstruck. Blood! was my first thought, blood! my last. I run home foaming with rage, pick myself a three-edged sword, and off like a fury to the minister's house, for he, he alone was the infernal pander. I must have been seen in the street, for when I got there all the rooms were locked. I hunted, I asked for him: he was with the prince, I was told. I hurry there straightaway, they denied that they had seen anything of him. I go back, break down the doors, find him, was on the point—but then five or six of his men sprang out of hiding and robbed me of my sword.

SCHWEITZER *(stamping on the ground)*: And he got off scot-free, and all your efforts were in vain?

KOSINSKY: I was arrested, charged, tried for my life, banished—do you hear?—as a mark of special consideration, banished from the country with ignominy, my estates confiscated and given to the minister. My Amalia is still in the tiger's clutches, sighing and mourning her life away, while my vengeance must go hungry and bow beneath the yoke of despotism.

SCHWEITZER *(standing up, whetting his sword):* Here is grist for our mill, Captain! Here is a fire to be lit!

MOOR *(who has been pacing up and down in violent agitation, starting suddenly, to the* Robbers*):* I must see her!—away! strike camp!—you shall stay with us, Kosinsky—pack up quickly!

THE ROBBERS: Where? What?

MOOR: Where? who can ask, where? *(violently, to* Schweitzer*)* Traitor, would you hold me back? But by every hope of heaven!—

SCHWEITZER: I, a traitor?—lead us to hell and I will follow you!

MOOR *(embracing him):* Brother of my heart! you shall follow me— she weeps, she mourns her life away. Up! away! all! to Franconia! Within the week we must be there! *(exeunt)*

Act 4

Scene 1

A country scene, by Old Moor's *castle.*

*(*Robber Moor, Kosinsky *in the distance.)*

MOOR: Go before and announce me. You remember everything you have to say?

KOSINSKY: You are Count Brand, from Mecklenburg, and I am your groom—have no fear, I shall play my part well enough, good-bye! *(exit)*

MOOR: Soil of my fatherland, I salute you! *(he kisses the ground.)* Sky of my fatherland! Sun of my fatherland! meadows and hills and rivers and forests! I salute you, from my heart I salute you all!—how sweet the breezes blow from the mountains of my home! with what joyous balm you greet the poor outcast! Elysium! a world of poetry! Stop, Moor! your feet tread the floor of a holy temple. *(coming closer)* See there, the swallows' nests in the castle courtyard—the little gate that leads to the garden!—and the corner by the palisade, where so often you would lie listening and mock your pursuer—and there below, the valley with its meadows, where as Alexander the hero you led your Macedonians into the battle of Arbela, and the hill hard by, where you repulsed the Persian satraps—and your victorious banner fluttered on high! *(smiling)* Those golden years of boyhood's May come to life again in an outcast's soul—Oh, you were so happy, so full of pure unclouded joy—and now—there lie the ruins of your schemes! Here you were one day to wander, a great man, dignified and renowned—here to live your boyhood once more in Amalia's blossoming children—here! here, the idol of your people—but the enemy scowled at your plans! *(starting up)* Why did I come here? To hear like a prisoner the clanking chain wake me with a start from dreams of freedom—no, let me return to my exile and misery!—the prisoner had forgotten the light, but the dream of freedom flashed past him like the lightning in the night, leaving it darker than before. Farewell, you valleys of my fatherland! once you saw Karl the boy, and Karl the boy was a happy and fortunate boy—now you have seen the man, and he was in despair. *(he turns and goes quickly to the farthest part of the scene, where he suddenly stops, stands still, and gazes across at the castle with an expression of grief.)* Not to see her, not one glance?—And but a single wall between myself and Amalia—No! I must see her—and him—and let me be annihilated! *(turning round)* Father! father! your son is coming—away, black, reeking blood! away, fearful, hollow, convulsive stare of death! This single hour I beg of you—Amalia! father! your Karl is coming! *(he goes quickly towards the castle)*—Torment me when the daybreak comes, do not leave me when the night has fallen—torment me with dreams of horror! but do not poison this my one last joy! *(at the gate)* What feelings are these? what is it, Moor? Be a man!—Pangs of death—horror and foreboding—*(he goes in)*

Scene 2

A gallery in the Castle.

(Enter Robber Moor *and* Amalia*)*

AMALIA: And do you believe that you can recognize his likeness amongst these pictures?

MOOR: Oh yes, quite certainly. His image was always fresh in my memory. *(going round looking at the pictures)* This is not he.

AMALIA: Rightly guessed! This is the first count, the founder of the line, who was ennobled by Barbarossa when he served under him against the corsairs.

MOOR *(in front of the pictures):* Nor is *this* he, nor *this*—nor *that* one there—he is not among them.

AMALIA: Why, look more closely!—I thought you said you knew him—

MOOR: I should not know my own father better! He lacks that cast of gentleness about the lips that would distinguish him among thousands—it is not he.

AMALIA: You amaze me. What? Not seen him for eighteen years, and yet—

MOOR *(quickly, his face suddenly flushed):* This is he! *(he stands as if thunderstruck)*

AMALIA: A fine figure of a man!

MOOR *(gazing rapt at the portrait):* Father, father, forgive me!—Yes, a fine figure of a man!—*(wiping his eyes)* A godlike figure of a man!

AMALIA: It seems you are deeply moved to think of him.

MOOR: Oh, a fine figure of a man! and he is gone?

AMALIA: Gone! as all our purest joys must go—*(gently taking his hand)* Dear Count, there is no happiness upon this earth.

MOOR: True, very true—and can it be that you have already found out that sad truth? You cannot be twenty-three years old.

AMALIA: And I have found it out. Everything that lives, lives but to die a sorrowful death; nothing we care for, nothing we make our own, but one day we must grieve at its loss.

MOOR: And what can you have lost already?

AMALIA: Nothing. Everything. Nothing.—Shall we not go further, my Lord?

MOOR: In such haste?—Whose is that portrait on the right? I seem to read ill luck in his features.

AMALIA: The portrait on the left is the count's son, the present holder of the title—will you not come?

MOOR: But the portrait on the right?

AMALIA: Will you not see the garden?

MOOR: But the portrait on the right?—you are weeping, my Amalia?

(Exit Amalia in haste)

MOOR: She loves me, she loves me!—her whole being began to stir, the telltale drops flowed down her cheeks. She loves me!—Wretch, was this what you deserved? Am I not standing here like a condemned man before the fatal block? Is that the couch where at her bosom I dissolved in rapture? Are these my father's halls? *(catching the eye of his father's portrait, as if transfixed)* You, you—

Flames of fire from your eye—Curses, curses, and rejection!—
Where am I? Night before my eyes—the terrors of God—I, I have
killed him. *(he rushes off)*

(Enter Franz von Moor, *deep in thought)*

FRANZ: Away with this vision! away, miserable coward! why, are you
are afraid, and of whom? does it not seem, these few hours that
the count has trodden these floors, as if a spy of hell were creeping
at my back—I ought to know him! There is something grand,
something familiar in his wild sunburnt face, something that
makes me tremble—and Amalia is not indifferent to him! Does
she not linger upon the fellow with greedy, pining glances, of a
kind of which she is otherwise so miserly?—Did I not see her let
fall a few furtive tears into his wine, that he gulped down behind
my back as hastily as if he would have swallowed the glass as well?
Yes, I saw it, saw it in the mirror with my own two eyes. Ho there,
Franz! beware! there lurks some monster pregnant with ruin! *(he
stands studying* Karl's *portrait)* His long gooseneck—his black,
fiery, flashing eyes—hmm, hmm!—his dark, overhanging, bushy
eyebrows! *(with a sudden seizure)* Cunning, malicious hell! is it
you who prompt me with this suspicion? It is *Karl!* Yes! all his
features spring to life once more—it is he! despite his disguise—it
is he! Death and damnation! *(pacing violently up and down)* Was
it for this that I sacrificed my nights—leveled rocks and filled in
yawning chasms—rebelled against every instinct of humanity, all
for this giddy vagrant to come blundering through my cunningest
coils.—Gently, gently! All that remains is child's play.—Have I not
already waded up to the ears in mortal sin?—it would be folly to
swim back when the shore lies so far behind me.—There can be
no thought of turning back—heavenly grace itself would be reduced to beggary, and God's infinite mercy bankrupted, if all that
I have incurred should be paid.—Forward then, like a man! *(he
rings the bell)* Let him be coupled with his father's ghost and
come, I care nothing for the dead.—Daniel! hey, Daniel!—What
do you bet that they've not already stirred him up against me,
too? He looks like a man with a secret.

(Enter Daniel)

DANIEL: What is your command, my lord?

FRANZ: Nothing. Go, fill this cup with wine, but hurry!

(Exit Daniel)

Just wait, old man! I will catch you, I will look you in the eye, I will fix you so that your startled conscience will pale beneath your mask!—He shall die!—A poor workman he, who leaves a job half-finished and stands back idly watching for what will happen next.

(Enter Daniel *with wine)*

FRANZ: Put it down here! Look me straight in the eye! How your knees are shaking! How you tremble! Confess, old man! What have you done?

DANIEL: Nothing, your lordship, as true as God's alive, and my poor soul!

FRANZ: Drink this wine! drain it!—What? You hesitate?—Out with it, quickly! What did you put in this wine?

DANIEL: So help me God!—What? I—in the wine?

FRANZ: Poison you put in the wine! Are you not as white as a sheet? Confess, confess! Who gave it to you? The count, wasn't it, the count gave it to you?

DANIEL: The count? Mary and Jesus! the count didn't give me anything.

FRANZ *(seizing him violently):* I will throttle you till you are blue in the face, you grizzled old liar! Nothing! And what were you doing with your heads together like that? You and he and Amalia? And what have you been whispering together? Out with it all! What were the secrets, what were the secrets he confided to you?

DANIEL: That God knows who knows everything. He didn't confide any secrets to me.

FRANZ: Will you deny it? What plots have you been hatching to get *me* out of the way? It's true, isn't it? You're going to strangle me in my sleep? Cut my throat when you are shaving me? Put poison in my wine or my chocolate? Out with it, out with it!—Send me to eternal rest with my soup? Out with it I say! I know everything!

DANIEL: Then may God help me in my hour of need, but it's nothing but the truth I'm telling you!

FRANZ: This time I will forgive you. But isn't it true he put money in your purse? He shook your hand more firmly than the custom is? Firmly, as he were greeting an old friend?

DANIEL: Never, my lord.

FRANZ: He said to you, for example, that he thought he knew you of old?—that you ought almost to recognize him? That the time would come when the scales would fall from your eyes—that— what? Are you telling me he never said such things?

DANIEL: Not a word of them.

FRANZ: That circumstances prevented him—that one often had to wear a mask to get within range of one's enemy—that he would take revenge, take the most terrible revenge?

DANIEL: Not a breath of any such thing.

FRANZ: What? Nothing at all? Think carefully—that he knew your former master well—knew him exceptionally well—that he loved him—loved him uncommonly—loved him like a son—

DANIEL: Something of the kind I do remember I heard him say.

FRANZ *(turning pale):* He did, he did, indeed? What, let me hear! He said he was my brother?

DANIEL *(taken aback):* What, your lordship? No, he didn't say that. but when the young lady took him through the gallery—I was just dusting the frames of the pictures—suddenly he stood still before the late master's portrait, as if he was thunderstruck. Her ladyship pointed to it, and said: a fine figure of a man! Yes, a fine figure of a man! he answered her, and wiped his eye as he did so.

FRANZ: Listen, Daniel! You know I have always been a good master to you, I have fed you and clothed you, I have spared you tasks that were too hard for you in your old age—

DANIEL: And may God reward you for it!—and I have always served you well.

FRANZ: That was what I was going to say. You have never refused me anything all the days of your life, for you know too well that you owe me obedience in all that I command.

DANIEL: In everything and with all my heart, as long as it's not against God and my conscience.

FRANZ: Nonsense, nonsense! Are you not ashamed? An old man, still believing in Christmas fairy tales! Away with you, Daniel! that was a foolish thought. I am your master. It is I who God and conscience will punish, if there are such things as God and conscience.

DANIEL *(clasping his hands together):* Merciful heavens!

FRANZ: By the obedience you owe me! Do you understand? By the obedience you owe me, I tell you, by tomorrow the count must no longer be in the land of the living.

DANIEL: Help, holy God! Why not?

FRANZ: By the *blind* obedience you owe me!—and I tell you, I shall depend on you.

DANIEL: On me! Help me, holy Mother of God! On me? What wrong has an old man like me done?

FRANZ: There is no time to think about it. Your fate is in my hand.

Would you sigh out the rest of your days in my deepest dungeon, where hunger will drive you to gnaw the flesh from your own bones, and burning thirst to drink your own water? Or would you rather eat your bread in peace and have a quiet old age?

DANIEL: What, Master? Peace, and a quiet old age—and a murderer?

FRANZ: Answer my question!

DANIEL: My gray hairs, my gray hairs!

FRANZ: Yes or no!

DANIEL: No!—God grant me mercy!

FRANZ *(about to go):* Good, you shall have need of it.

(Daniel *holds him back and falls on his knees before him*)

DANIEL: Mercy, my lord, have mercy!

FRANZ: Yes or no!

DANIEL: Your lordship, I am seventy-one years old today, and honored my father and mother, and never knowingly cheated anyone of a penny all the days of my life, and have stood by my faith like a true and honest man, and have served in your house for four and forty years, and look to die in peace and with a clear conscience, oh my lord, my lord! *(embracing his knees violently)* And you would rob me of my last comfort at my end, and have the sting of conscience stifle my last prayer, and have me enter the next life as an abomination in the sight of God and men.—No, no, my dear good dear gracious lord and master, you wouldn't do that, you couldn't want to do that to an old man of seventy-one.

FRANZ: Yes or no! What is this babbling?

DANIEL: I will be an even better servant from this day on, I will work my poor old fingers to the bone in your service like a common laborer, I will get up earlier, I will go to bed later—oh, and I will say a prayer for you too in the morning and in the evening, and God will not refuse to hear an old man's prayer.

FRANZ: To obey is better than sacrifice. Did you ever hear of the hangman putting on airs when he had a sentence to carry out?

DANIEL: Oh, no, no, I know! but to slaughter innocence—to—

FRANZ: Am I accountable to you? may the ax ask the executioner, why strike here and not there?—But see how patient I am—I shall reward you for the loyalty you have sworn to me.

DANIEL: But I hoped to stay a Christian man when I swore loyalty to you.

FRANZ: No contradictions! look, I will give you one more whole day to consider! Think on it again. Happiness and misery—do you hear, do you understand? The greatest happiness—and the depths of misery! I shall perform miracles of torture.

DANIEL *(after a little reflection):* I will do it, tomorrow I will do it. *(exit)*

FRANZ: Temptation is strong, and *he* was not born to be a martyr for his faith.—Your health then, Sir Count! It looks very much as though tomorrow morning you will be eating your hangman's breakfast!—Everything depends on how one looks at these things; and the man who does not look according to his own advantage is a fool. The father perhaps has drunk another bottle of wine, and—feels the itch; and the result is—one man more, and the man was surely the last thing to be thought of in the whole Herculean labor. Now it so happens that I feel the itch; and the result is—one man less, and surely there is more intelligence and intention in the loss than there ever was in the increase.—Is not the existence of the most of mankind largely the result of a hot July afternoon, or the tempting sight of bed linen, of the horizontal position of some sleeping kitchen nymph, or the putting out of a light? And if a man's birth is the work of an animal desire, of a mere chance, who is to think that the negation of his birth is any very important matter? A curse on the folly of our nursemaids and governesses, who corrupt our fantasy with horrific fairy tales and impress our soft brains with hideous images of judgments and punishments, so that involuntary shudders will seize a grown man's limbs with the chill of dread, bar the way to our boldest resolutions, bind our awakening reason in fetters of superstitious darkness—Murder! a whole hell full of furies swoops about the very word—nature forgot to make another man—they didn't tie the umbilical cord—the father's guts were running on his wedding night—and the whole shadow play* is gone. There was *something* and there is *nothing*—is that not just the same as: there was nothing and there is nothing and about nothing there is not a word to be said—man is born of filth, and wades a little while in filth, and makes filth, and rots away again in filth, till at the last he is no more than the muck that sticks to the soles of his great-grandson's shoes. That's the end of the song—

---

*A shadow play is a puppet play in which the audience can see only the shadows of the puppets on a screen.

the filthy circle of human destiny, and so it goes—a pleasant journey, brother dear! Our gouty, splenetic moralist of a conscience may chase wrinkled hags out of brothels and torture old usurers on their deathbeds—it will never get a hearing with me. *(exit)*

Scene 3

Another room in the castle.

(Enter Robber Moor *from one side,* Daniel *from the other)*

MOOR *(hurriedly):* Where is the lady?
DANIEL: Your lordship! Will you permit an old man to make one request of you?
MOOR: It is granted. What do you want?
DANIEL: Nothing, and everything, only a little, and yet so much—let me kiss your hand!
MOOR: That you shall not, good old man! *(embracing him)* Would that I might call you father!
DANIEL: Your hand, your hand! I beg you.
MOOR: You shall not.
DANIEL: I must! *(he seizes Karl's hand, looks at it quickly, and falls on his knees before him)* My beloved, my precious Karl!
MOOR *(startled, but coldly and with self-control):* What are you saying, my good man? I do not understand you.
DANIEL: Yes, deny it, disguise yourself! Very well, very well! You are still my own dear good young master.—Merciful God! I am an old man, and live to see—fool that I was, straight away I should have—oh, Father in heaven! So you have come back, and the old master is under the ground, and there you are again—what a jackass I was, blind I must have been, *(beating his forehead)* not to know you the very—well, well, well! Who would have dreamed it—all that I prayed for—Christ Jesus! here he is, as large as life, in these old rooms again!
MOOR: What is this talk? Have you got up in a raging fever, or is it a part in some comedy you are rehearsing?
DANIEL: Oh for shame, for shame! It's not right to play such tricks on your old servant.—This scar! Look, you remember—Great

God, how you frightened me! I was always so fond of you, and the pain you could have caused me—you were sitting on my lap—you remember? There in the round room? You've forgotten that, haven't you—and the cuckoo clock that you liked to hear so much—think of it! the cuckoo clock's gone, smashed to smithereens—old Susie knocked it flying when she was cleaning the room—yes, that's right, there you were sitting on my lap, and called out "Horsey!" And I ran off to fetch your horsey for you— oh sweet Jesus! why did I have to run off so, old donkey that I am—and how it ran hot and cold down my back—hear the crying and shouting out there in the passageway, come running in, and there is the blood all bright, and you on the floor, with—holy mother of God! I felt as if a bucket of icy water was poured over me—but that's what happens with children, if you don't watch them all the time. Great God, if it had gone in your eye—and it was your right hand, too. As long as I live, I said, never again will I let a child get hold of a knife or a pair of scissors or anything sharp like that, I said—thanks be, my lord and lady away—yes indeed, I shall let that be a warning to me, all the days of my life, I said—My godfathers! I could have lost my position, I could, may the Lord forgive you, you godless child! but praise be! it all healed up well, but for that wicked scar.

MOOR: I do not understand a word of what you are saying.

DANIEL: Oh yes, those were the days, weren't they? Many's the cake and biscuit and sweetmeat I've tucked into your hand, you were always my favorite, and do you remember what you said, down there in the stable, when I put you on the old master's sorrel horse and let you gallop all round the great meadow? "Daniel," you said, "just wait till I'm a great man, Daniel, and you shall be my bailiff, and ride with me in my coach."—"Yes," I said and laughed, "if the good Lord give life and health, and if you're not ashamed of an old man," I said, "then I shall ask you to let me have the cottage there in the village that's been standing empty for so long, and lay in a cask of wine, and play tavernkeeper in my old age."—Yes, go on, laugh! Forgotten all about it, hadn't you, young master—don't want to know an old man, behave like a stranger, so grand—and still you're my precious young gentleman—a bit of a wild one you were, to be sure—don't take it amiss! Young blood will have its day—and it can all turn out well in the end.

MOOR *(throwing his arms around his neck):* Yes, Daniel! I'll not conceal it any longer! I am your Karl, your long-lost Karl! And what about my Amalia?

DANIEL *(beginning to weep):* Oh, that I should live to see this happy day, old sinner that I am!—and the master—God rest his soul!—wept for nothing! Down, down, old white head and weary old bones, go to your grave rejoicing! My lord and master is alive, I have seen him with my own eyes!

MOOR: And he will keep the promises he made—take this, you honest graybeard, for the sorrel horse in the stable. *(thrusts a heavy purse of money into his hand)* No, I had not forgotten you, old man.

DANIEL: Stop, what are you doing? Too much! You didn't mean it!

MOOR: Yes, I meant it, Daniel! *(Daniel is about to fall on his knees)* Stand up, tell me, what about my Amalia?

DANIEL: God reward you! God reward you! Oh, good Lord!—Your Amalia, oh, it will be the end of her, she will die of joy!

MOOR *(eagerly):* She has not forgotten me?

DANIEL: Forgotten? What talk is that? Forgotten you?—you should have been there, you should have seen her when she heard the news that you were dead, the news his lordship gave out—

MOOR: What did you say? my brother—

DANIEL: Yes, your brother, his lordship, your brother—I will tell you about it another day, when there is time—and how neatly she cut him off every time he came, day after day, paying her his compliments and wanting to make her his lady. Oh, I must go, I must go, I must tell her, bring her the news. *(going)*

MOOR: Stop, stop! she must not know, no one must know, nor my brother either—

DANIEL: Your brother? No, not he, heaven forbid that he should know, he of all people!—If he doesn't already know more than he ought to—oh, let me tell you, there are wicked people, wicked brothers, wicked masters—but for all my master's gold I wouldn't be a wicked servant—his lordship thought you were dead.

MOOR: Hmm! What are you muttering?

DANIEL *(more softly):* And to be sure, with you coming alive again so uninvited—Your brother was the late master's only heir—

MOOR: Old man! What are you mumbling between your teeth, as if some monstrous secret was on the tip of your tongue, not wanting to come out—and yet it should come out! Speak more clearly!

DANIEL: But I would rather gnaw the flesh from my old bones for hunger, and drink my own water for thirst, than earn a life of plenty by murder. *(he hurries off)*

MOOR *(starting up, after a pause of horror):* Betrayed, betrayed! it flashes upon my soul like lightning!—*A villain's trickery!* Heaven and hell! not you, my father! *A villain's trickery!* A robber, a murderer, through a villain's trickery! Slandered by him! my letters forged, intercepted—full of love his heart—oh, monstrous fool that I have been—full of love his father's heart—oh, knavery, knavery! It would have cost me a single step, it would have cost me a single tear—oh, fool, fool, fool, blind fool that I have been *(running against the wall)* I could have been happy—oh villainy, villainy! my life's happiness vilely, vilely betrayed. *(raging up and down)* A murderer, a robber through a villain's trickery!—He was not even angry. Not the thought of a curse in his heart—oh, fiend! unbelievable, creeping, loathsome fiend!

(Enter Kosinsky)

KOSINSKY: Captain, where are you? What is it? You want to stay here longer, I see?

MOOR: Up! Saddle the horses! Before sunset we must be over the borders.

KOSINSKY: You are joking.

MOOR *(imperiously):* Hurry, hurry! Do not hesitate, leave everything here! and let no man catch sight of you.

(Exit Kosinsky)

I must flee from within these walls. The slightest delay could drive me to frenzy, and he is my father's son—oh, my brother, my brother! You have made me the most miserable outcast upon earth, I have done nothing to offend you, it was not a brotherly deed.—Reap the fruits of your wickedness in peace, my presence shall no longer sour your enjoyment—but truly, it was not a brotherly deed. Let it be ever veiled in darkness, and let not death disturb it!

(Enter Kosinsky)

KOSINSKY: The horses are saddled, you may mount as soon as you will.

MOOR: Such haste, such haste! Why do you harry me so? Am I not to see her again?

KOSINSKY: I will unharness again straightway if you bid me; you made me run, head over heels.

MOOR: Once more! one more farewell! I must drain this poisoned bliss to the last drop, and then—stop, Kosinsky! Ten minutes more—behind, by the courtyard gate—and we will gallop away!

Scene 4

The garden.

(Amalia)

AMALIA: *You are weeping, Amalia?*—and his voice as he said it! his voice! I felt as if nature were reborn—all the happy springtimes of love awakened again in his voice! The nightingale sang as it did then—the blossoms breathed perfume as they did then—and I lay in ecstasy upon his breast. Ah, false, faithless heart! how you seek to flatter your treachery! No, no, away, flee from my soul, deceitful image!—my own, my only one, I have not broken my oath! Flee from my soul, treacherous, godless desires! in the heart where Karl reigns there is no place for mortal man.—But why, my soul, why do you seek this stranger against my will? Why does he stand so close beside the image of my own, my only one? why is he his constant companion? *You are weeping, Amalia?* Ah, I will flee him, flee him! Never shall my eye behold this stranger more!
(Moor opens the garden gate.)
AMALIA *(with a shudder):* Hark, hark! did I not hear the gate? *(she sees Moor, and springs to her feet)* He?—where?—what?—here I stand rooted and cannot flee—do not forsake me, God in heaven!—No, you shall not rob me of my Karl! My soul has not room for two divinities, and I am a mortal maid! *(taking out Karl's portrait)* O you, my Karl, be my angel to guard me against this stranger, this intruder on my love! You, you, let me gaze at you unceasing—no more these blasphemous glances at the other—*(she sits in silence, her gaze fixed upon the portrait)*
MOOR: You here, my lady?—and in sorrow?—and a tear upon this picture?—
(Amalia does not answer)
And who is the fortunate man for whose sake an angel's eye will glisten? may I see the idol of your—*(trying to see the portrait)*

AMALIA: No, yes, no!

MOOR *(starting back):* Ah!—and does he deserve such adoration?—does he deserve it?

AMALIA: If you had known him!

MOOR: I should have envied him.

AMALIA: Worshiped him, you mean!

MOOR: Ah!

AMALIA: Oh, you would have loved him so—there was so much, in his face—in his eyes—in the tone of his voice—so much like you—so much that I love—

(Moor *stands with downcast eyes)*

AMALIA: Here, where you are standing, he stood a thousand times—and beside him she who at his side forgot all heaven and earth—here his eyes feasted on the glorious scene about him—nature seemed to feel his generous, approving gaze, and to grow yet more beautiful in the approbation of her masterpiece—here he would make heavenly music, and hold an airy audience ca;· ·e—here from this bush he would pluck roses, would pluck roses for me—here he lay upon my bosom, here his burning lips touched mine, and the flowers were glad to be crushed beneath the feet of lovers—

MOOR: He is no more?

AMALIA: He sails upon stormy seas—Amalia's love sails with him—he treads the pathless sandy desert—Amalia's love makes the burning sand grow green beneath him, and the thorny bushes blossom—the noonday sun scorches his bare head, the arctic snows blister his feet, hailstorms beat about his brow, and Amalia's love soothes him in the tempest—oceans and mountains and horizons between the lovers, but their souls escape the dusty prison, and are united in the paradise of love.—You seem sorrowful, Count?

MOOR: These words of love stir my love too to life.

AMALIA *(turning pale):* What do I hear? You love another?—Alas for me, what have I said?

MOOR: She believed me dead, and was true to him she thought dead—she learned that I was alive, and would sacrifice for me the diadem of a saint. She knows that I roam an outcast, a wanderer in the desert, and her love flies through exile and desert to be with me. And her name is Amalia like yours, my lady.

AMALIA: How I envy your Amalia!

MOOR: Oh, she is an unhappy lady, she gives her love to one who is lost, and never in all eternity will she be rewarded.

AMALIA: No, no, she will be rewarded in heaven. Are we not told that there is a better world, where the sorrowful shall rejoice, and lovers recognize each other again?

MOOR: Yes, a world where all veils are rent, and love sees itself again, in terror.—Eternity is its name—my Amalia is an unhappy lady.

AMALIA: Unhappy, and she loves you?

MOOR: Unhappy because she loves me! Why, what if I were a murderer? What, my lady? What if your lover could count a man killed for each one of your kisses? Alas for my Amalia! she is an unhappy lady.

AMALIA *(joyfully, springing to her feet)*: Ah! and I, I am happy! My only one is like the light of heaven itself, and heaven is grace and mercy! He could not bear to hurt the merest insect—his soul is as far from thoughts of blood as the pole of day from midnight.

(Moor *turns quickly away between the bushes, gazing fixedly into the distance*)

AMALIA *(takes her lute, plays, and sings):*

    Hector, wilt thou bid farewell forever,

    Now Achilles with his murd'rous quiver

    Fearful vengeance for Patroclus swears?

    Who will teach thy tender son to fight,

    To cast his spear, and fear the Gods of right,

    When thy corpse grim Xanthus downward bears?

MOOR *(takes the lute silently from her, and plays):*

    Dearest wife, go, fetch the fateful lance,

    Let me go—to tread—war's horrid dance—

(he *throws down the lute, and rushes off*)

Scene 5

A nearby forest: night. In the center, a dilapidated old castle.

(the Robbers *encamped on the ground, singing.)*

CHORUS:

>Thieving, whoring, killing, fighting,
>So we live from day to day,
>For every one the hangman's waiting,
>Let's be merry while we may.

>We lead a life of liberty,
>A life of merry joys,
>Our lodging is the forest free,
>In gale and tempest us you'll see,
>The moon's our sun, my boys!
>To Mercury we say our prayer,
>The god of thieves, and light as air.

>Today we'll be the farmer's guest,
>Tomorrow the priest's so fat,
>And for the next, we think it best
>To let the Lord take care of that!

>And every time the tale is told
>Of drinking and of toasting,
>We're fellows stout enough and bold
>To join the enemy of old,
>Who sits in hell a-roasting!

>The stricken father's cries and groans,
>The anguished mother's fearful moans,
>The lonely bride's despairing tears,
>Are joy and music to our ears!

>Ha! see them twitch when their heads we lop,
>Like oxen they bellow, like flies they drop,
>That's a pleasure to our sight,
>That's what gives our ears delight!

And when at last the tide has turned,
Then let the hangman take us,
It is but our reward we've earned,
We'll be gone before they make us.
A drop of Bacchus's juice to speed us as we go,
And up, my lads, away! and swifter than you know!

SCHWEITZER: It will soon be night, and the captain is not yet back!

RATZMANN: And he promised he'd be here with us again on the stroke of eight.

SCHWEITZER: If anything has happened to him—comrades! we'll burn the place down and kill every man, woman, and child.

SPIEGELBERG (*taking* Ratzmann *on one side*): A word in your ear, Ratzmann.

SCHWARZ (*to* Grimm): Shouldn't we be sending out scouts?

GRIMM: Let him be! He will come back with a prize to shame us all.

SCHWEITZER: No, I swear by hell you're wrong there! He didn't look like a man planning a trick of that kind when he left us. Have you forgotten what he told us as he led us over the heath? "Let one of you steal as much as a turnip from the field, if I find out then his head will fall on the spot—as sure as my name is Moor."—He has forbidden us to rob!

RATZMANN (*softly, to* Spiegelberg): What are you driving at? Speak plainer.

SPIEGELBERG: Hush!—I don't know what sort of a price you or I put on our freedom, straining away like oxen at a wagon, and holding forth all the time about our independence—I don't like it.

SCHWEITZER (*to* Grimm): What do you think that windbag is brewing now?

RATZMANN (*softly to* Spiegelberg): Do you mean the captain?

SPIEGELBERG: Hush, I say! He has his informers among us all the time.—Captain, did you say? Who made him our captain? Didn't he usurp a title that by rights belongs to me?—What? is that why we gamble our lives—is that why we let fortune vent her spleen on us, to count ourselves lucky at the last to be the bondsmen of a slave? Bondsmen, when we might be princes? By God, Ratzmann—I never liked it.

SCHWEITZER (*to the others*): Yes, you're a hero—good for squashing frogs with a stone.—Why, the sound of him blowing his nose would knock you flying—

SPIEGELBERG (*to* Ratzmann): Yes—and for years now I've been thinking: things will have to change. Ratzmann—if you're the

man I've always taken you for—Ratzmann—he's disappeared—
half given up for lost—Ratzmann—I do believe his hour of doom
has struck—what? Not a flush, not a flicker when you hear the
bells of freedom ring? Have you not the spirit to take the hint?

RATZMANN: Ah, Satan! what snares are you laying for my soul?

SPIEGELBERG: Have I caught you?—Good! then follow me! I made
note of which way he crept—come! Two pistols rarely miss, and
then—we shall have struck the first blow! *(he is about to drag*
Ratzmann *away with him)*

SCHWEITZER *(drawing his knife in fury)*: Ha! Vermin! Just in time
you remind me of the forests of Bohemia! Were not you the
coward whose teeth began to chatter when they cried "The enemy
is here!" That day on my soul I swore—away with you, assassin.
(stabs Spiegelberg *to death)*

ROBBERS *(in agitation)*: Murder! Murder! Schweitzer! Spiegelberg!
Separate them!

SCHWEITZER *(throwing his knife down on the body)*: There! and
that is the end of you! Calm now, comrades—take no notice of
him—the vermin, he was always jealous of the captain, and he
hadn't a scar on his body—never mind, lads!—ah, the scoundrel!
would he stab a man in the back? he, a man, in the back? Is that
why we have felt the sweat glowing on our cheeks, to slink out of
the world like rats? Vermin! Is that why we made our beds amidst
fire and smoke, to die like rats in the end?

GRIMM: But the devil—comrade—what was it between you? The
captain will be furious.

SCHWEITZER: Let me take care of that. And you, you scoundrel *(to*
Ratzmann*)*—you were his right-hand man! Out of my sight with
you—Schufterle tried that trick too, but now he is hanging there
in Switzerland, as the captain prophesied he would.

(A shot is heard)

SCHWARZ *(jumping up)*: Hark! a pistol shot!

(Another shot is heard)

   Another! Hurrah! The captain!

GRIMM: Patience! He must fire a third shot.

(Another shot is heard)

SCHWARZ: It is, it is! Look out for yourself, Schweitzer—let us
answer him!

(They fire)

(enter Moor *and* Kosinsky*)*

SCHWEITZER *(going to meet them)*: Welcome, Captain!—I have been a little hasty while you were away. *(leading him to the body)* You shall be judge between the two of us—he wanted to stab you in the back.

ROBBERS *(in amazement)*: What? The captain?

MOOR *(gazing for a while at the body, then bursting out furiously)*: O inscrutable hand of avenging Nemesis!—was it not he who sang me the siren song?—Let this knife be consecrated to that dark spirit of retribution!—It was not you who did this, Schweitzer.

SCHWEITZER: By God! it was I who did it, and by the devil I swear it is not the worst thing I have done in my life. *(exits indignantly)*

MOOR *(reflectively)*: I understand—guiding hand of heaven—I understand—the leaves are falling from the trees—and for me too it is autumn.—Take this from my sight.

(Spiegelberg's body is removed)

GRIMM: Give us the word, Captain—what are we to do now?

MOOR: Soon—soon all shall be accomplished.—Give me my lute.— I have lost myself since I went in there—my lute, I say—I must nurse myself back to strength.—Leave me.

ROBBERS: It is midnight, Captain.

MOOR: But those were only tears at a play—I must hear the Roman's song, to wake my sleeping spirit once more—my lute.— Midnight, you said?

SCHWARZ: If not past already. Sleep weighs on us like lead. Three days since we closed an eye.

MOOR: What, does the balm of sleep fall even on the eyes of knaves? Why then should I not feel it? I have never been a coward or a base fellow.—Lie down and sleep—tomorrow at daybreak we go on.

ROBBERS: Good night, Captain! *(they lie down on the ground and go to sleep)*

(profound silence)

MOOR *(takes up the lute and plays)*:

BRUTUS

Be ye welcome, fields of peace and calm,
Where the last of Romans seeks his rest.
From Philippi* with its wild alarm
I come, with shame and anguish in my breast.

*The town where the armies of Brutus and Cassius were defeated by those of Antony and Octavian in 42 B.C., and where Cassius, and later Brutus, committed suicide. Karl's poem depicts Brutus's encounter with his victim Caesar in hell.

Cassius, where art thou? Rome is gone,
My band of brothers lying in their gore,
To death's dark gate my steps are hurried on,
The world no place for Brutus more.

CAESAR

Who is that with steps so fierce and bold
Comes to meet me from the rocks ahead?
Can it be the truth my eyes have told?
That must be a Roman's tread.
Son of Tiber—whence has come thy way?
Stands the city on her seven hills?
Often I have mourned the grievous day
That she lacks a Caesar for her ills.

BRUTUS

Ah, thou with wounds from three-and-twenty hands?
Who summoned thee from death to light?
Reel in horror, back where hell's gate stands!
Triumph not, proud mourner, in thy spite!
Upon Philippi's brazen altar smokes
The final sacrifice of freedom's blood;
While Rome upon the bier of Brutus chokes.
Brutus to Minos goes—Sink in thy flood!

CAESAR

O fatal blow that Brutus's sword should deal!
Thou also, Brutus, thou?
My son—thy father—son, didst thou not feel,
The earth entire to thee should homage vow?
Go—thou as the noblest Roman art renowned,
Since in thy father's breast thou plunged thy sword.
Go—howl it till the gate of hell resound.
Brutus the noblest Roman is renowned
Since in his father's breast he plunged his sword!
Go—for now thou knowest by what hand
I was kept on Lethe's strand;
Come, dark ferryman, leave this land!

BRUTUS

Father, stay!—Upon the earth so wide
I have never known but one
Fit to stand at mighty Caesar's side:
It was he whom you called son.
Only Caesar could have sought Rome's doom,
Only Brutus Caesar would not fight.
Where Brutus lives, for Caesar is no room,
Go leftward, let me pass upon the right.

(he lays down the lute and paces up and down, deep in thought)
Who would be my surety?—All is so dark—labyrinths of confusion—no way out—no star to guide—if it were *over* with this
last drawn breath—*over* like a shallow puppet play—But why this
burning hunger for happiness? Why this ideal of unattained perfection? This looking to another world for what we have failed to
achieve in this—when one miserable touch of this miserable object *(holding his pistol to his forehead)* will make a wise man no
better than fool—a brave man no better than a coward—a noble
man no better than a rogue? There is such divine harmony in the
world of inanimate nature, why such discord in the world of
reason?—No! no! there is something more, for I have not yet
known happiness.

Do you think that I shall tremble? Spirits of my slaughtered
victims! I will not tremble. *(trembling violently)* The terror of
your dying moans—the blackness of your strangled faces—the
hideous gaping of your wounds are but links in an unending chain
of fate, and depend at the last on my idle moments, on the whims
of my tutors and nursemaids, on my father's temperament and my
mother's blood—*(shuddering)* Why not did my Perillus make a
brazen bull of me, to roast mankind in my glowing belly?* *(he
aims the pistol)*

Time and eternity—linked together by a single moment!—O
thou fearful key that will lock the prison of life behind me, and
unbar before me the dwelling of eternal night—tell me—tell me—
where, oh where wilt thou lead me?—Strange, undiscovered
country!—See, mankind grows weak before such visions, the

*In the fifth century B.C., Perillus of Agrigentum, in Sicily, fashioned a bull in which
humans could be cremated.

tensile force of finitude is relaxed, and fancy, willful ape of our senses, spins strange shadows to deceive our credulous mind.— No, no! A man must not stumble—be what thou wilt, nameless *beyond*—if but my own self to me is true—be what thou wilt, let me only take *myself* with me—externals are but the varnish upon a man—I am my heaven and my hell. If Thou wouldst leave me nothing but some smoking desert banished from Thy sight, where lonely night and everlasting desolation all I might behold?—Then I would people the silent emptiness with my imagination, and should have all eternity to pick apart the tangled webs of universal misery.—Or wilt Thou lead me born and reborn again, through ever-changing scenes of misery step-by-step—to utter destruction? Can I not snap the threads of life that are woven for me there beyond as easily as this present one?—You can make of me— nothing; of this freedom you cannot rob me. *(he loads the pistol. Suddenly he pauses)* And am I to die out of a fear of suffering? Am I to grant misery this victory over me?—No! I will endure it! *(throwing the pistol away)* Let suffering yield before my pride! It shall be accomplished!

(the darkness deepens. Enter Hermann *through the forest)*

HERMANN: Hark, hark! fearful the owl's cry—twelve has struck in the village beyond—all is well, all is well—villainy sleeps—no spies listening in this wilderness. *(he comes to the ruined castle and knocks)* Come out, man of sorrows, dungeon dweller! Your meal is ready.

MOOR *(drawing back quietly)*: What can this mean?

A VOICE *(from the tower)*: Who knocks? Ho, Hermann, my raven, is it you?

HERMANN: I, Hermann, your raven. Climb up to the grating and eat. *(owls hoot)*
A dreary song they sing, the companions of your sleep.—Is it good, old man?

THE VOICE: I was much hungered.—Thanks be to thee, sender of ravens, for this bread in the wilderness!—And what news of my dear child, Hermann?

HERMANN: Silence—hark—a sound like snoring! can you not hear it?

VOICE: What? can you hear something?

HERMANN: The wind sighing in the crannies of your prison—a

lullaby to make your teeth chatter and your nails turn blue.—But hark again—I keep thinking that I hear men snoring—you have company, old man!—oh, oh!

VOICE: Can you see anything?

HERMANN: Fare you well—fare you well—a fearful place is this—down into the hole—above, on high your help and your avenger—accursed son! *(fleeing)*

MOOR *(emerging, with horror)*: Stand!

HERMANN *(cries out)*: Ah!

MOOR: Stand, I say!

HERMANN: Mercy! mercy! mercy! now all is betrayed!

MOOR: Stand! Speak! Who are you? What business have you here? Speak!

HERMANN: Have pity, have pity on me, gracious Master—hear one word before you kill me.

MOOR *(drawing his sword)*: What am I to hear?

HERMANN: I know you forbade me on pain of death—I could not help—I could do nothing else—a God in heaven—your own father there—I took pity—strike me down!

MOOR: Here is some mystery—out with it! Speak! I will hear everything.

THE VOICE *(from the ruin)*: Alas, alas! Is it you, Hermann, speaking there? Who is it you are speaking to?

MOOR: Someone drawn there too—what is happening here? *(running up to the castle)* Is it some captive men have cast aside?—I will release his chains.—Voice! again! Where is the door?

HERMANN: O have mercy, my Lord—do not press further, my Lord—for pity's sake, go by on the other side! *(blocking his way)*

MOOR: A fourfold lock! Away!—It must out.—Now for the first time, tricks of the thief's trade, come to my assistance. *(he takes housebreaking instruments and forces the lock of the grating. From below an* Old Man *emerges, emaciated like a skeleton)*

OLD MAN: Have pity on a miserable wretch! Have pity!

MOOR *(starting back in terror)*: That is my father's voice!

OLD MOOR: Thanks be to you, O God! The hour of my deliverance is come.

MOOR: Spirit of Count Moor! What has disturbed you in your grave? Did you take a sin with you into the other world that has barred you entry to the gates of paradise? I will have masses read that shall speed the wandering spirit to its home. Did you take the gold of widows and orphans and bury it in the earth to drive you howling from your resting place at this midnight hour—then I will tear the buried treasure from the enchanted dragon's claws, and if he should vomit a thousand crimson flames upon me and bare his pointed teeth against my sword—or have you come at my request, to answer the riddles of eternity? Speak, speak! I am no man to pale with fear.

OLD MOOR: I am not a spirit—touch me, I live, oh, a life of misery and wretchedness!

MOOR: What? Were you not buried?

OLD MOOR: I was buried—that is to say, a dead dog is lying in the vault of my fathers; and I—for three months and more I have lain languishing in this dark underground chamber, with not a glimmer of light, with not a breath of warm air, with not a friend to visit me, with the croak of wild ravens about me and the hoot of owls at midnight.

MOOR: Heaven and earth! Who could do such a thing?

OLD MOOR: Do not curse him!—It was my son Franz who did it.

MOOR: Franz? Franz?—oh, everlasting chaos!

OLD MOOR: If you are a man, and have the heart of a man, oh my unknown deliverer, then hear, hear a father's sorrow, the sorrow his sons have brought upon him—for three months I have cried it to these unhearing rocky walls, but there was only a hollow echo to mock my lamentations. And so, if you are a man, and have the heart of a man—

MOOR: A challenge to bring the wild beasts from their lairs!

OLD MOOR: There I lay upon my sickbed, and had scarcely begun to recover my strength after my grave illness, when they brought a man to me who told me my firstborn was dead on the field of battle, and with him brought a sword stained with his blood, and his last farewell, and that it was my curse that had driven him to battle and death and despair.

MOOR (*turning away with a violent movement*): It is revealed!

OLD MOOR: Hear me further! I fell into a swoon at the message. They must have thought I was dead, for when I came to my senses again, I was lying in my coffin and wrapped in my shroud like a dead man. I scratched at the lid of the coffin, and it was opened. It was the dead of night; my son Franz stood before me.—"What?" he cried, in a terrible voice, "Will you live forever?"—and straightway the lid was slammed shut again. The thunder of those words had robbed me of my senses; when I awoke once more I felt the coffin being lifted up and taken in a carriage, half an hour's journey. At last it was opened—I found myself at the entrance to this dungeon, my son before me, and the man who had brought me Karl's sword with his blood—ten times I clasped his knees, and pleaded and implored him—his father's pleadings did not touch his heart.—"Down with him, the bag of bones!" his lips thundered. "He has lived for long enough," and down I was thrust without pity, and my son Franz locked the door behind me.

MOOR: It is not possible, not possible! You must have been mistaken.

OLD MOOR: I may have been mistaken. Hear me further, but do not be angry! So I lay for a day and a night, and no man thought of me in my need. Nor did any man set foot in this wilderness, for the story goes that in these ruins the ghosts of my forefathers drag their rattling chains, and make deathly moan at midnight. At last I heard the door open again, this man brought me bread and water, and told me that I had been condemned to die of hunger, and that his life would be in danger if it were known that he was feeding me. And so I have clung feebly to life these many days, but the unrelenting cold—the foul air of my own filth—the boundless grief—my strength ebbed from me, my body withered, a thousand times with tears in my eyes I pleaded with God for death, but the measure of my punishment cannot yet be accomplished—or some joy must yet await me, that I have been so miraculously preserved. But my sufferings are earned—my Karl, my Karl!—and there was not a gray hair upon his head.

MOOR: It is enough. Up, you blocks, you lumps of ice! you dull unfeeling sleepers! Up! will none of you awake? *(he fires a pistol shot over the sleeping robbers' heads)*

THE ROBBERS *(aroused)*: Ho! hallo! hallo! What is it?

MOOR: Did not this tale stir you in your slumbers? sleep everlasting had roused to wakefulness! Look, look! the laws of creation are made a game of dice, the bonds of nature are rent asunder, the ancient strife is let loose, the son has struck his father dead.

THE ROBBERS: What is the captain saying?

MOOR: No, not struck him dead! the words are too kind! A thousand times the son has racked his father, flayed him, spitted him, broken him upon the wheel! no, these are words of men—has done what makes sin blush, what makes the cannibal shudder, what no devil in eons could conceive.—His own son, his father—oh see, see, he has fallen in a swoon—his son, his own father, here in this dungeon he—cold—nakedness—hunger—thirst—oh look, oh see—he is my own father, it is the truth.

THE ROBBERS *(running and gathering round the old man):* Your father? your father?

SCHWEITZER *(approaches reverently and falls down before him):* Father of my captain! I kiss your feet! my dagger is yours to command.

MOOR: Vengeance, vengeance, vengeance shall be yours! venerable old man, so offended, so profaned! Thus from this moment I rend forever the band of brotherhood. *(rending his garment from top to bottom)* Thus I curse every drop of brother's blood before the face of heaven! Hear me, moon and stars! Hear me, midnight heavens! who look down upon this deed of shame! Hear me, thrice-terrible God, You who reign above the moon and sit in judgment and retribution above the stars, and flame with fire above the night! Here I kneel—here I stretch forth my three fingers in the horror of the night—here I swear, and may nature spew me forth from her creation like a venomous beast if I break this oath, swear never to greet the light of day again, until the blood of my father's murderer, spilt before these stones, shall smoke beneath the sun. *(standing up)*

THE ROBBERS: The very devil! Call us villains! No, in Belial's name! we never did the like of this!

MOOR: Yes! and by the fearful groans of all who ever died beneath your daggers, of those my flames consumed and those my falling tower crushed—no thought of murder or robbery shall find its place within your breasts, till all your garments are stained scarlet with the reprobate's blood—did you ever dream that you were the arm of a greater majesty? the tangled knot of our destinies is unraveled! Today, today an invisible power has conferred nobility upon our handiwork! Bow down in adoration before him who decreed you this sublime fate, who led you to this place, who deemed you worthy to be the terrible angels of his dark judgment! Uncover your heads! Kneel in the dust, that you may stand up sanctified!

(they kneel)

SCHWEITZER: Your command, Captain! what are we to do?

MOOR: Stand up, Schweitzer! and touch those hallowed locks! *(he leads him to his father, and makes him hold a lock of his hair)* Do you remember how you split the skull of that Bohemian cavalryman, just as he was raising his saber over my head, and I had sunk to my knees, breathless and exhausted from my work? I promised you then that you should have a kingly reward, but till this moment I could not pay my debt.—

SCHWEITZER: You swore it, it is true, but let me not claim that debt from you in all eternity!

MOOR: No, I will pay it now. Schweitzer, no mortal man till this day was so honored.—Be my father's avenger!

SCHWEITZER *(standing up):* My great Captain! Today you make me proud for the first time! Your command! Where, when, how shall he be struck down?

MOOR: Minutes are precious, you must hurry now—choose the worthiest men of our band, and lead them straight to the count's castle! Snatch him from his bed if he is asleep or lying in the arms of pleasure, drag him from table if he is gorged, tear him from the crucifix if you find him on his knees in prayer! But I tell you, and make no mistake of this! I do not want him dead! Scratch his skin, or harm one hair of his head, and I will tear your flesh in pieces, and cast it to the hungry vultures for food! Alive and whole I must have him, and if you bring him to me alive and whole, you shall have a million for your reward, I will steal it from a king at the risk of my own life, and you shall go as free as the air.—If you understand me, hurry!

SCHWEITZER: Enough, Captain—here is my hand on it: either you shall see the two of us return, or neither. Schweitzer's angel of death is approaching! *(exit, with a troop of robbers)*

MOOR: You others, disperse in the woods—I shall remain.

Act 5

Scene 1

A long vista of rooms—a dark night.

(Enter Daniel *with a lantern and a bundle.)*

DANIEL: Good-bye, dear old home—so much joy and happiness I've seen here, when the good old master was still alive—tears on your moldering bones! To ask such a thing of an old and faithful servant—it was a refuge for every orphan, and a haven for all with no one to care for them, and this son has made it a den of murderers.—Good-bye, old floor! How many times Daniel has swept you—good-bye, old stove, it's hard for Daniel to take his leave after all these years—everything so familiar—it will be painful, faithful old Eliezer*—But may God in his mercy protect me from the snares and wiles of the Evil One—Empty-handed I came—empty-handed I go—but my soul is saved.

(as he is about to go, Franz *rushes in, in his dressing gown)*

DANIEL: God be with me! The master! *(blowing out his lantern)*

FRANZ: Betrayed! betrayed! Spirits spewed from their graves—roused from eternal sleep the kingdom of the death cries to my face *Murder! murderer!*—Who's there?

DANIEL *(nervously):* Holy Mother of God! Is it you, my Lord, screaming through the passages so horribly that everyone starts from their sleep?

FRANZ: Sleep? Who bade you sleep? Off with you, and bring a light!

(Exit Daniel. *Enter another* Servant)

No one is to sleep tonight. Do you hear? Everyone must be up,

---

*The Eliezer to whom Daniel alludes is probably Abraham's steward, mentioned in Genesis 15:2.

and armed—all weapons loaded.—Did you see them, there, along the gallery?

SERVANT: Who, your lordship?

FRANZ: Who, you fool, who? So coldly, so emptily you ask who? Why, it took hold of me like a fit! Who, you mule, who? Spirits and devils! How far on is the night?

SERVANT: The watchman has just called two o'clock.

FRANZ: What? will this night last till the Day of Judgment? Did you not hear a tumult close at hand? No shouts of triumph? No galloping horses' hooves? Where is Ka—I mean the count?

SERVANT: I don't know, Master!

FRANZ: You don't know? You are one of them as well? I will kick your heart out from between your ribs! You with your accursed *I don't know!* Be off, and fetch the pastor!

SERVANT: My Lord!

FRANZ: Do you grumble? do you hesitate?

(Exit Servant, *hurriedly)*

What? Rogues and beggars conspired against me, too? Heaven, hell, all conspired against me?

DANIEL *(coming with a light):* Master—

FRANZ: No! I shall not tremble! It was nothing but a dream. The dead are not yet risen—who says that I am pale and trembling? I feel quite well, quite calm.

DANIEL: You are as pale as death, and your voice is quaking with fear.

FRANZ: I have a fever. Tell the pastor when he comes that I have a fever. I will have myself bled tomorrow, tell the pastor.

DANIEL: Shall I bring you some drops of balsam and sugar?

FRANZ: Some drops of balsam and sugar! The pastor will not be here for a little while. My voice is weak and quaking, yes, balsam and sugar!

DANIEL: Give me the keys, so that I can go and open the cupboard—

FRANZ: No, no, no! Stay! Or I shall go with you. You see, I cannot bear to be alone! How easily I might—you see—faint, if I am alone. No, let me be, let me be! It will pass, you must stay.

DANIEL: Oh, you are sick, in earnest.

FRANZ: Yes, of course, of course! That is all.—And sickness turns the brain, and hatches strange fantastic dreams—but dreams mean nothing, Daniel, do they? Dreams come from the belly, and dreams mean nothing—why, just now I had a merry dream—*(he collapses in a faint)*

DANIEL: In the name of Jesus, what is this? George! Conrad! Sebastian! Martin! don't just lie there! *(shaking him)* Oh, Joseph and Mary Magdalene! Can you not be sensible? They will say I murdered him, God have pity on me!

FRANZ *(in confusion):* Away—away! Why do you shake me like that, you hideous death's head?—The dead are not yet risen—

DANIEL: Oh, everlasting mercy! He is out of his mind.

FRANZ *(raising himself feebly):* Where am I?—You, Daniel? What have I been saying? Take no notice! I was lying, whatever it was—come, help me up!—it was nothing but a fit of giddiness—because—I did not sleep properly.

DANIEL: If only Johann was here! I will call for help, I will send for a doctor.

FRANZ: Stay! sit here beside me on this sofa—there—you are a sensible man, a good man. Let me tell you about it!

DANIEL: Not now, another time! I will put you to bed, rest will be better for you.

FRANZ: No, I beg you, let me tell you about it, and make fun of me!—See, I dreamed I had feasted like a king, and my heart was merry within me, and I lay drunken amidst the lawns of the castle gardens, and suddenly—it was the middle of the day—suddenly—but I tell you, make fun of me!

DANIEL: Suddenly?

FRANZ: Suddenly a fearful thunderclap struck my slumbering ear, shuddering I leaped up, and behold, I thought I saw the whole horizon stand ablaze with fiery flames, and mountains and cities and forests melted like wax in a furnace, and a howling whirlwind swept away the sea and the earth and the sky—and a voice rang out as of a brazen trumpet: "Earth, give up thy dead, give up thy dead, O sea!" and the bare ground was in labor, and began to cast up skulls and ribs and jaws and all manner of bones that joined together and made bodies of men, and they gathered in a great stream, more than the eye could see, a living torrent! Then I looked up, and behold, I stood at the foot of Sinai, the mountain of thunder, and a throng above me and below, and on the summit of the mountain upon three smoking thrones three men before whose glance all creatures fled—

DANIEL: That is the very image of the Day of Judgment.

FRANZ: Yes! the fantasies of a madman! Then there came forth one who was like the starry night, and he had in his hand a signet of iron, and he held it between the place of sunrise and of sunset and spoke: "Everlasting, holy, just, and incorruptible! There is but one truth and there is but one virtue! Woe, woe, woe to the creature that still dwells in doubt!"—Then there came forth another, who had in his hand a looking glass, and he held it between the place of sunrise and of sunset and spoke: "This glass is truth; masks and hypocrisy shall be no more."—Then I was afraid, and all the people, for we saw the faces of serpents and tigers and leopards in the terrible glass reflected.—Then there came forth a third, who had in his hand a balance of brass, and he held it between the place of sunrise and sunset and spoke: "Come forth, ye generation of Adam—for I shall weigh your thoughts in the balance of my wrath! and your works with the weight of my anger!"

DANIEL: God have mercy on me!

FRANZ: All stood as white as death, and each breast beat with fearful expectation. Then it was as if I heard my name named first in the thunder of the mountain, and the marrow of my bones froze, and my teeth chattered aloud. Then straightway the balance began to ring, and the rocks to thunder, and the hours went by, one by one, by the scale that hung on the left, and each one after the other cast in a deadly sin—

DANIEL: Oh, may God forgive you!

FRANZ: But He did not!—And the scale was piled high like a mountain, but the other filled with the blood of atonement kept it up still in the air—at the last there came an old man, bent double with grief, his own arm gnawed in his hunger, all eyes were cast down in awe before him, I knew that man, he cut a lock from the silvery hairs of his head, and cast it upon the scale of sins, and lo! it sank, sank suddenly into the pit, and the scale of atonement flew up aloft!—Then I heard a voice that spoke from the fiery rocks: "Forgiveness, forgiveness for every sinner upon earth and in the pit! thou only art cast out!" *(pause, profound silence)* Well, why do you not laugh?

DANIEL: How can I laugh, when you make my flesh creep? Dreams come from God.

FRANZ: Pah, nonsense! do not say that! Tell me that I am a fool, a crazy senseless fool! Say so, good Daniel, I beg of you, mock me!

DANIEL: Dreams come from God. I will pray for you.

FRANZ: It is a lie, I say.—go this instant, hurry, run, see where the pastor is, tell him to make haste, haste, but I tell you, it is a lie.

DANIEL: God be merciful to you! *(exit)*

FRANZ: Peasant's wisdom, peasant's fears!—No one has yet discovered whether the past is not past, or whether there is an eye watching beyond the stars—hmm! Who prompted me to such thoughts? Is there an Avenger there beyond the stars?—No, no! Yes, yes! I hear a fearful hissing about me: there is a Judge beyond the stars! To go this very night to face the Avenger beyond the stars! No, I say!—a miserable corner where your cowardice seeks to hide—empty, desolate it is beyond the stars, and none to hear you—but if there should be something more? No, no, there is not! I command it not to be!—but if it were? Woe to you if all has been accounted! if it should be counted up before you this very night!—why do my bones shiver?—To die!—why does the word catch my throat so? To answer for myself to the Avenger beyond the stars—and if He is just, the widows and the orphans, the tortured and the oppressed cry out to Him, and if He is just?— Why did they suffer? for what did you triumph over them?

(Enter Pastor Moser)

MOSER: You sent for me, my lord. I am astonished. The first time in my life! Do you have it in mind to make mock of religion, or are you beginning to tremble at its message?

FRANZ: To mock or to tremble, according to how you answer me.— Listen, Moser, I will show you that you are a fool, or that you are making a fool of the whole world, and you shall answer me. Do you hear? By your life you shall answer me.

MOSER: It is One greater than I to whom you issue your summons; one day He will surely give you your answer.

FRANZ: Now I will have it, now! this instant, so that I do not commit a shameful folly and call on the peasants' idol in my desperation, so often I have shouted and laughed to you as the wine flowed: There is no God!—Now I am talking to you in earnest, I tell you, there is none! and you are to muster all the arguments you have at your command, but I shall blow them away with the breath of my lips.

MOSER: But if you could so easily blow away the thunder that will fall on your proud soul with a weight like ten thousand tons! that all-seeing God whom you, fool and villain, would banish from the midst of His creation, has no need of justification from the lips of common dust. For His greatness is as surely seen in your tyrannies as in any smile of triumphant virtue.

FRANZ: Very good, Priest! I like you like this.

MOSER: I stand here in the name of a greater master and speak with one a mere worm like myself, and have no business to be liked. Indeed I should have to be able to work miracles to wring confession from your obstinate wickedness—but if your convictions are so firm, why did you send for me? Tell me this—why did you send for me, at this hour of midnight?

FRANZ: Because I am bored and can find no pleasure at the chessboard. I want to amuse myself with a little priest baiting. You will not unman my courage with your empty terrors. I know very well that those who have come off badly in this life put their trust in eternity; but they will find themselves horribly cheated. I have always read that our being is but a motion of the blood, and when the last drop of blood has ebbed, with it go mind and spirit too. They suffer all the infirmities of our body, will not they also cease when it is destroyed? go up in vapor as it rots? Let a drop of water find its way into your brain, and your life makes a sudden pause, and that pause is like the end of being, and its continuation is death. Our sensibility is the vibration of certain chords—and a broken instrument will sound no more. If I have my seven palaces demolished, if I smash this Venus to pieces, then symmetry and beauty have ceased to exist. Look! there is your immortal soul for you!

MOSER: That is your philosophy of despair. But your own heart, which beats with anxious dread against your ribs even as you utter your proofs, gives the lie to them. These spiders' webs of systems can be torn to pieces with the single word: you must die!—I challenge you, that shall be the proof. If you still stand firm in death, if your principles do not desert you even then, then the victory is yours; but if in the hour of death you feel but the slightest qualm, then woe unto you! you have been deceived.

FRANZ *(in confusion):* If in the hour of death I feel a qualm—?

MOSER: Oh, I have seen many such wretches, who until that moment had defied the truth like giants, but in death their delusions fluttered away. I will stand by your bedside when you are dying—I should so like to see a tyrant die—I will stand there and look you straight in the eye when the doctor takes your cold, damp hand

and can scarcely feel the limping, dwindling pulse, and with that fearful shrug of his shoulders looks up and says: "Mortal assistance is in vain!" Then beware, oh then beware, that you do not look like a Nero or a Richard!*

FRANZ: No, no!

MOSER: Even this no will then be turned into a howl of yes—a tribunal within, that your skeptical speculations will not be able to silence, will then awake and sit in judgment upon you. But it will be an awakening as of one buried alive in the bowels of the churchyard, it will be a reluctant stirring—like that of the suicide who repents after the fatal stroke; it will be a flash of lightning that illuminates the midnight of your life, it will be a revelation, and if you still stand firm, then you will have won!

FRANZ *(pacing up and down in agitation):* Priest's gossip, priest's gossip!

MOSER: Now for the first time the sword of eternity will cut through your soul, and now for the first time it will be too late.—The thought of God will arouse a fearful neighbor who is called the Judge. Moor, the lives of thousands hang upon your fingertips, and of each of those thousands nine hundred and ninety-nine you have made a misery. You would have been a Nero in the days of ancient Rome, in Peru a Pizarro. And now do you suppose that God will allow one man to dwell in His creation like a raging demon, and turn His works to nothing? Do you suppose that those nine hundred and ninety-nine were only there to be destroyed, puppets only for your devilish play? Oh, do not believe it! Every minute of theirs that you have murdered, every joy that you have poisoned, every perfection that you have kept from them, shall be demanded of you then, and if you can answer, Moor, then you will have won.

FRANZ: No more! not a word more! am I to be at the mercy of your liverish fancies?

MOSER: See, the destinies of men are held in a balance, fearful but beautiful to behold. Where the scale of this life falls, the scale of that will rise; where this rises, that will sink to the ground. But that which here was but temporal affliction will there be made eternal triumph, that which here was mortal triumph will there be made everlasting despair.

---

*Shakespeare's Richard III, who in act 5 sees the ghosts of the people he has killed.

FRANZ (*rushing at him furiously*): May the thunder strike you dumb, lying spirit! I will tear out your accursed tongue by the roots!

MOSER: Do you feel the weight of truth so soon? But I have said nothing of proof as yet. Let me come to the proofs—

FRANZ: Be silent, go to hell with your proofs! The soul is annihilated, I tell you, I will hear no more of it!

MOSER: So the spirits of the pit do whimper, but He in Heaven shakes His head. Do you think you can escape the arm of His retribution in the empty realm of nothingness? ascend up into heaven, and He is there! make your bed in hell, and He is there! say to the night: hide me! and to the darkness: cover me! but the darkness shall be made bright round about you, and the midnight shall be day about the damned—but your immortal spirit will refuse to hear the word, and shall be victorious over the blind thought.

FRANZ: But I will not be immortal—let those who will live forever, I will not seek to hinder it! But I will compel him to annihilate me, I will provoke him to rage, that in his rage he will annihilate me. Tell me, what is the greatest sin, the sin that stirs him to the greatest wrath?

MOSER: I know but two. But they are not such as men commit, nor even dream of.

FRANZ: These two!—

MOSER (*with a weight of meaning*): Parricide the one is called, fratricide the other—But why do you suddenly turn so pale?

FRANZ: What did you say, old man? Are you in league with heaven or with hell? Who told you that?

MOSER: Woe unto him who has both upon his conscience! Better it were for him that he had never been born! But be at ease, you have neither father nor brother more!

FRANZ: Aha!—what, you know of none greater? Think again—death, heaven, eternity, damnation hang upon your lips—none greater than these?

MOSER: None greater than these.

FRANZ (*collapsing into a chair*): Annihilation! annihilation!

MOSER: Rejoice, rejoice and be glad!—for all your abominations, you are still a saint compared with the parricide. The curse that will light upon you, compared with that awaiting him, is a song of love—the retribution—

FRANZ *(leaping up):* Away! may a thousand catacombs swallow you up, screech owl! who sent for you? go, I say, or I will run you through and through!

MOSER: Can priest's gossip put a philosopher in such a rage? Blow it away with the breath of your lips! *(exit)*

(Franz writhes on his chair in fearful convulsions. Profound silence. Enter a Servant, *in haste)*

SERVANT: Amalia has flown, the count has suddenly disappeared.

(Enter Daniel, *terrified)*

DANIEL: Your Lordship, a troop of fiery horsemen galloping down the hill, crying murder, murder—the whole village is aroused.

FRANZ: Go and have all the bells rung at once, get everyone to church—on their knees, everyone—they must pray for me—all the prisoners shall be freed—at liberty—the poor shall have their goods restored, everything twice, thrice over, I will—I will—go, go, call the confessor to bless my sins away, are you not gone yet?

(The tumult becomes more audible)

DANIEL: God have mercy on me, sinner that I am! How am I to make sense of this? You've always refused to hear a word of the comfort of prayer, thrown Bible and prayer book at my head so often when you caught me praying—

FRANZ: No more of that—To die! You see? Die? It will be too late.

(Schweitzer is heard making a furious noise)

Pray, I tell you, pray!

DANIEL: I always told you—you can be so scornful of the comfort of prayer—but look out, look out! when your hour of need is come, when the waters rise about your soul, you will give all the treasures of this world for a whisper of Christian prayer.—Do you see? You cursed at me, but now do you see?

FRANZ *(embracing him wildly):* Forgive me! Daniel, dear, good, precious, golden Daniel, forgive me! I will clothe you from head to foot—will you not pray—I will make you a bridegroom—I will—will you not pray—I beseech you—in the devil's name! will you not pray!

(Tumult in the street outside, cries, knocking)

SCHWEITZER *(in the street):* Take them by storm! Kill them! Break the doors down! I can see a light! he must be there.

FRANZ *(on his knees):* Hear me pray, O God in Heaven!—It is the first time—and shall never happen again—hear me, God in heaven!

DANIEL: Mercy, what are you saying? That is a godless prayer!

PEOPLE *(rushing in):* Robbers! murderers! who is it making such a din at midnight?

SCHWEITZER *(still outside):* Push them aside, comrade—it's the devil come to fetch your master—where are Schwarz and his band?— Surround the castle, Grimm—storm the walls!

GRIMM: Brands and torches here—it's us up or him down—I will set his rooms alight.

FRANZ *(praying):* Lord God, I have been no common murderer— Lord God, I have never stooped to trifles—

DANIEL: God have mercy on us, his prayer itself's a sin.

(stones and flaming brands fly through the air. The windows are broken. The castle is set on fire)

FRANZ: I cannot pray—here, here! *(beating his breast and forehead)* All dry, all withered *(standing up).* No, nor will I pray—heaven shall not have this victory, hell will not make this mockery of me—

DANIEL: Mary and Jesus! help—save us—the whole castle is in flames!

FRANZ: Here, take this sword. Quickly. Thrust it into my ribs from behind, so that these villains cannot come and abuse me.

(the fire gains ground)

DANIEL: God forbid, God forbid! I don't want to send anyone to heaven before his time, still less to—*(he runs away)*

FRANZ *(staring wide-eyed after him. After a pause):* To hell, were you going to say? In truth, I can smell something like—*(in a frenzy)* Are those its twitterings? do I hear you hissing, serpents of the pit?—They are forcing their way up—attacking the doors— why am I so afraid of this sharp steel?—the doors give way—crash down—no way out.—Ha! you then, take pity on me! *(he tears the golden cord from his hat and strangles himself. Enter* Schweitzer *with his men)*

SCHWEITZER: Murdering scum, where are you?—Did you see how they ran?—has he so few friends? Where has he crept to, the vermin?

GRIMM *(coming upon the body):* Stop! what's this in the way? Bring a light here—

SCHWARZ: He's stolen a march on us. Put up your swords, here he is, laid out like a dead cat.

SCHWEITZER: Dead? What? dead? Without me, dead? It's a lie, I tell you—see how quickly he will jump up!—*(shaking him)* Hey, you there! There's a father to be murdered.

GRIMM: Spare yourself the trouble. He's as dead as a rat.

SCHWEITZER *(leaving the body)*: Yes! That's the end of him—he is as dead as a rat.—Go back and tell the captain: He is as dead as a rat—he will not see me again. *(shoots himself)*

Scene 2

The setting as in the last scene of the preceding act.

(Old Moor *seated upon a stone*—Robber Moor *opposite him*—Robbers *scattered in the woods.*)

ROBBER MOOR: He is not yet back? *(he strikes a stone with his dagger, making sparks)*

OLD MOOR: Forgiveness be his punishment—my vengeance redoubled love.

ROBBER MOOR: No, by the anger of my soul. It shall not be. I will not have it so. Such a deed of shame he shall drag behind him into eternity!—Why else should I have killed him?

OLD MOOR *(bursting into tears)*: O my child!

ROBBER MOOR: What?—you weep for him? here by this dungeon?

OLD MOOR: Mercy! O have mercy! *(wringing his hands violently)* At this moment—at this moment my child is judged!

ROBBER MOOR *(in fright)*: Which?

OLD MOOR: Ah! what do you mean by that?

ROBBER MOOR: Nothing. Nothing.

OLD MOOR: Have you come to laugh in mockery at my grief?

ROBBER MOOR: Oh, my treacherous conscience!—Take no notice of what I say!

OLD MOOR: Yes, I had a son whom I tormented, and so a son must torment me in turn, it is the finger of God—O my Karl! my Karl! if you hover about me in the raiment of peace, forgive me! O forgive me!

ROBBER MOOR *(quickly)*: He forgives you. *(checking himself)* If he is worthy to be called your son—he must forgive you.

OLD MOOR: Ah, he was too glorious for me—but I will go to meet him with my tears, with my sleepless nights and my torturing dreams, I will embrace his knees and cry—will cry aloud: I have sinned in the sight of heaven and before you. I am not worthy to be called your father.

ROBBER MOOR *(deeply moved):* He was dear to you, your other son?

OLD MOOR: Heaven is my witness! Why did I let myself be deceived by the wiles of a wicked son? Praised as a father I went among the fathers of men. Fair about me blossomed my children full of promise. But—Oh, unhappy the hour!—the evil spirit entered into the heart of my youngest, I believed the serpent—lost my children, both of them. *(covering his face)*

ROBBER MOOR *(going away some distance from him):* Lost forever.

OLD MOOR: Oh, I feel it so deeply, what Amalia said, the spirit of vengeance spoke through her lips. In vain your dying hands you will stretch out to touch your son, in vain you will think you grasp the warm hand of your Karl, who will never come to stand at your bedside—

*(*Robber Moor *holds out his hand to him, with averted gaze)*

OLD MOOR: Would that this were my Karl's hand! But he lies far away in his narrow dwelling, is already sleeping his iron sleep, cannot hear the voice of my grief—woe to me! To die in the arms of a stranger—no son more—no son more to close my eyes—

ROBBER MOOR *(in the most violent agitation):* Now it must be—now—leave me *(to the* Robbers*).* And yet—can I give him back his son again?—I can no longer give him back his son—No! I will not do it.

OLD MOOR: What, my friend? What were you saying to yourself?

ROBBER MOOR: Your son—yes, old man—*(stammering)* your son—is—lost forever.

OLD MOOR: Forever?

ROBBER MOOR *(looking up to heaven in anguish):* O but this once—let not my soul be weakened—but this once sustain me!

OLD MOOR: Forever, you say?

ROBBER MOOR: Ask no more. Forever, I said.

OLD MOOR: Stranger! Stranger! Why did you drag me out of my dungeon?

ROBBER MOOR: And what then?—What if I were to snatch his blessing—snatch it like a thief, and creep away with that godlike prize—a father's blessing, they say, can never be lost.

OLD MOOR: And my Franz lost too?

ROBBER MOOR *(prostrating himself before him)*: It was I who broke the locks of your dungeon—Give me your blessing.

OLD MOOR *(with grief)*: That you had to destroy the son, to save the father!—See, the divinity is unwearying in its mercy, and we poor worms let the sun go down on our wrath. *(laying his hand on the* Robber's *head)* Be happy, according as you are merciful.

ROBBER MOOR *(standing up, tenderly)*: Oh—where is my manhood? My sinews grow slack, the dagger slips from my hand.

OLD MOOR: How good and how pleasant for brethren to dwell together in unity, as the dew of Hermon, and as the dew that descended on the mountains of Zion*—Learn to deserve such bliss, young man, and the angels of heaven will bask in the glory that shines about you. Let your wisdom be the wisdom of gray hairs, but your heart—let your heart be the heart of an innocent child.

ROBBER MOOR: Oh, a foretaste of such bliss. Kiss me, godlike old man!

OLD MOOR *(kissing him)*: Imagine that it is a father's kiss, and I will imagine I am kissing my son—can you also weep?

ROBBER MOOR: I thought it was a father's kiss!—Alas for me if they should bring him now!

(Enter Schweitzer's *companions in silent mourning procession, with lowered heads and faces covered)*

ROBBER MOOR: Heavens! *(drawing back anxiously, and trying to hide. The procession passes him. He looks away from them. Profound silence. They stop.)*

GRIMM *(in a subdued voice)*: Captain!

*(*Robber Moor *does not answer, and draws further back)*

SCHWARZ: Beloved Captain!

*(*Robber Moor *draws still further back)*

GRIMM: We are innocent, Captain.

ROBBER MOOR *(without looking at them)*: Who are you?

GRIMM: You will not look at us. We are your true and faithful band.

ROBBER MOOR: Woe to you if you have been true to me!

GRIMM: The last farewell of your trusty servant Schweitzer—he will come no more, your trusty servant Schweitzer.

---

*When brothers live together "it is like the dew of Hermon falling upon the hills of Zion. There the Lord bestows His blessing, life for evermore" (Psalms 133:3).

ROBBER MOOR *(springing to his feet):* Then you did not find him?

SCHWARZ: Found him dead.

ROBBER MOOR *(leaping up with joy):* Thanks be to Thee, guider of all things.—Embrace me, my children—mercy is the password from now on—so, even that might be overcome—all, all overcome!

(Enter more Robbers, *and* Amalia)

ROBBERS: Hurrah, hurrah! A catch, a magnificent catch!

AMALIA *(with hair flowing free):* The dead, they cry, are resurrected at the sound of his voice—my uncle alive—in these woods— where is he? Karl! Uncle! Ah! *(rushing over to the old man)*

OLD MOOR: Amalia! My daughter! Amalia! *(holding her tightly in his arms)*

ROBBER MOOR *(starting back):* Who conjures up this vision before my eyes?

AMALIA *(tears herself away from the old man, runs to* Karl *and embraces him with rapture):* He is mine, O you stars! he is mine!

ROBBER MOOR *(tearing himself loose, to the* Robbers*):* Strike camp, all of you! The fiend has betrayed me!

AMALIA: Oh, my bridegroom, you are raving! Ah, for rapture! Why am I so unfeeling, in this whirl of joy so cold?

OLD MOOR *(drawing himself upright):* Bridegroom? Daughter! daughter! A bridegroom?

AMALIA: His forever! Mine forever and forever and forever!—O you heavenly powers, take from me this joy unto death, or I shall faint beneath its burden!

ROBBER MOOR: Tear her from my neck! Kill her! Kill him! me, yourselves! Everything! The whole world falls in ruins! *(trying to escape)*

AMALIA: Where are you going? what is it? Love, eternity! Rapture unending, and you would flee?

ROBBER MOOR: Away, away! Unhappiest of brides! See for yourself, ask for yourself and hear! Unhappiest of fathers! Let me flee this place forever!

AMALIA: Take me, in God's name, take me in your arms! It is as night before my eyes—He is running away!

ROBBER MOOR: Too late! In vain! Your curse, Father—ask me no more! I am, I have—your curse—your curse, as I thought!—Who lured me to this place? *(drawing his sword and rushing at the* Robbers*)* Which of you lured me to this place, you creatures of the pit? Swoon then, Amalia!—Die, Father! Die through me a third time!—These your rescuers are robbers and murderers! Your Karl is their captain!

(Old Moor *expires*. Amalia *is silent, and stands like a statue. The whole band pauses in silent horror*)

ROBBER MOOR *(running against an oak tree):* The souls of those I strangled in the ecstasy of love—those I shattered in their blessed sleep—those—ha! Do you hear the powder magazine exploding over the beds of those women in labor? Do you see the flames licking at the cradles of their nurselings?—our nuptial torch, our wedding music—oh, he does not forget, he knows how to join the links—so, not for me the joy of love! so, for me love a torment! it is retribution!

AMALIA: It is true! Great Lord in heaven, it is true! What have I done, innocent lamb that I was! I loved him!

ROBBER MOOR: This is more than a man can bear. Have I not heard death whistling towards me from more than a thousand musket barrels, and without yielding a foot, and I am now to learn to quake like a woman? to quake before a woman?—No, no woman shall shake my manhood.—Blood! blood! It is only something caught from a woman—give me blood to swill, and it will pass. *(trying to escape)*

AMALIA *(falling into his arms):* Murderer! Devil! Angel—I cannot leave you.

ROBBER MOOR *(hurling her away from him):* Away, you serpent, you would mock a madman with your scorn, but I defy the tyrant destiny—what, you are weeping? Oh you wicked, wanton stars! She is pretending to weep, pretending there is a soul that weeps for me.

(Amalia *throws her arms about his neck*)

Ah, what is this? She does not spit at me, she does not thrust me from her—Amalia! Have you forgotten? do you know who it is you are embracing, Amalia?

AMALIA: My only one, I shall never leave you!

ROBBER MOOR *(in ecstatic joy):* She forgives me, she loves me! I am pure as the heavenly ether, she loves me! Tears of gratitude to you, merciful God in heaven! *(he falls on his knees, convulsed with weeping)* Peace has returned to my soul, the raging torment is past, hell is no more.—See, O see, the children of light weep upon the neck of the weeping devil—*(standing up, to the* robbers*)* Why do you not weep too? weep, weep, for you are so blessed. Oh, Amalia! Amalia! Amalia! *(They kiss and remain in silent embrace)*

A ROBBER *(approaching angrily)*: Stop, traitor!—Let go this arm straightway, or I shall tell you a word that will make your ears ring and your teeth chatter with horror! *(he parts them with his sword)*

AN OLD ROBBER: Remember the forests of Bohemia! Do you hear, do you hesitate—then remember the forests of Bohemia! Faithless man, where are your oaths? Do you forget wounds so quickly? When we risked fortune, honor and life itself for you? When we stood round you like ramparts, bore like shields the blows that were aimed at your life—did you not then raise your hand and swear an iron oath *never to forsake us,* as we had never forsaken you?—Have you no honor? have you no faith? will you abandon us for a whining whore?

A THIRD ROBBER: Shame on your perjury! the spirit of Roller that died for you, Roller whom you summoned from the dead to be your witness, will blush for your cowardice and rise armored from his grave to punish you.

THE ROBBERS *(all together, tearing open their clothes)*: Look, look here! Do you recognize these scars? you belong to us! We bought you for our bondsman with our heart's blood, you belong to us, and if the archangel Michael should fight with Moloch for you!—march with us, one sacrifice for another! Amalia for the band!

ROBBER MOOR *(letting go of her hand)*: It is finished!—I sought to mend my ways and turn again to my father, but heaven spoke, and said it should not be. *(coldly)* Fool, and why did I seek it? Can so great a sinner still mend his ways? So great a sinner cannot mend his ways, that I should have known long ago.—Be calm, I beg you, be calm! it is as it should be—when he sought me, I would not, now when I seek him he will not—what could be more just than that?—Do not roll your eyes like that—he has no need of me. Has he not creatures in abundance, he can so easily let one go, and that one am I. Come, comrades.

AMALIA *(dragging him back)*: Stop, stop! One stroke, one fatal stroke! Forsaken anew! Draw your sword, and have pity on me!

ROBBER MOOR: Pity is flown to the wild beasts—I will not kill you!

AMALIA *(clasping his knees)*: Oh, in the name of God, in the name of all mercies! I ask no more for love, I know that our stars above flee one another in enmity—death is my only wish.—Forsaken, forsaken! Think of it in all its horror, forsaken! I cannot bear it. You can see, a woman cannot bear it. Death is my only wish! See, my hand is trembling! I have not the heart to strike. I am afraid of the flashing steel—for you it is so easy, you are a master in the art of slaughter, draw your sword, and I shall be happy!

ROBBER MOOR: Would you alone be happy? Away with you, I kill no woman.

AMALIA: Ah, assassin! you can only kill those who are happy, those who are tired of life you pass by. *(crawling to the* robbers) Then you must take pity on me, you hangman's apprentices!—There is such bloodthirsty pity in your looks, that is comfort for the wretched—your master is a vain fainthearted braggart.

ROBBER MOOR: Woman, what are you saying?

(The robbers *turn away from her)*

AMALIA: No friend? not a friend among these either? *(standing up)* Then let Dido* teach me to die!

(She is going, one of the robbers *takes aim)*

ROBBER MOOR: Stop! Would you dare—Moor's love shall die by Moor's hand alone! *(he kills her)*

ROBBERS: Captain, Captain! What have you done, are you mad?

ROBBER MOOR *(with gaze fixed on the body):* She is hit! This last convulsion, and it is over.—Now, see! what more can you demand? You sacrificed to me a life that you could no longer call your own, a life of horror and disgrace—I have slaughtered an angel for you. Look, look, I say! Are you satisifed now?

GRIMM: You have paid your debts with interest. You have done more than any man would do for his honor. And now come with us!

ROBBER MOOR: You say that? The life of a saint for the lives of rogues, it is an unequal bargain, is it not?—Oh, I tell you, if every one of you were to walk the scaffold and have your flesh torn from your bones, piece by piece with red-hot pincers, that your torments should last eleven summer days long, it would not make good these tears. *(with bitter laughter)* The scars, the forests of Bohemia! Yes, yes! of course, that had to be repaid.

SCHWARZ: Be calm, Captain! Come with us, this is no sight for you. Lead us on!

---

*Dido took her life to escape marriage to King Iarbas. In Virgil, this occurs after her lover Aeneas sails from Carthage.

ROBBER MOOR: Stop—one word before we go.—Listen, you all too zealous executioners of my barbaric command—from this moment I cease to be your captain.—With shame and loathing I lay down this bloodstained baton under whose sway you thought yourselves entitled to sin, and to affront the light of heaven with works of darkness.—Draw aside to left and right—we shall never make common cause in all eternity.

ROBBERS: Ha! have you lost your courage? Where are your high-flying plans? Were they but soap bubbles that burst at a woman's breath?

ROBBER MOOR: Oh, fool that I was, to suppose that I could make the world a fairer place through terror, and uphold the cause of justice through lawlessness. I called it revenge and right—I took it upon myself, O Providence, to smooth the jagged edges of your sword and make good your partiality—but—oh, childish vanity—here I stand at the limit of a life of horror, and see now with weeping and gnashing of teeth, that *two men such as I would destroy the whole moral order of creation.* Mercy—mercy for the youth who sought to anticipate Thy judgment—Thine alone is vengeance. Thou hast no need of man's hand. And now, truly, it is no longer in my power to make up for the past—what is ruined is ruined—what I have overthrown will never rise again. But still something remains that can reconcile me to the laws against which I have offended, and restore the order which I have violated. They must have a sacrifice—a sacrifice that will make manifest their invulnerable majesty to all mankind—and I myself shall be the victim. For them I must surely die.

ROBBERS: Take his sword from him—he is going to kill himself.

ROBBER MOOR: You fools! Damned to eternal blindness! Do you suppose a mortal sin can cancel out mortal sins, do you suppose the harmony of creation will be restored by such blasphemous discord? *(throwing his weapons contemptuously at their feet)* He shall have me alive. I shall go and give myself up into the hands of the law.

ROBBERS: Tie him up, chain him! He is raving mad.

ROBBER MOOR: Not that I doubt they would find me soon enough, if the powers above so will it. But they might surprise me in my sleep, or catch me as I fled, or surround me by force and with swords, and then I should have lost my one remaining merit, of dying for justice of my own free will. Why should I still seek like a common thief to keep hidden a life that in the eyes of heaven has long been forfeit?

ROBBERS: Let him go! These are fantasies of greatness. He will stake his life on empty admiration.

ROBBER MOOR: I might be admired for it. *(after some reflection)* I remember speaking to a poor wretch as I came here—a wage earner with eleven children—they are offering a thousand–louis d'or reward for handing over the great robber alive—I can help that man. *(exit)*

Translated by F. J. Lamport

Schiller's Preface
to *The Robbers*

Consider this play no more than a dramatic narrative which, catching the soul in its most secret operations, makes use of the stage, while neither limiting itself to the rules of drama nor coveting the dubious rewards available to writers of theater adaptations. It would be absurd, as I think you will agree, to try to develop three extraordinary human beings fully within three hours—figures whose actions depend on the turning of perhaps a thousand little wheels—just as in real life it is impossible for even the most penetrating intellect to provide a complete analysis of three extraordinary human beings even within twenty-four hours. Writing this play meant dealing with an abundance of interwoven realities that I could not fit within the all-too-narrow rules of Aristotle and Batteux.*

Yet what will keep it from the stage is not so much this abundance as its content. The overall economy of the piece made it necessary to present several characters who offend the finer feelings of virtue and offend our delicate manners. This is a position in which every painter of human beings is put whenever the aim is to produce a copy of the real world, and not merely textbook characters with idealistic affectations. It just so happens that in this world good is eclipsed by evil—and virtue, when contrasted with vice, takes on the most lively colors. Whoever takes on the task of toppling vice and avenging religion, morality, and civil laws on its enemies must unveil vice in its naked horror and place it before the eye of humanity in its full proportions. And that person must personally wander through those dark labyrinths and force himself to experience feelings whose perversity causes him to bristle.

Here vice is unfolded together with all its inner workings. In

---

*Charles Batteux (1713–80), author of *Traité des beaux-arts réduits à un seul principe* (The fine arts reduced to a single principle, 1747).

Franz, vice dissolves intricate terrors of conscience into powerless abstractions, reduces higher sentiments to a skeleton, and mocks away the grave voice of religion. For a person who, like Franz, has gone so far in refining his understanding at the expense of his heart (a notoriety we do not envy), the most holy is no longer holy; humanity and heaven amount to nothing in his eyes. I have attempted to sketch an accurate likeness of such a miscreant, laying out the entire mechanism of his vice and putting its power to the test. The public will have to judge to what extent I succeed in this task; I believe I have copied nature true to life.

Next to Franz stands another figure, one who will put many of my readers in an awkward position: a spirit who finds the worst vice attractive only because of its monumental stature, only because of the power *(Kraft)* that it demands, only because of the dangers that accompany it. He is a striking, serious human being, armed with every power, who could become either a Brutus or a Catiline, depending how that power was wielded. Unfortunate circumstances decide for the latter, and not until this man's monstrous straying is over does he arrive at the former. Erroneous attitudes toward activity and power, and a plenitude of energy that overflows all law had, of course, to come to nothing as it shattered against civil society. To his enthusiastic dreams of the monumental and the efficacious there needed only to be added a bitterness toward the unideal world— thus was born the strange Don Quixote who, in Robber Moor, we hate and love, admire and lament. I hope I do not have to point out that this portrait is no more a warning only to robbers than the satire of Don Quixote is a warning only to knights-errant.

These days it is in such good taste to exercise one's sarcasm at the expense of religion that it is practically impossible to pass for a genius without deriding its most sacred truths. In daily assemblies of the so-called wits, the noble simplicity of the holy scripture is mishandled and made to look ridiculous. Yet what is so holy and serious that, when one twists it around, it cannot be made fun of? I hope to have provided religion and morality no small revenge in depicting these malicious despisers of the holy scripture in the form of my most abominable robbers.

But there is more. These immoral characters also had to shine in certain respects, even win from the perspective of the spirit what they lose from the perspective of the heart. Here I did no more than copy nature verbatim. Every person, even the most wicked, is made to a certain extent in God's image, and it might even be that the greater villain has a shorter path to righteousness than the lesser. For morality keeps even pace with one's powers: the greater one's capabilities, the greater and more monstrous are one's errors—and the more blameworthy is the misuse of those powers.

Klopstock's Adramelech* inspires a feeling in us in which admiration is blended with disgust; we follow Milton's Satan with shuddering awe through pathless chaos; the Medea of the ancient stage remains, for all her atrocities, a great and wondrous woman; and certainly we admire Shakespeare's Richard as much as a literary figure as we would hate him in reality. If it is my task to depict whole human beings, then I have to include their strong points, which are never lacking even in the most evil of people. If I want to provide a warning against tigers, then I cannot forget to mention their dazzling, spotted coats so that the animals are not overlooked. At any rate, the human being who is completely evil is simply not a proper subject of art, repelling rather than attracting interest: the reader would simply turn the page. A noble soul can no more put up with uninterrupted moral dissonance than with the scratching of a knife on glass.

Precisely for these reasons I am probably ill-advised to bring my play to the stage. A certain strength of mind is needed both on the part of the writer and the reader: the former must be careful not to glorify vice; the latter must not be so captivated by some attractive aspect of that vice that its essential ugliness goes unrecognized. Others will have to judge my own role in this; I am not entirely sure about my readers. The vulgar—and here I mean not just street sweepers—strike root (just between us) all over, and unfortunately they set the tone. Too nearsighted to take in the whole picture I present, too small-minded to understand its importance, too spiteful to allow me a moral aim, that person will, I fear, thwart my intentions and perhaps even see in my work an apology for the vice that I topple—all making the poor poet, to which one is willing to grant everything except justice, pay the penalty for the stupidity of others.

*A devil in Friedrich Gottlieb Klopstock's biblical epic *Der Messias* (The Messiah, 1751–73).

Once again it is the old story of Democritus and the Abderans,* and to rid us of this nuisance our good Hippocrates would use up whole plantations of hellebore. As many friends of the truth as you like might stand up and instruct their fellow citizens from the pulpit and the stage; still, the vulgar will never cease to be vulgar, even if the sun and the moon changed course, and heaven and earth went out of style like a dress. Perhaps, for the sake of the weak of heart, I should have been less true to nature. But if that beetle with which we are all familiar can extract manure from pearls, and if it has been shown that fire burns and water drowns, should pearls and fire and water all be confiscated?

In light of its remarkable dénouement, I can rightfully claim for my drama a place among moral books; vice leads to the outcome it deserves. The one who strayed is back on the track of the law. Virtue goes away victorious. Those who are fair to me and read my work through with the desire to understand, from such readers I expect not that they will admire the poet, but that they will esteem my honesty and righteousness.

Translated by Alan C. Leidner

---

*Abdera, a Greek city on the coast of Thrace, was the birthplace of Democritus. Reference is to a tale told by Christoph Martin Wieland in his novel *Die Abderiten, eine sehr wahrscheinliche Geschichte* (The history of the Abderites, 1744–80, excerpted in The German Library volume 10) in which Hippocrates, asked by the proverbially simpleminded Abderans to cure Democritus, whom they thought deranged because they could not understand him, prescribes a concoction made of hellebore to the entire city.

Select List of Secondary Literature in English

Auerbach, Erich. "Miller the Musician." In *Mimesis: The Representation of Reality in Western Literature*, 434–53. Translated by Willard R. Trask. Princeton: Princeton University Press, 1953.

Blackall, Eric A. "The Language of Sturm and Drang." In *Stil- und Formprobleme in der Literatur*, 272–83. Edited by Paul Böckmann. Heidelberg: C. Winter, 1959.

Blunden, Allen. "J. M. R. Lenz." In *German Men of Letters*. Vol. 6, 209–40. Edited by Alex Natan and Brian Keith-Smith. London: Wolff, 1972.

Bruford, Walter H. *Germany in the Eighteenth Century: The Social Background of the Literary Revival.* Cambridge: Cambridge University Press, 1935.

Duncan, Bruce. "The Comic Structure of Lenz's *Soldaten*." *Modern Language Notes* 91 (1976): 515–23.

Ergang, Robert Reinhold. "Möser and the Rise of National Thought in Germany." *Journal of Modern History* 5 (1933): 172–96.

Kieffer, Bruce. *The Storm and Stress of Language: Linguistic Catastrophe in the Early Works of Goethe, Lenz, Klinger, and Schiller.* University Park: Pennsylvania State University Press, 1986.

Kistler, Mark. O. *Drama of the Storm and Stress.* New York: Twayne, 1969.

Koepke, Wulf. *Johann Gottfried Herder.* Boston: G. K. Hall, 1987.

Leidner, Alan C. "A Titan in Extenuating Circumstances: Sturm und Drang and the *Kraftmensch. PMLA* vol. 104 no. 2 (1989): 178–89.

Madland, Helga Stipa. *Non-Aristotelian Drama in Eighteenth-century Germany and its Modernity: J. M. R. Lenz.* Bern: Lang, 1982.

Magill, C. P. and L. A. Wilkinson. "Introduction." *Die Räuber: Ein Trauerspiel*, ix–lxvi. Oxford: Basil Blackwell, 1974.

McInnes, Edward. "The Sturm und Drang and the Development of Social Drama." *Deutsche Vierteljahrsschrift* 46 (1972): 61–81.

O'Flaherty, James C. *Johann Georg Hamann.* Boston: G. K. Hall, 1979.

Osborne, John. *J. M. R. Lenz: The Renunciation of Heroism*. Gottingen: Vandenhoeck & Ruprecht, 1975.

Pascal, Roy. *The German Sturm und Drang*. New York: Philosophical Library, 1953.

Ryder, Frank. "Toward a Revaluation of Goethe's *Götz:* Features of Recurrence." *PMLA* 77 (1962): 58–70.

Schmidt, Henry J. "The Language of Confinement: Gerstenberg's *Ugolino* and Klinger's *Sturm und Drang.*" *Lessing Yearbook* 11 (1979): 165–97.

Thorlby, Anthony. "From What Did Goethe Save Himself in *Werther?*" In *Versuche 3ᵘ Goethe: Festschrift für Erich Heller,* 150–66. Edited by Volker Dürr and Géza von Molnár. Heidelberg: Lothar Stiehm, 1976.

**Other Literature of Sturm und Drang
Available in English Translation**

Goethe, Johann Wolfgang von. *Götz von Berlichingen*. Translated by Charles E. Passage. Prospect Heights, IL: Waveland, 1991.

Goethe, Johann Wolfgang von. *The Sufferings of Young Werther*. In *"The Sufferings of Young Werther" and "Elective Affinities."* The German Library. Vol. 19. New York: Continuum, 1990.

Leisewitz, Johann Anton. *Julius of Tarento*. Translated by Betty Senk Waterhouse. In *Five Plays of the Sturm und Drang,* 191–229. Lanham, MD: University Press of America, 1986.

Lenz, J. M. R. *The Tutor*. In *"The Tutor" and "The Soldiers,"* 1–80. Translated by William E. Yuill. Chicago: University of Chicago Press, 1972.

Schiller, Friedrich. *Intrigue and Love*. Translated by Charles E. Passage. The German Library. Vol. 15, 2–101. Edited by Walter Hinderer. New York: Continuum, 1983.

ACKNOWLEDGMENTS

Every reasonable effort has been made to locate the owners of rights to previously published translations printed here. We gratefully acknowledge permission to reprint the following materal:

The Childmurderess by Heinrich Leopold Wagner and *Storm and Stress* by Friedrich Maxmilian Klinger from *Five Plays of the Sturm und Drang,* translated by Betty Senk Waterhouse (University of America, 1986). Reprinted by permission of the publisher.

J. M. R. Lenz, *The Soldiers,* translated by William E. Yuill in *"The Tutor" and "The Soldiers"* (Chicago, University of Chicago Press, 1972). Reprinted by permission of the publisher.

Friedrich Schiller, *The Robbers,* translated by F. J. Lamport from *"The Robbers" and "Wallenstein"* (Penguin Classics, 1979), Copyright © F. J. Lamport 1979. Reproduced by permission of the publisher, Penguin Books Limited.

*   *   *

The editor gratefully acknowledges a grant from the President's Office of the University of Louisville, which allowed partial course relief during the 1990–91 academic year.

Additional footnotes are by Betty Senk Waterhouse and William E. Yuill.

THE GERMAN LIBRARY
in 100 Volumes

Wolfram von Eschenbach
Parzival
Edited by André Lefevere

Gottfried von Strassburg
Tristan and Isolde
Edited and Revised by Francis G. Gentry
Foreword by C. Stephen Jaeger

German Mystical Writings
Edited by Karen J. Campbell
Foreword by Carol Zaleski

German Medieval Tales
Edited by Francis G. Gentry
Foreword by Thomas Berger

German Humanism and Reformation
Edited by Reinhard P. Becker
Foreword by Roland Bainton

Immanuel Kant
Philosophical Writings
Edited by Ernst Behler
Foreword by René Wellek

Friedrich Schiller
Plays: Intrigue and Love and Don Carlos
Edited by Walter Hinderer
Foreword by Gordon Craig

Friedrich Schiller
Wallenstein and Mary Stuart
Edited by Walter Hinderer

Johann Wolfgang von Goethe
*The Sufferings of Young Werther
and Elective Affinities*
Edited by Victor Lange
Forewords by Thomas Mann

German Romantic Criticism
Edited by A. Leslie Willson
Foreword by Ernst Behler

Friedrich Hölderlin
Hyperion and Selected Poems
Edited by Eric L. Santner

Philosophy of German Idealism
Edited by Ernst Behler

G. W. F. Hegel
*Encyclopedia of the Philosophical Sciences in Outline and Critical
    Writings*
Edited by Ernst Behler

Heinrich von Kleist
Plays
Edited by Walter Hinderer
Foreword by E. L. Doctorow

E. T. A. Hoffmann
Tales
Edited by Victor Lange

Georg Büchner
Complete Works and Letters
Edited by Walter Hinderer and Henry J. Schmidt

German Fairy Tales
Edited by Helmut Brackert and Volkmar Sander
Foreword by Bruno Bettelheim

German Literary Fairy Tales
Edited by Frank G. Ryder and Robert M. Browning
Introduction by Gordon Birrell
Foreword by John Gardner

F. Grillparzer, J. H. Nestroy, F. Hebbel
Nineteenth Century German Plays
Edited by Egon Schwarz in collaboration with
Hannelore M. Spence

Heinrich Heine
Poetry and Prose
Edited by Jost Hermand and Robert C. Holub
Foreword by Alfred Kazin

Heinrich Heine
The Romantic School and other Essays
Edited by Jost Hermand and Robert C. Holub

Heinrich von Kleist and Jean Paul
German Romantic Novellas
Edited by Frank G. Ryder and Robert M. Browning
Foreword by John Simon

German Romantic Stories
Edited by Frank Ryder
Introduction by Gordon Birrell

German Poetry from 1750 to 1900
Edited by Robert M. Browning
Foreword by Michael Hamburger

German Radio Plays
Edited by Everett Frost and Margaret Herzfeld-Sander

Hans Magnus Enzensberger
Critical Essays
Edited by Reinhold Grimm and Bruce Armstrong
Foreword by John Simon

All volumes available in hardcover and paperback editions at your bookstore or from the publisher. For more information on The German Library write to: The Continuum Publishing Company, 370 Lexington Avenue, New York, NY 10017.